Whitman's Que‹

Whitman's Queer Children
America's Homosexual Epics

Catherine A. Davies

B L O O M S B U R Y
LONDON · NEW DELHI · NEW YORK · SYDNEY

Bloomsbury Academic
An imprint of Bloomsbury Publishing Inc

1385 Broadway	50 Bedford Square
New York	London
NY 10018	WC1B 3DP
USA	UK

www.bloomsbury.com

Bloomsbury is a registered trade mark of Bloomsbury Publishing Plc

First published 2012
Paperback edition first published 2013

Library of Congress Cataloging-in-Publication Data
A catalog record for this title is available from the Library of Congress.

ISBN:	HB:	978-1-4411-9262-2
	PB:	978-1-6289-2318-6
	ePDF:	978-1-4411-0974-3

Typeset by Newgen Imaging Systems Pvt Ltd, Chennai, India

Contents

List of Abbreviations

CPHC   Hart Crane, *The Complete Poems of Hart Crane*, ed. Marc Simon (New York: Liveright, 2000).

FC   John Ashbery, *Flow Chart* (London: Carcanet, 1991).

GCP   Allen Ginsberg, *Collected Poems 1947–1980* (New York: Harper Row, 1984).

Acknowledgements

This book was begun during the term of a research studentship funded by the Arts and Humanities Research Council and a fellowship at University College, London. I would like to extend my thanks to Mark Ford, Peter Swaab and Hugh Stevens for their patient readings and advice during my time as a PhD candidate. Their generous readings of chapters and encouraging discussions contributed greatly to the progress of the project. My thanks especially to Mark for first introducing me to the work of Hart Crane and so many of the poets discussed here. My wonderful friends, Rachel Parker, Lytton Smith and Michael Mellor were not only generous in their readings of various drafts of the chapters in progress but also offered invaluable support and advice during the writing process. I would also like to thank Stephen Yenser who went 'above and beyond' in assisting with the acquisition of permissions from the estate of James Merrill. Thank you to Roberto Foddai for permission to use his beautiful photograph as the cover image. I am also most grateful to David Trotter for his early encouragement of my academic pursuits. My parents also provided unwavering support on a path that was strange and unfamiliar to a family such as ours. Without them, the public library and the literary signposts of the Manic Street Preachers, this book would not have been possible.

Extracts from *Flow Chart* by John Ashbery. © 1998 by John Ashbery. Reprinted by permission of Georges Borchardt, Inc, on behalf of the author.

Extracts from *Flow Chart* by John Ashbery. © 1991 by John Ashbery. Reprinted by permission of Carcanet Press Ltd.

Excerpts from *Selected Poems* by John Ashbery. © 1998 by John Ashbery. Reprinted by permission of Carcanet Press Ltd.

Excerpts from 'Soonest Mended' from *The Double Dream of Spring*, by John Ashbery. © 1966, 1970 by John Ashbery. Reprinted by permission of Georges Borchardt, Inc, on behalf of the author.

Excerpts from 'Houseboat Days' from *Houseboat Days,* by John Ashbery. © 1975, 1976, 1977, 1999 by John Ashbery. Reprinted by permission of Georges Borchardt, Inc, on behalf of the author.

Excerpts from 'The Thinnest Shadow' from *Some Trees,* by John Ashbery. © 1956 by John Ashbery. Reprinted by permission of Georges Borchardt, Inc, on behalf of the author.

Excerpts from *Collected Poems 1947–1997,* by Allen Ginsberg. © 1984, 1996. Reprinted by permission of the Wylie Agency (UK) Ltd, on behalf of the author.

Excerpts from *'Why I Am Not a Painter' and Other Poems* by Frank O'Hara. Edited by Mark Ford. © 2003. Reprinted by permission of Carcanet Press Ltd.

Excerpts from 'Clearing the Title' from *Selected Poems* by James Merrill. © 1996. Reprinted by permission of Carcanet Press Ltd.

Excerpts from 'The Broken Home' from *Selected Poems* by James Merrill. © 1996. Reprinted by permission of Carcanet Press Ltd.

Excerpts from *The Changing Light at Sandover* by James Merrill. © 1980, 1982 by James Merrill. Used by permission of Alfred A. Knopf, a division of Random House, Inc.

Excerpts from *Collected Poems* by James Merrill, edited by J. D. McClatchy and Stephen Yenser. © 2001 by the literary estate of James Merrill at Washington University. Used by permission of Alfred A. Knopf, a division of Random House, Inc.

Introduction

(i) The homosexual epic

This book examines a series of twentieth-century poems that reimagined the epic for a modern age. I use the term 'homosexual epic' to demarcate a group of poems written by male poets who are also homosexual but whose sexuality is not necessarily reflected explicitly in the contents of their poems. Rather, this study proposes that these poets' sexuality problematizes the contractual pact of the epic mode. This is a pact based on the representability presumed of the epic poet, which, by virtue of his outsider status, the homosexual is excluded from.[1]

The idea of a 'homosexual epic' fundamentally problematizes the traditional aims of the genre. As Bakhtin suggests, the job of epic is to 'accomplish the task of cultural, national, and political centralization of the verbal-ideological world'.[2] How can the homosexual poet renegotiate the epic poem to create a new idea of representability that bypasses or reimagines the central tenets of the mode? Undertaking a series of readings of these poems, I argue for the existence of a genealogy of American epic poems that renegotiate the conventions governing the relationship between the public and the private – a genealogy that I trace back to Walt Whitman's *Leaves of Grass* and his radical suggestion, as Robert Creeley so eloquently notes, that 'the common is personal'.[3] Whitman's epic-lyricism forms the foundations of the tradition I trace here, paving the way for Crane, Ginsberg, Merrill and Ashbery to fashion new kinds of epic voices to speak with in their poetry.

---

[1] For an account of approaches to the contractual nature of the epic genre, see Adeline Johns-Putra, *The History of the Epic* (Hampshire & New York: Palgrave Macmillan, 2006), 3–4.

[2] M. M. Bakhtin, *The Dialogic Imagination: Four Essays*, ed. Michael Holquist, trans. Caryl Emerson and Michael Holquist (Austin, TX: University of Texas Press, 1981), 273.

[3] Robert Creeley, introduction to *Whitman: Poems Selected by Robert Creeley* (Baltimore, MD: Penguin Books, 1973), 7.

In addition to the poets' sexuality, the selection of texts was determined by a number of other criteria. I use the term 'epic' in reference to these poems in so far as they distinguish themselves from other long poems by all exhibiting, in different quotients, a concern to engage with ideas of American nationhood (most explicitly seen in the case of Hart Crane's and Allen Ginsberg's poems). These poems also share an awareness of their relationship to the various traditions of epic, in terms of their intertextual dialogue, both with one another and with their epic precursors; all, in their very different ways, emulate the formal ambition and encyclopaedic scope of the traditional epic.[4]

Any attempt to define concisely the nature of the 'epic' is made difficult by the imprecise use made of the term as an adjective in contemporary culture to describe novels, films and television series. Its use as a literary term is also complicated by the need for it to encompass such diverse poems as *The Odyssey*, *The Iliad*, *The Divine Comedy*, *Paradise Lost*, *The Prelude* and *The Cantos*. However, the difficulties of defining the epic are arguably common to any genre that incorporates and absorbs mutations and aberrations. It is in the evolution of the epic tradition that this study locates its interest, considering such questions as: How have issues of nationhood been reinvigorated by the development in popular culture and its representation in poetry? How has the epic voice been reconsidered in the postmodern era?

All four poets examined here consider themselves to be in some way contributing to the tradition of epic. Crane set out explicitly to rethink the epic for the modern age in *The Bridge*, speaking of a desire to express in poetry the 'mystical synthesis of America'.[5] Similarly, Ginsberg imagined *The Fall of America* to be an epic 'about present-day politics'; it was his attempt at a '*dis*-sociated thought stream which includes politics

[4] With the exception of 'Howl', all the poems considered here have been published in book-length form. *The Changing Light at Sandover* was originally published as three individual poems: 'The Book of Ephraim' in *Divine Comedies* (1976), *Mirabell's Books of Number* (1978) and *Scripts for the Pageant* (1980). The poems were collected together as *The Changing Light at Sandover* and published in a single book-length volume with an additional coda, 'The Higher Keys', in 1982. The publication in 1995 of the 'Original Draft and Facsimile' edition of 'Howl' also arguably qualifies Ginsberg's earlier poem for inclusion under this criteria. See *'Howl': Original Draft Facsimile, Transcript & Variant Versions, Fully Annotated by Author, with Contemporaneous Correspondence, Account of First Public Reading, Legal Skirmishes, Precursor Texts & Bibliography*, ed. Barry Miles (New York: Harper Perennial, 1995).

[5] Hart Crane to Gorham Munson, 18 February 1923, *O My Land, My Friends: The Selected Letters of Hart Crane*, ed. Langdon Hammer and Brom Weber (New York & London: Four Walls Eight Windows, 1997), 131.

and history'.[6] *The Changing Light at Sandover* is also clearly indebted to a Dantesque epic vision of the afterlife, while Ashbery's *Flow Chart* develops its dialogue with Wordsworthian self-reflection, as an autobiographical epic that taps into the 'bloodstream of our collective memory'.[7]

My study begins by assessing Hart Crane's epic, *The Bridge* (1930), focusing on its uneasy marriage of a Whitmanian heritage with Crane's modernist aspirations. I follow this with a discussion of Allen Ginsberg's 'Howl' (1956) and *The Fall of America* (1972), developing readings of these poems that stress their use of the tradition of the epic's descent into the underworld. The fourth chapter examines James Merrill's *The Changing Light at Sandover* (1982), which is here read as establishing an elaborate cosmology that radically places the homosexual and the childless at its very centre. My final chapter on John Ashbery approaches *Flow Chart* (1991), his longest poem, as a postmodernist version of Wordsworth's attempt in *The Prelude* to present the 'growth of a poet's mind'.

In considering the field of epic, I follow both Brian Wilkie and Adeline Johns-Putra in approaching 'epic'[8] as what Johns-Putra calls 'an accumulation of definitions'.[9] Both Wilkie and Johns-Putra see the category of 'epic' as being endlessly redefined by the works that seek to extend the boundaries of the mode and redefine its nature, and are concerned in their work to concentrate on the variety *within* the epic terrain rather than to attempt the difficult task of setting out strict boundaries which are persistently being redrawn.

(ii) The history of the epic poem

The epic poem, historically, has been the literary genre through which ideas of nationhood have been most notably formed and articulated. Brian Wilkie argues that Virgil's *Aeneid* introduced these 'moral and political messages' – a substantial modification of 'Homeric objectivity'.[10] In narrating the foundation of the Roman Empire, *The Aeneid* is important for establishing the nationalism of the epic mode as Virgil marries the

---

[6] Allen Ginsberg, 'Interview with Tom Clark', *Spontaneous Mind: Selected Interviews 1958–1996*, ed. David Carter (London: Penguin Books, 2001), 49–50.

[7] John Ashbery, *Flow Chart* (London: Carcanet, 1991), 27.

[8] Brian Wilkie, *Romantic Poets and Epic Tradition* (Madison, WI: University of Wisconsin Press, 1965), 8–9.

[9] Johns-Putra, *The History of the Epic*, 1.

[10] Wilkie, *Romantic Poets and Epic Tradition*, 12.

impulses of *The Odyssey* (*nostos*) and *The Iliad* (war) in a single narrative. However, in addition to establishing the nationalistic strain of the epic poem, Wilkie argues that Virgil created something new in *The Aeneid*, by introducing the 'individualistic . . . suggesting at almost every moment the presence of its author and his attitudes'.[11] Virgil's poem, Wilkie suggests, firmly establishes the dialectic between the public and the private in the epic mode, positing (as William Rowe has suggested of the epic at large) that 'the individual and the collective [are] extensions of one another'.[12]

In a journal entry from 1957, Charles Olson notes the advantages of the long poem:

> The advantage of a long poem is [that] like *pot au feu*, it creates its own juice . . . Or put it formally: the long poem creates its own situation. Which is its gain over the small poem, which, each time, must make its own way, and thus loses, to itself, a character of reality which the long poem creates for itself – a continuity in time which is both *massa confusa* and the prolongation of life itself. When you got that meat stock the poem's got more to work with.[13]

Writing just as the stock of his own *Maximus* poems was beginning to thicken, Olson goes some way at least to suggesting the attraction of the size and scale of the long poem to the ambitious American poet. Marrying this scale to the epic's ideological aims, one can see how the epic has, historically speaking, tended to define a poet's ambition to distinguish himself in his art. From Milton's pursuit of 'Things unattempted yet in Prose or Rhyme'[14] to Pound's attempt to 'write Paradise',[15] the epic poem has been figured as the great challenge by many of the greatest poets of Western civilization.

While Olson is right to note that the long poem can create 'its own juice', the immense demands it places upon both knowledge and invention require substantial resources to sustain the scope, grandeur and

[11] Ibid.

[12] William Rowe, *Poets of Contemporary Latin America: History and the Inner Life* (Oxford: Oxford University Press, 2000), 23.

[13] , Unpublished journal (1957), quoted in Tom Clark, *Charles Olson: The Allegory of a Poet's Life* (Berkeley, CA: North Atlantic Books, 2001), 270.

[14] John Milton, *Paradise Lost*, ed. Christopher Ricks (London & New York: Penguin Books, 1989), 5.

[15] Ezra Pound, 'Notes for Canto CXVII', *The Cantos* (London: Faber, 1986), 816.

variety required in order to 'create its own situation', as well as to encapsulate the culture of its time. In his *Poetics*, Aristotle deemed the epic second only to tragedy in his 'hierarchy' of genres, and it remained a relevant force in the twentieth-century literature as a form that could offer hope of order and coherence in times of tumultuous cultural change.

With its roots in oral poetic traditions, the epic mode is deeply entangled with the diffusion and maintenance of a nation's history, passed on from generation to generation. The literary epic continued in this tradition; the classical epic poems of Homer (*The Odyssey* and *The Iliad*) and Virgil's *Aeneid* set out to narrate the long and perilous journeys of their nation's heroes, and their protagonists represented a culture's heroic ideal. With their invocations to the muse, their openings *in medias res*, and their episodic accounts of heroic battles and journeys, these poems suggest distinguishing formal characteristics of the epic form.

However, as the tradition has evolved and progressed, the term 'epic' has also come to be applied to works that manifest, as E. M. W. Tillyard has suggested, the epic 'spirit', either in their scale or scope.[16] As Brian Wilkie has remarked, the term 'epic' can be used to denote a family of texts with physiognomic similarities, rather than a strictly definable genre,[17] and it is in this sense that I return to the term 'epic' as a framework under which to evaluate the poems considered here. In this broader sense, works of prose fiction such as Melville's *Moby-Dick* are now also widely accepted as examples of 'epic', with Melville's work often heralded as the epitome of the 'American Epic Novel', which has arguably come to rival the epic poem as the form of choice for America's national literature. The homoerotic pairings of Ishmael and Queequeg in *Moby-Dick* cannot pass without comment in a study concerned with the intersection of the national identity and homosexual identity.[18] However, while such examples will be considered in brief as literary precedents for Crane's own version of what Leslie Fiedler called 'a kind of counter-matrimony',[19] for the purposes of my study I have limited the parameters of my discussion to the field of the twentieth-century American epic

---

[16] Tillyard proposes four main characteristics of the epic: high quality and seriousness, inclusiveness or amplitude, control and exactitude commensurate with exuberance, and an expression of the feelings of a large group of people. See E. M. W. Tillyard, *The English Epic and its Background* (London: Chatto & Windus, 1954), 5–12.

[17] Wilkie, *Romantic Poets and Epic Tradition*, 3–10.

[18] For a compilation of Melville's homoerotic passages, see *The Gay Herman Melville Reader*, ed. Ken Schellenberg (Arlington, VA: Gival Press, 2002).

[19] Leslie Fiedler, *Love and Death and the American Novel* (New York: Criterion, 1960), 209.

poem. My use of the term 'epic' is therefore restricted in the same way, and throughout the book I use it to refer to its poetic incarnation.

As this study makes no claims to document a social history of male homosexuality, I have generally avoided using historically specific epithets to talk about same-sex desire, and have chosen to use the term 'homosexuality' and 'homosexual' throughout the book to denote male-to-male sexual relationships, except where it has been necessary to note the historical problems of the terminology.[20] I also rejected the term 'queer' as both too inclusive of various homo-, bi-, trans-, inter- and asexual communities, and as having too many socio-political connotations to suit the terms of my enquiry here. The popularity of the term 'gay' to speak about homosexuality from the 1960s onwards would arguably make this term preferable in some ways to 'homosexual' for speaking about the texts dating from the latter half of the twentieth century. It is certainly true that the clinical connotations of 'homosexual' are unhelpfully evocative of the medicalization and pathologization of same-sex desire. However, while I might have termed the later poems 'gay epics', this term is not without its problems for speaking (e.g.) about Crane's experience as a 1920s homosexual, or Whitman's 'manly attachments'. There is certainly no unproblematic terminology that does not erase the historical specificity of same-sex desire. However, as the texts discussed in this book are drawn from across what David Halperin has called the 'one hundred years of homosexuality',[21] I have found the term 'homosexual' helpful for consistency of reference, carrying the fewest disadvantages and objections for the majority of the texts discussed here.

(iii) Homosexuality and the epic

With the centrality of its homoerotic representation of Gilgamesh and Enkidu, *The Epic of Gilgamesh* both predates and surpasses the examples

---

[20] In 1869, Karl-Maria Kertbeny anonymously published a pamphlet entitled 'Paragraph 143 of the Prussian Penal Code of 14 April 1851 and its Reaffirmation as Paragraph 152 in the Proposed Penal Code for the Norddeutscher Bund. An Open and Professional Correspondence to His Excellency Dr. Leonhardt, Royal Prussian Minister of Justice'. In it, Kertbeny used the term 'homosexual', which later became part of his broader system for the classification of sexual types. Kertbeny's 'homosexual' was distinct from Karl Ulrich's 'Urning' in distancing the classification from effeminate behaviour or characteristics.

[21] David Halperin, *One Hundred Years of Homosexuality, and Other Essays on Greek Love* (New York & London: Routledge, 1990).

of Western classical epics as a contender for the title of proto-homosexual epic. Although the relationship between the two male characters is not explicitly sexual, the intensity of their bond and kinship and their representation as two complementary halves whose union is necessary to the health of the kingdom, gives much credence to subsequent queer readings of the text and the status it has achieved as a potent gay myth.[22]

Discussions of the place of homosexuality in the history of the epic poem, however, have tended to focus upon the presence of same-sex desire in primary epics such as Homer's *Odyssey* and *Iliad*. The arguments for the acceptance of 'Greek love' (as male-to-male sexual relations were referred to in the Victorian era) as only post-dating Homer's texts are certainly supported by *The Odyssey*'s focus upon the heterosexual exploits of Odysseus. Even John Addington Symonds – an otherwise ardent supporter of the homosexual cause – argued that the classical epics had no place for homosexuality as we have now come to know it, with the intense male friendship of Achilles and Patroclus having no sexual component but that which was imposed by the interpretations of 'later generations'.[23] However, while the narrative drama of *The Iliad* undeniably turns upon the intensity of two men's heterosexual love for Helen of Troy, the relationship between Achilles and Patroclus is also integral to its story: Achilles is only persuaded to fight after the death of Patroclus, and his passion for the youth remains one of the most potent examples of same-sex desire in Greek literature, even if *The Iliad* itself could not be called a 'homosexual epic' in the sense that I use the term in relation to this study.

Regardless of its treatment in classical epic literature, homosexuality encounters some fundamental ideological problems in the context of the modern epic genre. From its roots in oral poetic traditions, the epic has undergone perhaps the most radical redefinition of any genre in literary history. What remains, however, is the totalizing impulse of the epic to constitute itself as the narrative of its audience's historical heritage by providing heroic models of conduct. As Borges notes, 'the important

---

[22] Thorkild Jacobsen was the first scholar to argue that the relationship between Gilgamesh and Enkidu should be understood as sexual in nature. See Thorkild Jacobsen, 'How did Gilgamesh oppress Uruk?', *Acta Orientalia* 8 (1930), 62–74. For a more recent exposition of Jacobsen's interpretation, see Neal Walls, *Desire, Discord and Death: Approaches to Ancient Near Eastern Myth* (Boston, MA: Asor Books, 2001).

[23] See John Addington Symonds, 'The Dantesque and Platonic Ideals of Love' (1893), reprinted in *Hidden Heritage: History and the Gay Imagination*, ed. Byrne R. S. Fone (New York: Irvington, 1981), 148.

thing about epic is a hero – a man who is a pattern for all men'.[24] These models of conduct are the site of implicit narratives that sanction the exclusion of minorities from power, and it is this tendency that has seen critics such as Bernard Schweizer argue for epic as the paradigmatic genre of patriarchy. As Schweizer notes in his discussion regarding the exclusion of the feminine from the epic mode:

> Formally, epic has long been considered the crowning achievement of the 'timeless' poetic genius, the repository of sublime diction, and even the product of 'divine' inspiration – all attributes carrying connotations of masculinity.[25]

However, as this study will demonstrate, whereas until the arrival of sub-genres such as 'social history' and 'oral history', History (as a discourse) has tended to focus upon a handful of emblematic public figures, the American epic poem has typically moved towards the inclusion of the lowest ranks and classes, as epitomized by Whitman's ambition to speak for and through the Everyman figure in *Leaves of Grass*. In this respect one might argue that the totalizing impulse of the epic has shifted (in the example of American literature) towards one of *inclusivity*. Rather than retaining the focus of the classical epics on the single heroic and exemplary individual, American epics more often reflect the ideology of the melting pot: this has dictated a poetics that has moved towards a more representative approach to the epic poem. As Alan C. Jalowitz notes:

> For the United States . . . with its multiple ethnicities, spacious geography, and continuing influx of a variety of foreign languages, the possibility to achieve *the* national epic must give way to the production and acceptance of numerous epics, not all of which would be by majority voices.[26]

In the first half of the twentieth century, Pound defined the modern epic as 'a poem including history' and 'the tale of the tribe',[27] while Eliot

---

[24] Jorge Luis Borges, 'The Telling of the Tale', *The Atlantic Monthly* 86.3 (September 2000), 63–5.

[25] Bernard Schweizer, *Approaches to the Anglo and American Female Epic, 1621–1982* (Aldershot: Ashgate, 2006), 1.

[26] Alan C. Jalowitz, 'The Daughters of Penelope: Tradition and Innovations in American Epics by Women', *Approaches to the Anglo American Epic*, ed. Bernard Schweizer (Aldershot: Ashgate, 2006), 141.

[27] Ezra Pound, *ABC of Reading* (London: Faber, 1951), 46.

believed that the 'mythical method' developed by Joyce might make sense of the 'immense panorama of futility and anarchy that is contemporary history'.[28] The difficulties presented by epic's foundations in the commonality of the 'tribe' constitute the starting point for my discussion of those homosexual poets who have risen to the ideological challenge the genre presents for the minority voice. Working from Pound's assumption that epic channels 'the voice of a nation through the mouth of one man', this book looks to examine the nature or sound of that voice when it emanates from the mouth of a homosexual man, following Robert Martin in asking, 'what cultural authority does the openly gay man possess that he can draw upon to write the poem of the nation?'[29]

Although my field of enquiry is that of the epic poem, as already noted, my main concern with genre is with its establishment of cultural imperatives. As epic takes 'the definition of cultural value as its conscious center',[30] this study is interested in the literary effects of challenges to cultural values: If genres have a historical component, how might the epic poem show itself to be modified in the service of queer content? Although two of the four poems considered here were not conceived of as epic poems in the strictest sense of the genre, both John Ashbery's *Flow Chart* and James Merrill's *The Changing Light at Sandover* engage with many of the questions examined by Crane and Ginsberg in their more consciously epic projects. In continuing the dialogue about what it means to be American, as well as maintaining the breadth and scope of the traditional epic, Merrill's and Ashbery's poems come to stand in my genealogy as excellent examples of the way in which the epic was transformed in the latter half of the twentieth century.

Further to the earlier discussion of homosexual terminology, I have restricted the remit of my enquiry to the work of several key *male* homosexual poets. The differences between lesbian and gay experience are too large to be conflated here: psychoanalytic discourse, for example, considers lesbianism as an aetiology distinct from male homosexuality, and the conditions of living as both a homosexual *and* as a woman, alongside the absence of legislative history regarding female homosexuality,

[28] T. S. Eliot, 'Ulysses, Order, and Myth', *Selected Prose of T. S. Eliot*, ed. Frank Kermode (New York: Harcourt Brace Jovanovich, 1975), 177.

[29] Robert K. Martin, 'Myths of Native Masculinity: Hart Crane and the Poem of the Nation', *American Modernism across the Arts*, ed. Jay Bochner and Justin D. Edwards (New York & Canterbury: Peter Lang, 1999), 213.

[30] Thomas E. Yingling, *Hart Crane and the Homosexual Text: New Thresholds, New Anatomies* (Chicago & London: University of Chicago Press, 1990), 194.

necessitate a clear division.[31] Furthermore, epic is often envisioned as
a distinctly 'masculine' tradition, to the point where 'epic may well be
the most exclusively gender coded of all literary genres; so much so that
epic and masculinity appear to be almost coterminous',[32] and all of the
poets explored here participate in some of those recognizably masculine
aspects of epic's scope and ambition; yet their homosexuality tempers it
with, in gender terms, something new.

I have also chosen to focus upon one American poet whose sexual orientation is not necessarily at the centre or forefront of the poetic choices
they make – John Ashbery being an excellent example of a poet who is
homosexual but who does not wish to be identified as a 'gay poet' as
such.[33] In addition, my study does not consider the more recent manifestations of programmatically gay poetry (such as the large body of
work responding to the HIV-AIDS epidemic), although Allen Ginsberg
forms a striking example of the ways in which homosexuality can be seen
to have acted as a catalyst for a poet's challenge to traditional Anglo-
American forms. I have also excluded a discussion of the work of immigrant American poets, whose cultural authority is further complicated by
diaspora, although Ginsberg may be considered as a second-generation
Jewish poet – an issue I address briefly in my third chapter.

My focus on a predominantly Whitmanian heritage has narrowed my
discussion to four American-born poets, rather than a more comprehensive account of the ways in which American poetry has engaged with
the epic tradition. A more wide-ranging approach would have included
the work of transatlantic figures such as W. H. Auden and Thom Gunn,
whose work would undeniably have contributed to a fuller picture of
how the homosexual poet has negotiated the idea of nationhood. I also
deal only tangentially with Frank O'Hara who might seem a prime candidate for inclusion in such a study. O'Hara worked hard to free his poetry
from the kinds of explicit 'seriousness' demanded by the epic genre,
and although his poems of significant length (such as 'In Memory of My
Feelings') might be included in a broader inquiry, he seemed to me to
evoke issues of 'American-ness' less strongly than John Ashbery whose

---

[31] For an influential discussion of the differences between the literary history of male and
female homosexuality, see Monica Wittig, *The Lesbian Body*, trans. David Le Vay (New
York: Viking Press, 1971), 9.
[32] Schweizer, *Approaches to the Anglo and American Female Epic, 1621–1982*, 1.
[33] Ashbery claims that, 'I do not think of myself as a gay poet' (conversation with John
Shoptaw, February 1993. Quoted in John Shoptaw, *On the Outside Looking Out: John
Ashbery's Poetry* (Cambridge: Harvard University Press, 1994), 4.

poetry, I felt, provided ample representation of the New York School of Poets.

My most significant exclusion is that of Robert Duncan. The long poems, such as *Passages 22–27: Of the War* (1966) and *Tribunals, Passages 31–35* (1970) resonate with many of the themes of this book and might, alongside O'Hara's work, have been included in another incarnation of this study. However, Duncan's most significant poems overlap, chronologically speaking, with those I consider here by Ginsberg. I wanted to retain a single poet focus for each chapter (with each reflecting, rather approximately, a distinct time period in the twentieth century) and consequentially, a consideration of Duncan's poetry is displaced by Ginsberg's more forceful evocations of the collisions of the themes of sexuality and the national in *The Fall of America*. Ginsberg's undoubted larger cultural footprint also played a part in this selection process, as well as the interconnections and cross-references I found between the poems of the four poets considered here.

Allen Ginsberg, James Merrill and John Ashbery all inherited similar critical and cultural markers. Ginsberg and Merrill were born in 1926, and Ashbery in 1927, all on the East Coast of America. Although they came from distinct economic, political and social backgrounds, all three poets were university educated – Ginsberg at Columbia, Ashbery at Harvard and Columbia and Merrill at Amherst. Despite these shared beginnings, three distinct paths emerge from the ways in which each of the poets explores his place within poetic traditions, and figures his sexuality in his writing. Where Ginsberg's coupling of an avant-garde aesthetic with his radical politics constructs a narrative that suggests that sexual liberation might be achieved via its expression through formally progressive means, Merrill's poetry remains wedded to a formal tradition, even when his work takes a more autobiographical turn.[34] Ashbery distinguishes himself yet again: while sharing Merrill's touchstones of Bishop, Stevens and Auden, he has repeatedly rejected any ghettoization of his work by refusing to style himself as a 'gay poet'. Preferring instead to mine the democratic source of popular culture, Ashbery is anxious to maintain a wide appeal, rather than subsume his poetic practices in minority politics.

Alongside their stylistic and political differences, each of the poems I have chosen to focus on develops out of very different historical moments. Although I make no claim to present a comprehensive history of

---

[34] With the 1962 publication of his collection *Water Street*, Merrill's poetry began to tackle more autobiographical subject matter.

homosexuality, in each chapter I try to anchor my readings to an analysis of the changing social climate. Writing in 1920s America, Crane experienced very different restrictions on his sexual behaviour and expression from those Ashbery experienced, writing *Flow Chart* over 60 years later. However, it is interesting to note that the homosexual content of the poems does not correlate to the relative acceptability of homosexuality at any given time. Of all the poets that I consider here, Ginsberg is the most explicit about his homosexuality, even though his revelations take place against the backdrop of 1950s McCarthyism, where the penalties for such disclosure were higher than those threatened in both Whitman and Crane's time.

Gregory Woods has pointed out that 'the canon would not look at all convincingly definitive without its gay content'.[35] However, it is perhaps not coincidental that those gay poets who have embarked upon the project of writing a long poem have been more successful in overcoming what Yingling has called the implicit homophobia of American literary criticism.[36] For all the poets considered here, I would argue that the epic poem has played a crucial role in securing their positions in the canon. Both Merrill's and Ashbery's critical reputations were arguably secured (if not founded) after the publication of *The Changing Light at Sandover* and 'Self-Portrait in a Convex Mirror' (1975) respectively. Ginsberg's poetic standing (as opposed to his iconic cultural status) also largely rests on his poems, 'Howl' and 'Kaddish'. As a form that connotes simultaneously both individual ambition and dialogue with a rich literary past, the epic guarantees its author a place in the illustrious history of poets that have, as Pound put it, tried to 'make it cohere'.[37]

Although a critical failure during his lifetime, Hart Crane's *The Bridge* is now generally considered to be a canonical work of American modernist poetry,[38] with its fusion of a Whitmanian myth of America with the poet's own anxious homoeroticism. As a pioneering work in the

---

[35] Gregory Woods, *A History of Gay Literature: The Male Tradition* (New Haven & London: Yale University Press, 1998), 11. Elsewhere, Woods has posited that the 'strength of the literature of homosexuality' (as thus its often canonical status) 'lies in obliquity, arising from the need to resort to metaphor to express sexual meaning' (*Articulate Flesh: Male Homoeroticism and Modern Poetry* (New Haven & London: Yale University Press, 1987), 2).

[36] Yingling has spoken about the intellectual dishonesty at work in American literary criticism, where, despite the canonical status of figures such as Whitman, Robert Duncan, John Ashbery and Frank O'Hara, there is a persistent 'absence of male homosexuality as a central topic of investigation' (Yingling, *Hart Crane and the Homosexual Text*, 1).

[37] Pound, 'Canto CXVI', *The Cantos*, 810.

[38] Crane's poem appears in full in the sixth edition of the *Norton Anthology of American Poetry* (2002) and in the second volume of the Library of America's *American Poetry: The Twentieth Century* (2000).

project of realizing a modern homosexual epic, Crane's poem constitutes the focus of my first chapter, opening my discussion of the renewal
of Whitman's politics and vision for the new century. Each subsequent
chapter examines, in chronological order of their composition, a long
poem written in the post-war period, considering the ways in which the
work might be seen to engage with the shifting context of what it means
to be a homosexual man in America. By virtue of the similar birth dates
of three of the poets I have chosen to discuss, my study does not offer a
progressive narrative of liberation, but rather an approach to homosexual literature that does not attempt to homogenize the diverse methods
of the poets. Although I propose that the responses to Whitman's legacy
may amount to a genealogy of sorts, it is important not to standardize
the rich and varied tradition these poems embody. I offer what I hope is
a representative selection, rather than an encyclopaedic approach to the
subject of the homosexual epic in American literature.

(iv) Sexual citizenship

So we are taking off our masks, are we, and keeping
our mouths shut? as if we'd been pierced by a glance![39]

Since the rise of postcolonial studies, the field of inquiry that surrounds
the concept of national identity has expanded voluminously. The reclamation of the many 'unofficial' histories of nations and peoples has
become a project that has taken in the exclusions of gender, as well as
those of ethnic, racial and religious minorities.[40] Despite the more recent
work of Stephen O'Murray, however, the issue of 'sexual citizenship' is
still relatively under-explored in a literary context.[41] Even in the midst
of the popular currency of the term 'queer nation',[42] the dynamics of

[39] Frank O'Hara, 'Homosexuality', *The Collected Poems of Frank O'Hara*, ed. Donald Allen (Berkeley, Los Angeles & London: University of California Press, 1995), 181.
[40] Michelle Wallace, 'Critical Fictions', *Critical Fictions: The Politics of Imaginative Writing*, ed. Philomena Mariani (Seattle: Bay Press, 1991), 139–42.
[41] Stephen O'Murray posits the idea of the 'lesbigay' community as 'a quasi-ethnic group' in *American Gay* (Chicago & London: Chicago University Press, 1996), 4.
[42] 'Queer nation' refers to direct-action organization founded in 1990 in the United States by members of ACT-UP. The term has subsequently gained currency in academic dis-course concerned with the legitimacy of queer nationalism. See, for example, Lauren Berlant and Elizabeth Freeman, 'Queer Nationality', *Boundary 2*, 19.1, 'New Americanists 2: National Identities and Postnational Narratives' (Spring 1992), 149–80.

the interaction of gay male subjectivity and national identity in America remains largely uncharted.[43]

The critical silence regarding homosexuality in literary criticism of the first half of the twentieth century has been slowly replaced over the last few decades, as gay and lesbian studies and queer theory have been accepted and absorbed into the academy. Queer theorists such as Eve Kosofsky Sedgwick have done much to reposition homosexuality at the centre of the discursive field.[44] However, any claim for this new-found visibility as an index of a more general sense of acceptance should also be accompanied by a questioning of the coincidence of this proposed new cultural dynamic with the endemic *in*visibility of the homosexual population that HIV-AIDS seemed to both promise and threaten in the late 1980s and early 1990s. As Leo Bersani has observed, while 'nothing has made gay men more visible than AIDS',[45] in once again transforming the homosexual male into a 'fascinating taboo', the visibility 'conferred on gay men by AIDS is the visibility of imminent death, of a promised invisibility'.[46]

The relation of queer sexuality to national identity in the context of Canadian literature was the subject of a 1999 book-length study.[47] Critical accounts of an equivalent American tradition in twentieth-century poetry, however, are notably still absent.[48] The aim of this book is to redress this critical oversight, turning to the particular historical anxieties surrounding the performance of homosexual subjectivity in the American poetic

---

[43] See George Mosse's study from 1985, *Nationalism and Sexuality: Middle-Class Morality and Social Norms in Modern Europe* (Madison, WI: University of Wisconsin Press, 1985) for an account of the formation of homosexual identity in Europe. Alongside Mosse's study, exceptions to this phenomenon include Jeffrey Escoffier's *American Homo: Community and Perversity* (Berkeley, Los Angeles & London: University of California Press, 1998), which offers a series of essays on the political life of homosexuality since 1945.

[44] For example, Eve Kosofsky Sedgwick has argued for the centrality of homosexuality to Western discourse, claiming that, 'many of the major nodes of thought and knowledge in twentieth-century Western culture . . . are structured – indeed, fractured – by a chronic, now endemic crisis of homo/heterosexual definition'. See Eve Kosofsky Sedgwick, *Epistemology of the Closet* (Berkeley, CA: University of California Press, 1992), 1.

[45] Leo Bersani, *Homos* (Cambridge & London: Harvard University Press, 1995), 19–21.

[46] Bersani, *Homos*, 20

[47] Peter Dickinson, *Here is Queer: Nationalisms and Sexualities in the Literature of Canada* (Toronto & London: University of Toronto Press, 1999).

[48] Robert Martin's *The Homosexual Tradition in American Poetry, Expanded* (Iowa City, IA: University of Iowa Press, 1998) is the most notable example of an attempt to fill this critical gap. However, Martin's study is more of an account of Whitman as a poetic forebear for other homosexual poets, and does not address in-depth ideas of the American nation and the homosexual.

epic.[49] Building upon the critical work of Robert Martin, James Miller and Thomas Yingling, I will be looking to understand the negotiation of the idea of 'America' by the homosexual poet. Focusing on how the homosexual subject is situated in relation to American national identity, I want to look at the implications of social exclusion or alienation for the articulation of community. If identity is constructed by a sense of origins, family and community (both sexual and otherwise), the crisis of these, in terms of hybridity, separatism or exclusion, must also be seen to bear upon the construction of the narrative of the self. Might these epic poems be seen to reflect anxieties regarding the negotiation of a national identity that can be reconciled to homosexuality? In seeking to interrogate the textual implications of the tensions between homosexual subjectivity and American national identity, the first chapter will concentrate on Hart Crane and the period over which he struggled to produce *The Bridge*.

While Thomas Yingling has proposed that the required commonality of the epic form is essentially opposed to the discourse of homosexuality, I will read the textual strategies of *The Bridge* as echoing the concerns of recent queer theorists by attempting to imagine Crane's sexual identity as neither oppositional nor marginal. Rather, I argue that *The Bridge* works to imagine the homosexual male as the very definition of the American citizen, employing the discourse of citizenship available to him at the time to recast the Pocahontas myth as a quasi-Girardian triangle that culminates in the union of the red and the white man.[50] Given that the epic typically claims cultural centrality, my reading focuses on Crane's strategy of exploring the fissures in American identity by examining the historic position of the Native American, so as to allegorize the contemporary erasure of the homosexual from the nation. By identifying America's native inheritance with a myth of homosexual origins, I explore the ways in which Crane's poetic strategies resonate with Eric Gans' stricture that 'the voice of lyric poetry is the unmediated voice of resentment'.[51] This chapter also begins to address how Crane follows Whitman's example in

---

[49] I use the term 'homosexual' to denote both the desiring subject and the field of discourse that surrounds and constructs the practices and mythologies of same-sex desire.

[50] For an account of the application of the Girardian triangle to a homosexual reading of a text, see Eve Kosofsky Sedgwick, *Between Men: English Literature and Male Homosocial Desire* (New York: Columbia University Press, 1985), 21–7.

[51] Eric Gans, *The End of Culture: Toward a Generative Anthropology* (Berkeley, Los Angeles & London: University of California Press, 1985), 271.

recasting the relations between the epic's concern with the public and the lyric's orientation towards the private realm.

The second chapter further examines the dynamic between the public and the private in the epic poem, by focusing on Ginsberg's queer rejoinder to an era dominated by McCarthyism and Cold War politics. Moving towards an understanding of Ginsberg's contribution to the homosexual epic, I focus on 'Howl' and *The Fall of America (1965–1971)* as poems that continue this genealogy. Treating the idea of the Jungian *nekyia* as an encounter with the collective unconscious, I look at the epic narrative of 'Howl' as a record of Ginsberg's descent into an underworld that fuses the horrors of contemporary America with Ginsberg's own personal psychodrama.

The third chapter focuses on two aspects of James Merrill's *The Changing Light at Sandover* – childlessness, and the fragmentation of the bardic voice. I argue that the reflections and refractions of Merrill's poetic avatar, 'JM', substantially modify the myth of Narcissus most commonly associated with the homosexual psyche, transforming the autobiographical weight of the poem from egotism into a grand act of self-dispersal and erasure. I also propose that Merrill's poetics present an alternative response to that of Ginsberg's rejection of traditional forms. Merrill's regard for the prosodic and lyric traditions as a means to explore homosexual subjectivity problematizes any simple equation that might be made between sexual liberation and formal innovation. As I unpack the significance of childlessness in the trilogy, I argue that Merrill's cosmology re-envisions a world-order where, excluded from the reproductive realm, the homosexual is uniquely privileged to produce 'meaningful' art.

The final chapter reads Ashbery's *Flow Chart* in the light of Harold Bloom's assertion that Ashbery is part of 'that American sequence that includes Whitman, Dickinson, Stevens and Hart Crane'.[52] Foregrounding the significance of sexuality in a way that Bloom's proposed genealogy does not, I consider Ashbery's democratic poetics as following in a Whitmanian tradition, inasmuch as *Flow Chart* registers the full range of American dictions, including 'multitudinous' ways of talking, in place of the 'multitudes' of types that populate Whitman's poetry. I consider *Flow Chart*'s intertextual engagement with both *The Prelude* and *The Bridge* to indicate some degree of intention on Ashbery's

---

[52] Harold Bloom, jacket copy, Ashbery, *Flow Chart* (London: Carcanet, 1991).

part to initiate a dialogue with a tradition of epic poetry, while the poem's invocation of ideas of America and nation also make it a useful text through which to trace the continuing Whitmanian impulses.

In place of an explicit exposition of 'the myth of America', Ashbery's poem foregrounds the problematics of subjectivity that were always implicit in the American epic project. Although there are moments where *Flow Chart* operates on similar terrain to the mock-epic, the collision between the transcendental vision and the banality of the everyday has a bathetic, rather than comic, effect. If on the one hand *Flow Chart* seems to turn its back on the grandiose ambitions of the epic because its author is more concerned with the anxieties of subjectivity, on the other, its exploration of a multitude of subjectivities can be seen as a redefinition, and expansion, of the epic genre.

(v) Homosexuality and the national

The cult of origins is a hate reaction. Hatred of those others who do not share my origins and affront me personally, economically, and culturally.[53]

The discourses of the national and the sexual both offer a model for conceiving of one's identity – the one founded upon geographical or racial origins, the other upon sexual practice or orientation. Alongside Foucault's dissection of the history of sexuality in the mid-1970s, sexuality emerged as an equally valid way of defining identity and origins.[54] Foucault's contribution to our understanding of the intersection of sexuality, power and knowledge has certainly done much to advance the idea of sexuality as both a public and a private discourse. It became, as David Evans notes, the 'central bearer of power relations in the second half of the twentieth century'.[55]

Edmund White observed in a 1980 essay that, 'with the collapse of other social values (religion, patriotism, family and so on) sex has been forced to take up the slack, to become our sole model of transcendence,

---

[53] Julia Kristeva, *Nations without Nationalism* (New York: Columbia University Press, 1993), 2.

[54] Foucault was also following Freud in his explorations of the history and anthropology of sexuality. See in particular *Totem and Taboo* (1913) and *Civilization and its Discontents* (1930).

[55] David T. Evans, *Sexual Citizenship: The Material Construction of Sexualities* (New York & London: Routledge, 1993), 12.

and our only touchstone of authenticity'.[56] White's statement emphasizes the colonization of the communal realm by the sexual, as is evident
from the increased focus on political and civil rights for sexual minorities and the sexualization of Western capitalist cultures over the last
three decades. Mapping out the displacement of 'religion, patriotism,
and family', White highlights the potential of sexuality to function as an
alternative communal order, operating as Eric Gans has suggested, as a
potentially competitive mode of 'significance' to the community.[57] White
laments the transformation of sex into 'a religion, a reason for being',
hoping for its restoration as 'a pleasure, a communication, and art'.[58]

Similarly, Benedict Anderson attributes the rise of alternative modes of
social cohesion to the decreasing importance of religion. As the foremost
proponent of the 'modernization model' of nationalism, Anderson's
Imagined Communities: Reflections on the Origin and Spread of Nationalism
(1983) locates the birth of the idea of the nation at the end of the eigh-
teenth century.[59] At the very centre of Anderson's account is the growth
of what he calls 'print capitalism', with the democratization of language
(particularly the reduction of privileged access to script languages such
as Latin) and the revolutions of print culture laying the foundations
for the creation of a national consciousness to fill the void left by the
increased secularization of society. These new fields of exchange and
communication provided the means by which national identities could
be constructed among the people themselves.

Part of the project of this inquiry will be to attempt to fuse together these
two models of conceiving of identity, looking at the 'enmeshment' (to borrow George Mosse's term) of the national and the sexual in the American
epic poem. In this respect the foundations of my discussion are much
indebted to the work of Mosse and Foucault, who have both been fundamental in questioning the heteronormative assumptions that had previously theorized national identity and sexuality as discrete, autonomous and

---

[56] Edmund White, *States of Desire* (London: André Deutsch, 1980), 282. Quoted in Evans,
Sexual Citizenship, 1.

[57] Gans conceives of sexuality as a 'dangerous force that must be brought within communal
order', with the importance of sexuality to a grand narrative of culture residing in its
potential as a 'rival source of significance' to that communal order. For Gans, however,
all forms of sexuality are potentially transgressive. His model does not account for the
systematic representation in modern culture of same-sex desire as inherently transgressive. See Gans, 'Originary Thoughts on Sexuality', *Chronicles of Love & Resentment* 220
(November 2000), www.anthropoetics.ucla.edu, site visited on 15 September 2011.

[58] White, *States of Desire*, 282.

[59] Benedict Anderson, *Imagined Communities: Reflections on the Origin and Spread of Nationalism*
(London: Verso, 1983).

historically transcendent categories. Mosse was the first to sketch a double history of both modern European nationalism and the emergence of bourgeois sexuality, highlighting the normative assumptions behind our understanding of these categories in his study of sexuality in Germany: 'what one regards as normal or abnormal behaviour, sexual or otherwise', he suggests, 'is a product of historical development, not universal law'.[60]

Both Foucault's analysis of the history of sexuality and Anderson's account of the origins of nations have argued for a discursive production of these categories that is neither geographically privileged, nor historically static. Following in the footsteps of Anderson's account of the nation state as a variable cultural artefact and collection of 'imagined communities', theorists such as Homi Bhabha have gone on to suggest that national identity be seen as a strictly relational term, whose characteristics are derived from a system of differences.[61] For Bhabha, national identity is determined not by the presence of intrinsic properties but 'as a function of what it (presumably) is not'.[62] This element of alterity is crucial to the modern definition of a nation, which is shaped by that which it opposes, as much as that which it embraces and represents.

The importance of this system of differences is echoed in Thomas Yingling's consideration of the nation in relation to the discursive construction of AIDS and homosexuality in the 1990s; 'national identity', he contends, 'requires an ideal conception of the [national] body and a rejection of accommodation to Otherness'.[63] In thinking about the importance of AIDS to the representation of homosexuality, David Caron also notes that, 'AIDS incorporated the metaphorical networks and narrative structures already in place in western cultures to depict, define, and make sense of homosexuality'.[64] Certainly, the figuring of AIDS as

---

[60] Mosse, *Nationalism and Sexuality*, 3.

[61] Homi K. Bhabha has encouraged a rigorous rethinking of nationalism and its representation, emphasizing the 'ambivalence' or 'hybridity' at the site of colonial contestation as the 'liminal' spaces in which cultural differences are articulated and, Bhabha argues, where 'imagined' constructions of cultural and national identity are actually produced. Critiquing essentialist narratives of nationhood, Bhabha proposed in *Nation and Narration* (1991) that nations are narrative constructions that arise from the interaction of these contending cultural constituencies.

[62] Andrew Parker, Mary Russo, Doris Sommer and Patricia Yaeger, 'Introduction', *Nationalisms and Sexualities*, ed. Parker, Russo, Sommer and Yaeger (New York & London: Routledge, 1992), 5.

[63] Thomas E. Yingling, *AIDS and the National Body* (Durham & London: Duke University Press, 1997), 25.

[64] David Caron, *AIDS in French Culture: Social Ills, Literary Cures* (Madison & London: University of Wisconsin Press, 2001), 3.

'anti-American, in its violation of heterosexually sanctioned erogenous
zones, familial bonds, and social formations of privacy and pleasure'[65]
reads like a Republican indictment of homosexuality. However, it could
also be seen as an updated version of René Girard's contention that 'sexual desire must be forbidden whenever its presence is incompatible with
communal existence'.[66]

The general congruence of Western attitudes in the 1980s and 1990s
towards AIDS and homosexuality (with their mutual narrative tropes
of invasion and contagion) complicates the process of unwrapping the
underlying ideology that drives the need to eject the homosexual subject
from the national corpus. Yingling's recasting of the medieval concept of
the body politic[67] uncannily echoes the deferral action of the scapegoat
mechanism as a ritual function of religious social systems, as delineated
in Girard's *Violence and the Sacred* (1972).

Girard's account of the myth-making underlying this ritual mechanism,
whereby society seeks to direct its inherent violence towards a relatively
arbitrary victim, is not translatable to the example of the HIV-positive
homosexual of the 1980s and 1990s without a caveat. In this scenario
the scapegoat in question is not random, but rather marked out by virtue of his or her seropositivity.[68] However, as the sacrificial substitution
depends in Girard's account on its 'ability to conceal the displacement
upon which the rite is based',[69] the normalization of the discrimination
and hatred directed towards what Yingling calls 'the homosexual AIDS
subject' comes to seem not merely politically motivated, but also ritual-
istic in character:

The fearful transgression of a single individual is substituted for the
universal onslaught of reciprocal violence . . . Oedipus is responsible

---

[65] Yingling, *AIDS and the National Body*, 3.
[66] René Girard, *Violence and the Sacred*, trans. P. Gregory (Baltimore & London: Johns
Hopkins University Press, 1972), 220.
[67] The notion of 'the king's two bodies' attempts to deal with the paradox of the mortality
of the monarch and the perpetuity of the state by endowing the monarch with a *body
natural* and a *body politic*. Derived from medieval political theology, it found the height
of its expression during the reign of Elizabeth I. See E. H. Kantorowicz, *The King's Two
Bodies* (Princeton, NJ: Princeton University Press, 1957).
[68] The distinctive lesions of Kaposi's sarcoma could be seen to act as a marker in this case,
although evidence of an individual's homosexuality alone was often enough to warrant
suspicion of HIV positivity. See Cindy Patton, *Sex and Germs: The Politics of AIDS* (Boston,
MA: Southend Press, 1985).
[69] Girard, *Violence and the Sacred*, 5.

for the ills that have befallen his people. He has become a prime example of the human scapegoat.[70]

The potency of Girard's model for the situation of the HIV-positive individual under the Reagan administration of the 1980s is palpable. Reading between the lines, one can transpose Girard's model onto the reinscription of the incidence of HIV-AIDS in the homosexual community as symptomatic of a moral 'transgression'. In this narrative, the homosexual community becomes 'responsible' for the 'ills that have befallen [the] people', in terms of the wider infection and incidence of HIV-AIDS in the population. This redirects and defers any threat of 'reciprocal violence' arising out of the government's powerlessness to control the epidemic and the gross negligence regarding education and prevention of further infection.

Theoretically speaking, however, the scapegoat or outsider is not completely without the ability to disrupt the community. Homi Bhabha's work has persistently sought to critique the authoritarian weight of Benedict Anderson's account of the origins of nations, by asserting that the 'margins of the modern nation' have, from the beginning, been in the process of inscribing themselves as a counter-narrative.[71] Bhabha's counter-force of 'national ambivalence' finds its queer analogue in Jonathan Dollimore's notion of 'sexual dissidence'.

Dollimore's 1991 study seeks to explain

> why in our time the negation of homosexuality has been in direct proportion to its symbolic centrality; its cultural marginality in direct proportion to its cultural significance; why, also, homosexuality is so strangely integral to the selfsame heterosexual cultures which obsessively denounce it.[72]

In this respect, although there are many visible examples of the ways in which homosexuality has been presented as incompatible with the interests of the nation (e.g. in the ways in which the fall of the Roman Empire has often been associated with its relative acceptance of homosexuality),

---

[70] Ibid., 77.

[71] Homi K. Bhabha, 'DissemiNation: Time, Narrative and the Margins of the Modern Nation', *Nation and Narration* (London & New York: Routledge, 1990), 300.

[72] Dollimore Jonathan, *Sexual Dissidence: Augustine to Wilde, Freud to Foucault* (Oxford: Clarendon Press, 1991), 28.

such negative equations have also been accompanied by an alternative strain of discourse which has in some ways sought to reconcile the nation and the homosexual.

(vi) 'I too/that am a nation':[73]
The homosexual in America

In order to consider the ways in which these American poets have engaged in their poems with ideas of national identity, one must make clear a considerable number of caveats involved in conceiving of the American national psyche as a monolithic or identifiable phenomenon. While it is necessary to deal with such terminology if one wishes to consider 'American poetry' as a manageable discursive construction, it is important to avoid transforming the terms 'homosexual' and 'America' into transhistorical categories. As David Halperin has argued, sexuality is both culturally variable and historically contingent. In this respect, my approach is much indebted to the work of Eve Kosofsky Sedgwick who has argued for homosexuality as a 'process of cultural differentiation', rather than as a fixed identity or essence.[74] However, while considering the historical contingencies of homosexuality in America, this study will also attend to the continuing ideological battle that deems the homosexual to be ineligible for full and complete citizenship of his country. The 'don't ask, don't tell' policy of the American military (repealed only in 2010) is a telling index of the irreconcilable spheres of America and homosexuality that these poets were writing under during the twentieth century. As Aaron Belkin has noted, the history of sexual minorities in the military is 'about full citizenship':

> If you look at the understandings and definitions of citizenship going back for more than a thousand years, you will see that a full citizen is almost always, in every society, someone who has the right to enter into contracts, someone who has the right to own property, someone who has the right to get married, and someone who has the right to serve in the military. Gays and lesbians will never be able to lock in

---

[73] Robert Duncan, 'Poem Beginning with a Line by Pindar', *Opening of the Field* (New York: Grove Press, 1960), 64.
[74] Sedgwick, *Epistemology of the Closet*, 1–3.

their hard-won citizenship rights in other areas as long as the largest employer in the country continues to fire them.[75]

As homosexuals in America are (at the time of writing) still excluded from entering fully into the contract of marriage, it is clear that their status as American citizens is still considered to be only partial, at best. However, the poetry of Walt Whitman, among others, bears witness to a notable drive in American literature, if not in its legislation, to integrate same-sex desire into a vision of the nation.

Oliver Buckton has argued that autobiographical texts such as Whitman's *Leaves of Grass* offer 'rich opportunities for apprehending the ways in which the self is conceived of . . . in specific historical periods and social contexts'.[76] While Buckton's praise for literature as an accurate barometer of the history of identity should be tempered with an awareness of the constructed nature of the textual self, his comments are pertinent here. Whitman's epic-lyricism has made autobiography an integral part of the American epic poem.

The evolution of modern homosexuality has both relied upon and resisted the circulation of texts such as Whitman's. The role of literature in the formation and development of gay identity is well documented: David Bergman has gone so far as to contend that 'homosexuality, it is almost true to say, is a literary construct for many people'.[77] Bergman concurs here with Richard Gilman who has observed that, 'like so many other categories of the "abnormal", homosexuality has made itself known to us, at least in the beginning, in the form of legend'.[78] Certainly, Oscar Wilde's construction as a figure of homosexual martyrdom after his 1895 trial, alongside the homoerotic tones of Whitman's epic verse, conspired to create a powerful cultural heritage on both sides of the Atlantic. For the would-be homosexual poet at the turn of the century, there was certainly no lack of literary precedent to turn to draw on. As David Bergman has noted, 'A literature which gives Whitman, Melville,

---

[75] Excerpted proceedings from a panel convened by the National Sexuality Resource Center at San Francisco State University, San Francisco, CA, January 22, 2004. See *Sexuality Research & Social Policy*, September 2004, 1.378, www.gaymilitary.ucsb.edu/PressClips/04_09_NSRC.htm, site visited on 4/4/11.

[76] Oliver Buckton, *Secret Selves: Confession and Same-Sex Desire in Victorian Autobiography* (Chapel Hill & London: University of North Carolina Press, 1998), 1.

[77] David Bergman, *Gaiety Transfigured: Gay Self-Representation in American Literature* (Madison, WI: University of Wisconsin Press, 1991), 6.

[78] Richard Gilman, *Decadence: The Strange Life of an Epithet* (New York: Farrar Straus & Giroux, 1979), 13.

Thoreau, and Henry James significant places cannot be said to under-represent homosexual writers'.[79] This study proposes that a genealogy might be traced in those epic poems that have engaged with this powerful legacy. The poets that I consider have sought not only to liberate the homosexual from the Wildean role of outsider, stranger and martyr, but also to place him at the very centre of America, as citizen and spokesperson.

Of those historical moments that have reflected how homosexuality has been constructed as a threat to the institutions of modern nationhood, Wilde's trial is exemplary for the ways in which it reveals how homosexuality can speak about what was going wrong with heterosexuality. If, at the turn of the century, homosexuality was figured as a threat to the realms of matrimony and the family, the perception of its increased incidence coincided with the mobility, anonymity, and demographic and cultural mixing that made the modern city a site where traditional value systems were increasingly being put in question. Amidst these cultural insecurities of a *fin de siècle* culture, the demarcations of gender, family and sexuality needed to be reasserted. The conjuring of this visible homosexual identity from the relative invisibilities of sexual practice in the late nineteenth century, however, also created an awareness of the emerging subculture that was resistant both to the cultural imperative for visibility, and to the strict classifications of the medical model of homosexuality.[80] As the evidence from the American Newport scandal of 1919–20 suggests,[81] the literature of sexologists such as Richard von Krafft-Ebing (which has been seen by so many theorists as crucial to the transformation of sodomy from a criminal act into a perverted identity), received only a relatively limited circulation through scholarly journals among the academic echelons of society.[82] In reality, such discourse played a relatively minor role (at most) in the shaping of the identities and categories of most

[79] Bergman, *Gaiety Transfigured*, 11.
[80] 'Anxieties about an escalating, or at least bolder deviant presence in twentieth-century America were containable precisely so long as those who didn't conform to type remained invisible, leaving the field to the detectable 'fairy', not the disguised but possibly ubiquitous 'homosexual' (John Loughery, *The Other Side of Silence: Men's Lives and Gay Identities* (New York: Henry Holt, 1998), 20).
[81] Between 1919 and 1920, the navy undertook an investigation of the incidence of homosexuality at the Newport Naval Training Station. See George Chauncey, *Gay New York: The Making of the Gay Male World, 1890–1940* (London: Flamingo, 1994), 145.
[82] Chauncey, *Gay New York*, 283.

of the individuals involved in a variety of homosexual practices at the time of World War I.[83]

Much more evocative for the poets considered here was the legacy of Whitmanian 'adhesiveness'. Whitman's belief that the 'hope and safety of the future' of America was only to be found in the 'intense and loving comradeship, the personal and passionate attachment of man to man'[84] was indebted to the popular nineteenth-century discourse of phrenology. 'Adhesiveness' was originally a term that had been used by phrenologists to denote a type of love that was distinct from 'amativeness', which referred to love that yielded reproduction. Defined by Orson Fowler as 'friendship, sociability, fondness for society; susceptibility of forming attachments; inclination to love and desire to be loved', adhesiveness was used to explain same-sex attachments, although it was not immune to the already burgeoning tendency to pathologize what was yet to be termed 'homosexual' behaviour. For example, an 1836 description of an adhesive relationship in the *Lancet* medical journal describes an 'excessive' attachment between two gentlemen that went so far 'as to amount to a disease':

> When the one visited the other, they slept in the same bed, sat constantly alongside of each other at table, spoke in affectionate whispers, and were, in short, miserable when separated.[85]

While the concept of adhesiveness enjoyed some social recognition in the mid-nineteenth century, by the 1870s psychiatric discourse had successfully merged adhesiveness with ideas of Uranianism or sexual inversion, as seen in the work of Karl Heinrich Ulrichs, Magnus Hirschfeld and Havelock Ellis. These new models of sexuality proposed that homosexuality was the result of some kind of congenital gender inversion.[86]

---

[83] 'Large numbers of sailors were able to have sex with men identified as "queers" without it affecting their image of themselves as normal men' (George Chauncey, 'Christian Brotherhood or Sexual Perversion? Homosexual Identities and the Construction of Sexual Boundaries in the World War I Era', *Hidden from History*, ed. Duberman, Vicinus and Chauncey (London: Penguin, 1989), 294).

[84] Walt Whitman, 'Democratic Vistas' (1871), *Complete Verse, Selected Prose*, ed. Emory Holloway (London: Nonesuch Press, 1938), 710.

[85] Robert Macnish, *Lancet*, August 1836, quoted in Michael Lynch, 'Here is Adhesiveness: From Friendship to Homosexuality', *Victorian Studies* 29 (Autumn 1985), 84.

[86] For an account of the medicalization of homosexuality, see David F. Greenberg, *The Construction of Homosexuality* (Chicago & London: University of Chicago Press, 1988), 410–14.

This shift in discourses surrounding same-sex desire goes some way to explaining Whitman's notes to his 1876 'Preface', where he explained the 'special meaning' of 'Calamus' as residing in its 'political significance',[87] with adhesiveness constituting the very binding force of democracy:

> In my opinion, it is by a fervent accepted development of comrade-ship, the beautiful and sane affection of man for man, latent in all the young fellows, north and south, east and west – it is by this, I say, and by what goes directly and indirectly along with it, that the United States of the future, (I cannot too often repeat), are to be most effectively welded together.[88]

For Whitman, 'the adhesive love, at least rivalling the amative love hitherto possessing imaginative literature', constituted the means to 'counter-balance and offset our materialistic and vulgar American democracy'.[89] Rather than the heterosexual foundations of family and reproduction, Whitman favoured such relationships as the 'most inevitable twin or counterpart' to democracy, 'without which it will be incomplete, in vain, and incapable of perpetuating itself'.[90]

The tradition of the homosexual epic is inextricably bound to the legacy bequeathed by Whitman's vision of an America bound together by 'loving comradeship'. Although one must be careful not to confuse Whitman's particular brand of homosocial and homoerotic citizenship with what would come to be known as modern homosexuality, his poetry did provide a powerful precedent for those seeking to reconcile their own desires with the requirements for cultural consensus demanded by the epic. As Robert Creeley has noted, speaking of the pioneering combination of private scope with public purpose in *Leaves of Grass*, 'if Whitman has taught me anything . . . it is that the common is personal'.[91] It is from here that this study takes its starting point, considering the legacy of Whitman's renegotiation of the dialectic between the public and the private for the modern gay poet, arguing that Whitman's original generic transgression paved the way for the homosexual poet to speak for the nation.

---

[87] Whitman, preface to *Leaves of Grass* (1876), *Complete Verse, Selected Prose*, 734.
[88] Ibid.
[89] Whitman, 'Democratic Vistas', *Complete Verse, Selected Prose*, 710.
[90] Ibid.
[91] Creeley, introduction to *Whitman: Poems Selected by Robert Creeley*, 7.

Whitman's importance to what we might call a homosexual tradition has been well documented, with Robert K. Martin's seminal study, *The Homosexual Tradition in American Poetry* (1979), setting out to delineate the poet's influence on 11 gay poets.[92] Although my book does not purport to be an account of a Whitmanian lineage, it owes much to the pioneering example of Martin, whose work in the late 1970s sought to outline a genealogy of 'gay liberation', rather than merely offering studies of 'any author who happens to be homosexual'.[93] Distancing itself from those studies composed of 'homosexual incidents' in literature,[94] Martin's project was one of the first to consider the extent to which a poet's 'awareness of himself as a homosexual . . . affected how and what he wrote'.[95] As Jared Gardner notes in his review of the 1998 expanded edition of *The Homosexual Tradition*, Martin's book 'reoriented completely the language in which American poetry was discussed', insisting that, 'if Whitman's love is silenced, the tradition that follows is unmoored'.[96]

Since first proposing his thesis in *A Critical Guide to Leaves of Grass* (1957), James E. Miller has devoted his academic career to advancing his belief that the distinct achievement of Whitman lies in the 'epic reach of his lyric voice'.[97] Miller proposes that, in writing *Leaves of Grass*, Whitman created a new American literary form that combines the intensely private with the expansively public mode of the epic – the 'personal epic'.[98] Over 20 years later, in *The American Quest for a Supreme Fiction: Whitman's Legacy in the Personal Epic* (1979), Miller continued to focus on Whitman's generic transgression. The focus of this new study was to trace the influence of the 'personal epic' on America's 'classic long poems', exploring the interrelationships between Whitman's work and poems such as John Berryman's *Dream Songs*.

---

[92] Robert K. Martin, *The Homosexual Tradition in American Poetry*. Martin published an expanded edition in 1998 to address the African American tradition as well as the impact of AIDS.

[93] Martin, introduction to *The Homosexual Tradition*, xv.

[94] Martin cites Leslie Fiedler's *Love and Death in the American Novel* as an example of such studies.

[95] Martin, *The Homosexual Tradition*, xv.

[96] Jared Gardner, review of *The Homosexual Tradition in American Poetry: An Expanded Edition* (Iowa City, IA: University of Iowa Press, 1998), *American Literature* 71.4 (1999), 817–18.

[97] Scott MacPhail, 'Lyric Nationalism: Whitman, American Studies, and the New Criticism', *Texas Studies in Literature and Language* 44.2 (Summer 2002), 136. See also James E. Miller Jr, *The American Quest for a Supreme Fiction: Whitman's Legacy in the Personal Epic* (Chicago, IL: University of Chicago Press, 1979), and *Leaves of Grass: America's Lyric Epic of Self and Democracy* (New York: Twayne, 1992).

[98] Miller, preface to *The American Quest*, ix.

This study is indebted to Miller's identification of Whitman's genre-bending for suggesting the ways in which this reimagining of the relationship between the public and the private makes it possible for homosexual poets to renegotiate the epic poem. Building on Miller's study, I explore the implications for a homosexual male tradition of what Miller calls Whitman's 'invention of the heroic tribal (or national) poem [that] incorporates both the private confession and the public chant, the lyric voice and the epic vision'.[99] By incorporating the private mode into the epic, I argue, Whitman's experiments opened up the epic to minority voices. However, in seeking to determine the extent to which Whitman's hybrid form opened up the discourse of epic to homosexual content, I depart from Miller, who pays only passing attention in *The American Quest* to the sexuality of both the homosexual and heterosexual poets he discusses.[100] In this sense, my methodology combines the parameters of Martin's venture with Miller's original thesis in order to address the omissions of both projects.

In his 2002 essay, 'Lyric Nationalism: Whitman, American Studies, and the New Criticism', Scott MacPhail continued the work of Miller and Martin. In seeking to account for the coincidence of Whitman's critical ascendance with the rise of New Criticism and its bias towards genre-based criticism, MacPhail's essay chimes with my own concerns in considering the issues attending to national poetry to be grounded in questions of genre and its ideological underpinnings. MacPhail's deconstruction echoes D. H. Lawrence's infamous reading of Whitman, which suggested that his reputation was due to a disproportionate swelling of his poetic achievement.[101] Similarly, Leslie Fiedler contended in 1955 that Whitman had been mistakenly adopted as the founding father of a tradition of American national poetry.[102] However, whereas Lawrence and Fiedler's readings of Whitman are distinctly iconoclastic, MacPhail's thesis is sympathetic, arguing that Whitman's elevation to the position of national poet is due to the impressive 'epic reach of his lyric voice'.

---

[99] Miller, *Leaves of Grass: America's Lyric Epic of Self and Democracy*, 10.

[100] The relative absence of commentary on homosexuality in *The American Quest* is noteworthy for the emphasis Miller places on homosexuality elsewhere, especially in his readings of T. S. Eliot's work. James E. Miller, *T. S. Eliot's Personal Waste Land: Exorcism of the Demons* (University Park, London: Pennsylvania State University Press, 1977); James E. Miller, *T. S. Eliot: The Making of an American Poet: 1888–1922* (University Park, London: Pennsylvania State University Press, 2005).

[101] D. H. Lawrence, *Studies in Classic American Literature* (Garden City, NY: Doubleday, 1953).

[102] Leslie Fiedler, *An End to Innocence: Essays on Culture and Politics* (Boston, MA: Beacon, 1955), 157.

With Whitman at the foundation, the tradition of American national poetry, MacPhail proposes, is based upon a breaking down of generic boundaries as opposed to an adherence to conventions. This reading concurs with my own analysis of the distinctiveness of the American epic poem. Whitman's 'lyric nationalism' (as MacPhail terms the resulting hybrid form) certainly has important implications for both the homosexual poet seeking to master the epic form, and for the American poetic tradition in general. If 'all American poetry . . . is, in essence if not in substance, a series of arguments with Whitman',[103] the tradition of the national epic is already compromised by its pivotal figure. The implications for my genealogy are substantial. In asserting that the success of Whitman's epic voice is founded upon generic confusion, MacPhail strikes at the heart of the construction of the American epic tradition. If *Leaves of Grass*, as America's unofficial national poem, is founded upon a generic transformation, then the strict conventions of the European epic tradition become anachronistic for judging the success of an American epic.

For MacPhail, the consequence of the habitual placement of Whitman and Dickinson at the opposite poles of American national literature is that poetry is given 'the task of neutralizing contradictions in the American identity'.[104] His analysis of the coincidence of Whitman's critical elevation and the rise of New Criticism, however, does not discuss what many critics have seen as the 'neutralizing' of Whitman's homosexuality.[105] As Thomas Yingling has noted:

Myth criticism enshrined Whitman as the national bard, but insisted that his homosexuality remain either invisible or extraneous to the

---

[103] Roy Harvey Pearce, *The Continuity of American Poetry* (Middletown, CT: Wesleyan University Press, 1987), 57.

[104] MacPhail, 'Lyric Nationalism: Whitman, American Studies, and the New Criticism', 133.

[105] Emory Holloway's Pulitzer-winning biography, *Whitman: An Interpretation in Narrative* (1926) revived discussion about the ambivalent sexuality expressed in *Leaves of Grass*, following Holloway's discovery in *The Uncollected Poetry and Prose of Walt Whitman* (1921) of the original manuscript for 'Once I Passed through a Populous City' wherein the word 'man' appears instead of 'woman'. After 1975, when Robert K. Martin published his essay 'Whitman's Song of Myself: Homosexual Dream and Vision' (that would later become incorporated into *The Homosexual Tradition*), the face of Whitman criticism was indelibly altered. Joseph Cady followed Martin's lead in his 1978 essay 'Not Happy in the Capitol: Homosexuality in the *Calamus* Poems', *American Studies* 19 (1978), 5–22. For a selection of recent queer readings of Whitman, see Donald D. Kummings, *Approaches to Teaching Whitman's Leaves of Grass* (New York: MLA, 1990), and Michael Moon's *Disseminating Whitman: Revision and Corporeality in Leaves of Grass* (London: Harvard University Press, 1991).

supposedly more important nationalist concerns the discipline took as its central agenda.[106]

In renegotiating the terms of epic (Yingling suggests), same-sex desire is sacrificed to the demands of nationalist ambition. In this sense, Crane's recognition of the disciplinary force of epic discourse to 'bind us throbbing with one voice'[107] speaks of not only the erotic undertones of Whitman's community of comrades, but also the restrictive parameters of a genre that would seem not to accommodate the homosexuality of the poet, but merely leave it 'throbbing' as a sublimated presence. For critics such as Yingling, this sublimated presence is constituted by the 'homotextual' trace that results from the fact that, for gay writers, literature has been 'less a matter of self-expression and more a matter of coding'.[108]

(vii) Homotextuality

The idea that homosexuality can encode itself as a style or semiotic system is highly problematic. Although I agree in part with Yingling's suggestion that homosexual poets write differently, I want to dwell briefly on the critical pitfalls of the notion of 'homotextuality' in order to make clear my methodological departures from his otherwise instructive approach to Crane's work. The issue of homotextuality brings with it similar argumentative baggage to that of the concept of a feminine *semiotique*. Michael Warner has also noted the problems with conceiving of a shared homosexual subjectivity or sense of community, observing that 'much of lesbian and gay history has to do with non-community and dispersal rather than localization'.[109] The pitfalls of essentialism that necessarily befall those who attempt to conceive of a 'homosexual style' are coupled with the cries of the poets themselves, unwilling to have their work overshadowed by their sexual orientation. The critical hostility towards such approaches is also palpable in Harold Bloom's introduction to the Centennial edition of Crane's *Collected Poems*:

So overt and harrowing is Crane's erotic quest that attempts to analyze it from the stance of a 'homosexual poetic' seem to me quite

---

[106] Yingling, *Hart Crane and the Homosexual Text*, 6.

[107] Hart Crane, 'Cape Hatteras', *The Complete Poems of Hart Crane*, ed. Marc Simon (New York & London: Liveright, 2000) (hereafter abbreviated as *CPHC*), 83.

[108] Yingling, *Hart Crane and the Homosexual Text*, 25.

[109] Michael Warner, 'Thoreau's Bottom', *Raritan* 11 (Winter 1992), 25.

redundant, and bound to fail. Critics of that persuasion repeat ineptly what Crane conveys with mordant skill.[110]

While I disagree with Bloom's characterization of Crane's 'erotic quest' as 'overt' (because Crane's modernist aspirations make his poetics necessarily obscure, both politically and aesthetically), Bloom's condemnation of such projects is not without foundation, as early attempts to conceive of a homosexual poetic were often heavy-handed and reductive.

Since Jacob Stockinger's seminal essay of 1978, in which he coined the term 'homotextuality',[111] the notion that homosexuality could offer a system of enquiry that moved beyond a question of thematics gained much ground. The notion that one could investigate homosexuality as a *textual* system evolved out of the biographical and thematic bias of early gay and lesbian studies in the 1970s. Stockinger's original thesis, however, remains rather unhelpfully anchored to the idea of homosexuality as a fixed identity or essence, by proposing that a distinct *semiotic* of homosexuality is predicated upon the pre-existence of a 'homotext':

> Before elaborating a critical construct to deal with particular forms of textual sexuality, however, there must be reason to believe that sexuality does in fact enter into the very fabric of the text. In short before defining 'homotextuality' the existence of the 'homotext' must be determined.[112]

Stockinger's problematic distinction between the 'homotext' and 'homotextual' produces an irreconcilable yoking of thematic and structural approaches, with his emphasis on the identification of the classic *topoi* of homosexual literature undermining his own case that 'gay studies' has evolved from 'little more than thematic studies' to embrace structuralism. However, although Stockinger's focus on thematic motifs weakens his case, his discussion of homosexual journeying as an idea that resonates both geographically and psychologically illustrates the potential for a continuum between a thematic and psychoanalytic approach. The extension of what Stockinger calls the 'homotextual space', from the confines of Genet and Proust to the 'open country side', leads him

[110] Harold Bloom, introduction to *CPHC*, ed. Marc Simon, xiii.
[111] Jacob Stockinger, 'Homotextuality: A Proposal', *The Gay Academic*, ed. Louie Crew (Palm Springs: Etc. Publications, 1979), 135–51.
[112] Stockinger, 'Homotextuality', 136.

to conclude that 'the external itinerary . . . corresponds to an internal journey of self-discovery'.[113] In detailing this 'quest for self', Stockinger comes close to formulating a model for homosexual identity based upon ego formation, pre-empting critics such as David Bergman who would subsequently employ such psychoanalytic models to describe a homosexual poetic based on egolessness.[114]

The problem with Stockinger, Yingling and Bergman's models is that they seem to reduce all experiences of same-sex desire to a singular phenomenon. As Crane himself asserted, homosexuality is 'modified in the characteristics of the image by each age in each civilisation'.[115] The experience of homosexuality in Ginsberg's poems cannot be conflated with that of Crane, or W. H. Auden, or Frank O'Hara: each inhabits a distinct subjectivity and cultural moment. However, it is the *intersections* of these divergent lines of gay experience that interest me when looking at the feasibility of positing a generalized 'homo-ness' (to borrow a phrase from Leo Bersani). As Bersani himself has said, 'the most varied, even antagonistic, identities meet transversely'.[116]

In examining these poems in some depth in the forthcoming chapters, I hope to draw some conclusions about the shared preoccupations of these men who have tried to write 'America' from the vantage point of the homosexual male poet. However, it is the *differences* between the poets' approaches to the epic project that draws my attention. I want to interrogate the changing social contexts that have made it more, or less, acceptable to speak about the American nation from a position of sexual minority. In arguing that the homosexual epic represents a distinct approach to a nation's most privileged literary mode, I am concerned, in particular, to highlight the ways in which poets might be seen to produce texts that reflect the ideological constraints of being a homosexual subject at different points in American history.

While the poets I consider here are united (by way of Whitman) in their re-evaluation of the relationship between the public and the private, each poem, as we shall see, demonstrates a distinct approach to issues of tradition and formal innovation, sexual candidness and the democratization of poetry. In this sense, I depart from Yingling's approach to Crane's epic; rather than mine his work for signs of coded confession, I attend

[113] Ibid., 144.
[114] Bergman, *Gaiety Transfigured*.
[115] Crane to Winters, 29 May 1927, *O My Land*, 338.
[116] Bersani, *Homos*, 9

to the ways in which his poetry engages in a dialogue with citizenship discourse of the 1920s as a way of talking about homosexuality.

It is from this point that I begin my study, opening with a discussion of Crane's avowedly epic project, *The Bridge*, before moving on to consider the more ambiguous examples of Ginsberg, Merrill and Ashbery's work. These poets, following Whitman in his call for the 'new' tradition of American epic poetry to be 'transcendent', discard the directness of the epics of 'other nations' and ascend to new heights of creativity.[117] Moving beyond the traditional retelling of wars, dynastic histories and the founding of cities, these poems illustrate a wide interpretation of the 'indirect' approach to the expression of the New World that Whitman prophesied, all developing distinctive and original idioms and reinvigorating old traditions in order to give voice to the New World.

---

[117] Whitman, preface to the 1855 version of *Leaves of Grass*, in *Complete Verse, Selected Prose*, 573.

Chapter 1

'Stranger in America': Hart Crane's Homosexual Epic

(i) *The Bridge*

This chapter explores the challenges involved in writing an epic poem by looking at the example of Hart Crane's *The Bridge* (1930). In the course of exploring the poem's genesis and production, I propose that there is a strong case for moving beyond pathological readings of the work, taking it out of its critical isolation as an example of a 'failed modernist project' and placing the poem within a broader tradition of, what I have termed, the homosexual epic. While Crane's homosexuality marginalized him during his lifetime, he has come to stand, if only posthumously, at the very centre of the tradition discussed here.[1] Within this pantheon, Crane is uniquely situated, writing with greater anxiety about his sexuality than his predecessors did, or successors would. In this way, *The Bridge* offers unique insight into the historical contingencies of writing an epic at a time when homosexuality was becoming increasingly visible, but was not yet visibly politicized.

As Christopher Nealon has argued, Crane is positioned at an important frontier in the history of homosexual writers. As a 'foundling' of American literature, Nealon argues that texts such as *The Bridge* express what he calls 'foundling' issues by focusing on issues of exile from traditional families, while simultaneously longing for nation and history.[2] Crane's poem stands as an important example in the history of homosexual

---

[1] For example, Allen Ginsberg cites the 'Atlantis' section of *The Bridge* as a 'Model Text' and 'Precursor' to 'Howl' (1956), in 'Appendix IV, Model Texts: Inspirations Precursor to "Howl"', *Howl: Original Draft Facsimile, Transcript & Variant Versions*, 175. We will see that the poem is also a significant influence for Ashbery's *Flow Chart*.

[2] Christopher Nealon, *Foundlings: Lesbian and Gay Historical Emotion before Stonewall* (Durham & London: Duke University Press, 2001).

writers, as a record of the poet's struggle to mediate between his poetic ambitions and the expression of his sexuality. Writing at a moment in history when the anxiety of revelation was a possibility that had not been available to Whitman (and would eventually, after a period of intensified persecution, dissipate significantly during the times of his successors), Crane's position in the homosexual epic tradition is unique.

Following Jared Gardner's reading of *The Bridge* through discourses of racial and sexual identity,[3] I address the position of Crane as a homosexual man in 1920s America by looking at contemporary discourses of citizenship and how these are reflected in, for example, the ways in which *The Bridge* imagines the narrative union of the poet with the Native American. I begin by looking at the dominant critical interpretations of Crane's poetry before moving on to consider the distinctive nature of the American epic, in relation to its European precedents. The second half of this chapter considers the ideological problems involved in writing a homosexual epic, exploring Whitman's legacy for Crane. Finally, I will undertake some close readings of sections from 'The Dance' section of *The Bridge* to illustrate the way Crane's poetic strategies seek to imagine the homosexual as the emblematic American citizen.

(ii) 'Stranger in America'[4]

The body of commentary that surrounds Crane's work has generally presented him as a figure of disappointment, occasionally casting this failure as 'important'[5] or even, paradoxically as 'splendid'.[6] Yvor Winters and Allen Tate were the first to propose these kinds of readings of Crane's work, which strongly partake of nineteenth-century medical constructions of homosexuality, linking Crane's suicide and poetic failure to a

---

[3] See Jared Gardner, '"Our Native Clay": Racial and Sexual Identity and the Making of Americans in *The Bridge*', *American Quarterly* 44.1 (March 1992), 24–50. Although Gardner's article does not explicitly address the idea of the epic, its project to define Crane's dialogue with American identity in the 1920s is crucial to my thinking about the ways in which Crane manipulates contemporary discourses of citizenship to construct the mythic narrative of *The Bridge*.

[4] Robert Lowell, 'Words for Hart Crane' (1959), *Robert Lowell: Collected Poems*, ed. Frank Bidart and David Gewanter (New York: Farrar, Straus and Giroux, 2003), 159.

[5] Jeffrey Walker, preface to *Bardic Ethos and the American Epic Poem* (Baton Rouge & London: Louisiana State University Press, 1989), xi.

[6] Edward Brunner, *Splendid Failure: Hart Crane and the Making of the Bridge* (Urbana, IL: University of Illinois Press, 1985).

neurosis that is seen as symptomatic of his sexuality.[7] These critical constructions perpetuate the myth of the homosexual *thanatos*, where same-sex desire is conflated with the desire (to paraphrase Thom Gunn) for one's own annihilation.[8]

After Leo Bersani's essay of 1987, 'Is the Rectum a Grave?', which firmly established queer theory's fascination with 'self-shattering', Crane became somewhat of a paradigm for what Michael Snediker calls 'queer self-dissolution', spawning a proliferation of narratives of self-destructive *jouissance*.[9] This tendency to turn to psychopathological readings of Crane's biography has given rise to the rather schizophrenic appearance of what we might call 'Crane studies'. Where once it had been occluded,[10] homosexuality has found its way to the centre of many of the most recent critical appraisals of Crane's work.[11] This critical emphasis on the Dionysian spectacle of Crane's conflicts in his romantic and creative life began with Yvor Winters' comments on the 'wreckage' of *The Bridge* in his review of the poem,[12] and is encapsulated in the title of Edward Brunner's 1985 study of Crane, *Splendid Failure: Hart Crane and the Making of The Bridge*.

While other modernist epics, such as Pound's *Cantos*, have received similar critical attention in terms of the emphasis upon their incoherencies and failings, *The Bridge* is unique in that its formal and thematic shortcomings are often cast as a symptom of Crane's sexuality, rather than attributed to his inability to achieve a successful poetic synthesis of his impulses towards the Modernist and the Whitmanian. However, if *The Bridge*'s final incoherencies are to be read in part as the product of the ideological

---

[7] For example, in 1965 Wallace Fowlie wrote, 'sexual aberration and drunkenness were the pitfalls in which [Crane's] spirit wrestled with a kind of desperation'. See Wallace Fowlie, *Love in Literature* (Bloomington, IN: Indiana University Press, 1965), 129.

[8] 'My thoughts are crowded with death/and it draws so oddly on the sexual/that I am confused/confused to be attracted/by, in effect, my own annihilation' (Thom Gunn, 'In Time of Plague', *Collected Poems* (London & Boston: Faber, 1993), 463).

[9] Michael Snediker, 'Hart Crane's Smile', *Modernism/Modernity* 12.4 (2005), 630.

[10] Woods comments on this critical bias, including a list of works on Crane that contain no reference to his homosexuality, in *Articulate Flesh*, 244, n. 3.

[11] Recent studies that consider Crane's poetry in light of his homosexuality include Peter Nickowitz's *Rhetoric and Sexuality: The Poetry of Hart Crane, Elizabeth Bishop and James Merrill* (New York: Palgrave Macmillan, 2006), where the author looks at the extent to which homosexual desire compels poets such as Crane to formulate new ways of expressing themselves as their 'poetic language serves simultaneously to reveal and to conceal a dramatization of the poet's sexual, personal and artistic identity' (7).

[12] 'With Mr. Crane's wreckage in view, it seems highly unlikely that any writer of comparable ability will struggle with [the Whitmanian inspiration] again' (Winters' review of *The Bridge*, cited in Weber, *O My Land*, 391).

impossibility of a homosexually authored epic (as Thomas Yingling has persuasively argued),[13] then Crane's poem makes a fine starting point for my discussion of the ways in which homosexuality has renegotiated its exclusion from the epic project of telling 'the tale of tribe'.

From Crane's conception in 1923 of a poem that would express the 'mystical synthesis of "America" ',[14] to its publication in 1930, *The Bridge* became the means through which Crane could attempt not only to re-conceive of what a truly modern epic might be, but, in doing so, also to rethink his sense of self, as both poet and American citizen.[15] By utilizing contemporary citizenship discourses, Crane transformed himself from a 'stranger in America' into an emblematic American citizen and epic hero.

Robert Lowell's peculiar elegy, 'Words for Hart Crane' (1959), introduces Crane as a biographical sketch – an approach that is typical of the critical treatment received by the poet since his suicidal leap into the Gulf of Mexico. In the inverted sonnet, Lowell sketches Crane 'stalking sailors' 'by the Place de la Concorde', 'wolfing the stray lambs',[16] echoing this image of Crane as a stereotypically tragic figure of predatory homosexuality who fulfilled the destiny of his alcoholic life and failed poetic ambitions by jumping from the deck of the *Orizaba* in 1932.[17] Reading somewhat like a potted biography, the poem can do much to introduce the uninitiated reader to the main plot-points of Crane's short existence. While Lowell's poem is complicit with much of the critical sensationalism surrounding Crane in placing much of its emphasis upon sexual exploits, in recognizing the performativity of Crane's homosexuality as a 'role' of expectation to be played ('I used to play my role/of homosexual, wolfing the stray lambs'), Lowell goes someway beyond the critics and friends (such as Allen Tate) who saw Crane's homosexuality as something fatal to his poetic ambitions.[18]

---

[13] See Yingling, *Hart Crane and the Homosexual Text*, 186–226.
[14] Crane to Gorham Munson, 18 February 1923, *O My Land*, 131.
[15] For a detailed discussion of Crane's status as an American poet, see Brian M. Reed, *Hart Crane: After His Lights* (Tuscaloosa: University of Alabama Press, 2006), 17–38.
[16] Lowell, *Collected Poems*, 159.
[17] Woods presents a telling summary of the critical commentary of the 1960s and 1970s that links Crane's alcoholism to his homosexuality. See Woods, *Articulate Flesh*, 140–1. Reed takes up from where Woods leaves off, in his re-evaluation of Crane in light of developments in modern humanities scholarship since the 1980s in his recently published study, *Hart Crane: After His Lights* (2006).
[18] See Langdon Hammer, introduction to *O My Land, My Friends: The Letters of Hart Crane*, ed. Brom Weber and Langdon Hammer (New York & London: Four Walls Eight Windows, 1997), xii.

Born in Garrettsville, Ohio, in 1899, Crane left for New York City at the age of 17 with the intention of preparing to enter college. His formal education, however, was never to be resumed, and the poet spent the next 7 years drifting from job to job and residence to residence, as the friends who generously offered up their hospitality quickly, and almost inevitably, grew tired of Crane's drinking and erratic behaviour.[19] His already desperate financial situation was not helped by his refusal to deviate for too long from his chosen vocation. As Lowell frames it, Crane's 'profit' for following his poetic vision was often a 'pocket with a hole', leaving the young poet looking for 'bed and board' with friends and fellow writers in a bid not to have to return to the stifling fold of his father's successful confectionery business in Ohio.

This constant sense of displacement is figured from the outset of *The Bridge*. Its opening epigraph, taken from the Book of Job, echoes Crane's own sense of unrelenting motion, through Satan's account of his restless wanderings 'going to and fro in the earth,/and from walking up and down in it' (*CPHC*, 41). Crane found himself journeying from his father's factory in Cleveland, Ohio, to New York, Paterson, the Isle of Pines, Hollywood, Europe, and finally to Mexico, and this almost constant travelling reflected a sense of not belonging that would come to figure strongly in his negotiation of the epic genre. As Yingling suggests, *The Bridge* issues from this 'problem of motion' (which is also the 'problem of the modern') and its proem is marked by its search for a 'point of stasis that will no longer be the point of dip and pivot'.[20] In a sense, Crane's quest for a model of citizenship that could deliver him from this and his role of 'stranger in America' comes to define his overall quest in writing *The Bridge*.

Lowell's poem for Crane revised an earlier version of the poem that was written in 1950 for Stephen Spender, whose sexual tastes, like Crane's, were an open secret in literary circles.[21] This earlier version was intended to be spoken to a 'Stranger from England',[22] and in this sense, the themes of outsider-hood, both in a national and sexual sense, are retained in the version for Crane that appeared in *Life Studies* in 1959. The continuity between the versions of the poems is significant in that it suggests Lowell's

---

[19] For a detailed account of Crane's life, see Clive Fisher, *Hart Crane: A Life* (New Haven, CT & London: Yale University Press, 2002).

[20] Yingling, *Hart Crane and the Homosexual Text*, 191.

[21] A version of Lowell's poem entitled, 'Epitaph for a Fallen Poet', appeared in *Partisan Review* 20 (1953), 39.

[22] Lowell, *Collected Poems*, 1037.

preoccupation in the poem with the figure of the outsider. In this respect Lowell's portrait of a 'stranger in America' is peculiarly resonant with Crane's sense of himself both as a homosexual threatened with exile from his literary community (for writing the 'wrong kind of modernism', as Tate might have called it),[23] and as an aesthetic exile from the high-modernist pessimism of 'soap-eaters' such as Eliot. Although this phrase is almost certainly spoken to one of Crane's imagined stray 'sailors', Lowell's figure introduces themes of nationhood and strangeness that are crucial to considering the problems of thinking about a homosexual epic. For if Crane was marginalized, economically speaking, by choosing the hand-to-mouth existence of the poet, his sexual identity also rendered him an 'alien' in the ideological eyes of 1920s America. As Thomas Yingling has noted, during Crane's lifetime, 'homosexuality [was] an inadmissible center from which to write about American life'.[24]

(iii) Redefining the epic for America

Writing in the same year as Lowell published his poem, Frank O'Hara's mock manifesto, 'Personism', testifies to the universality, rather than the marginality, of Crane's writing, quipping, 'after all, only Whitman and Crane and Williams, of the American poets, are better than the movies'.[25] Far from Yingling's 'inadmissible center',[26] O'Hara suggests, albeit rather playfully, that Crane's poetry issued from a place that could, alongside the formidable figures of fellow epic poets Whitman and Williams, issue a challenge to rival the universal attraction of mass entertainment.

Despite its camp deflation of poetry, O'Hara's one-liner also suggests much about the role of the poet in the modern world. In pitching poetry against the cinema, O'Hara highlights the ways in which the latest Hollywood epic might be seen to have displaced the role of poet as myth-maker, with the 'heavenly dimensions and reverberations and iconoclasms!'[27] of the silver screen becoming the more popular domain for articulating the exceptionalism of the nation, where once this epic

---

[23] See Langdon Hammer, preface to *Hart Crane & Allen Tate: Janus-Faced Modernism* (Princeton, NJ: Princeton University Press, 1993), xii.

[24] Yingling, *Hart Crane and the Homosexual Text*, 27.

[25] Frank O'Hara, 'Personism: A Manifesto', *'Why I am Not a Painter' and Other Poems*, ed. Mark Ford (Manchester: Carcanet, 2003), 89.

[26] Yingling, *Hart Crane and the Homosexual Text*, 27.

[27] O'Hara, 'To the Film Industry in Crisis', *'Why I am Not a Painter' and Other Poems*, 37–8.

project had been the task of the poet.[28] Crane had summed up this sense
of crisis for modern poetry in his lyric of 1920, 'Porphyro in Akron':
'In this town, poetry's a/Bedroom occupation', he laments (*CPHC*,
150). Where once the epic had been the domain for the articulation of
America's exceptionalism, now the latest Hollywood feature displaces it
as the medium for expressing the myth of the nation, and the poet is
relegated to the private domain of the 'Bedroom'.

O'Hara's words, however, rather than forecasting the death of poetry,
suggest in some way the distinctiveness of the new modern American
epic poem. The epic of the New World is, and must be, very different
from, those of its Old World European ancestors. The American epic
project was always about a new nation and its founding myths, but by the
twentieth century it had become a project concerned with the expression of new ages; it is the world of technological advance and the sexual
revolution that informs the epic projects of poets such as Crane and
Ginsberg. The articulation of this new age displaced (for Crane) the retrospective celebrations of Homer, Virgil and Milton, as the possibilities
for the 'mechanical manifestations of today as subject for lyrical, dramatic and even epic poetry' were suggested to him after reading Gorham
Munson's study of Waldo Frank.[29]

When, in 1930, Yvor Winters criticized what he saw as *The Bridge*'s epic
ambitions, he had firmly in mind the European traditions of Virgil and
Dante as the yardstick against which to measure Crane's efforts. Winters
claimed that:

> The book cannot be called an epic, in spite of its endeavour to create
> and embody a national myth, because it has no narrative framework
> and so lacks the formal unity of an epic.[30]

While Winters' criticism of the poem is part of the much broader
and more complex issue of his problems with Crane's relationship to
Whitman, his conception of the epic in this review does not take account

---

[28] 'Nobody should experience anything they don't need to, if they don't need poetry bully
for them. I like the movies too. And after all, only Whitman and Crane and Williams,
of the American poets, are better than the movies' (O'Hara, 'Personism: A Manifesto',
'Why I am Not a Painter' and Other Poems, 89).

[29] Crane to Gorham Munson, 18 February 1923, *O My Land*, 131.

[30] Yvor Winters, 'The Progress of Hart Crane', *Critical Essays on Hart Crane*, ed. David R.
Clark (Boston: G.K Hall & Co, 1982), 102. This review of *The Bridge* first appeared in
Poetry 36 (June 1930), 153–65.

of the need for the American epic to move beyond its European precursors. This kind of 'tick-box' classification of genre, where 'formal unity' is a requirement for a poem to qualify as an epic, is just the kind of rigid critical framework that is unhelpful when considering Crane's dialogue with the genre – rooted as it was in a reconsideration of the very feasibility of a modern epic which could discard the 'traditional qualifications and pedantic trappings' of the traditional epic form.[31]

Crane showed himself to be acutely aware of these problems of conceiving of a truly modern epic poem. In a letter of 4 June 1930, responding to Winters' scathing review of *The Bridge*, Crane asserts:

> Your primary presumption that *The Bridge* was proffered as an epic has no substantial foundation. You knew quite well that I doubt that our present stage of cultural development is so ordered yet as to provide the means or method for such an organic manifestation as that.[32]

Crane goes on to add that 'when we do have an "epic" it need not necessarily incorporate a personalized "hero" ', emphasizing his willingness to radically reconsider the form. He continues:

> Perhaps any modern equivalent of the old epic form should be called by some other name, for certainly, as I see it, the old definition cannot cover the kind of poem I am trying to write except on certain fundamental points . . . The old narrative form, then, with its concomitant species of rhetoric, is obviously unequal to the task.[33]

However, in a letter to his patron, Otto Kahn in September 1927, Crane had compared *The Bridge* to Virgil's *The Aeneid*, signalling, alongside the difficulties of its composition, a realization of the scope and the potential of his own poem as a national literary document. Crane writes:

> *The Aeneid* was not written in two years – nor in four, and in more than one sense I feel justified in comparing the historic and cultural scope of the Bridge to this great work. It is at least a symphony with an epic theme.

It is important to note that Crane speaks of an epic *theme*, rather than of form or structure. As his original intentions to present a history of

---

[31] Crane to Winters, 4 June 1930, *O My Land*, 428.
[32] Ibid., 427–30.
[33] Ibid.

his nation quickly became more organic and symphonic in form,[34] he found himself unable to write to the almost chronological structure he had originally imposed, aiming instead at 'an assimilation of this experience, a more organic panorama'.[35] The 'myth of America' that he saw the poem as 'handling' was comprised, he said, of 'thousands of strands [that] have had to be searched out, sorted, and interwoven. In a sense I have had to do a good deal of pioneering myself'.[36] In the same letter, Crane speaks quite clearly of writing 'an epic of the modern *consciousness*' (my emphasis), implying that he had come to think of *The Bridge* as no conventional epic poem. This is illustrated by his use of Pocahontas, not as a founding myth around which to build the narrative of his poem, but as just another element in his montage of historical and contemporary references to create this 'symphony' of American experience.

Comprised of 15 poems, *The Bridge* is divided into eight sections of differing lengths, with an additional prefatory proem, 'To Brooklyn Bridge'. With its unruly organization, Crane's poem would seem to share little in common with the organization of the classical epic. Its irregular structure certainly echoes Crane's wish to create a 'mystical synthesis' – the poem meanders through voices, themes and styles in a manner similar to that of Eliot's *The Waste Land*. However, the narrative refuses to anchor the reader in the dates and facts that would convey a nation's history, opting instead to 'accrete, modify, and interrelate moments of emotional vision'.[37] Turning away from existing taxonomies, Crane's poem stands as a record of his quest to reconsider the epic and he invokes the conventions of the genre in order to innovate and modify. His juxtaposition of the terms 'epic' and 'consciousness' suggests a scope for the poem that moves beyond the boundaries of the European epic poem; the traditional narrative and epic hero are displaced by a more organic form that presents Crane's own mind as the key to the modern consciousness.

---

[34] On discarding the chronological form, Crane commented to his patron, Kahn, 'It seemed altogether ineffective, from the poetic standpoint, to approach this material from the purely chronological historic angle – beginning with, say, the landing of The Mayflower, continuing with a resumé of the Revolution through the conquest of the West, etc. One can get this viewpoint in any history primer' (Crane to Otto Kahn, 12 September 1927, *O My Land, My Friends*, 345).

[35] Ibid.

[36] Ibid.

[37] R. P. Blackmur, 'New Thresholds, New Anatomies: Notes on a Text of Hart Crane' (1935), *Hart Crane: A Collection of Critical Essays*, ed. Alan Trachtenberg (London: Prentice Hall, 1982), 274.

In this sense, Crane's poetry might suggest a connection between generic 'perversity' and sexuality. As Brian Reed has noted, Crane's formal innovations are not offered for their own sake, but rather function as markers of sexual 'deviancy'.[38] This relationship between form and sexuality, however, should not be confused with the concept of homotextuality (as I touched upon in the introductory chapter). Instead, Reed proposes a historically specific relationship between Crane's generic experiments and the way in which the tropes of aestheticism had become unsafe after the Wilde trial.[39] Crane's move to distance himself from the now obsolete mode of *fin de siècle* camp echoes a broader cultural shift in early twentieth-century America, which saw a move away from European heritages, in favour of a distinctly American identity. Pioneering an American style of epic was just part of this political and cultural programme, although it has now come to signify a standard concept in American literature.

(iv) America versus Europe

The American epic differs from those of the European tradition by being about prospective nation-building, rather than retrospective celebration of the founding of an Empire. If the Virgilian mode of epic was all about the conquering of new territories, leading to the creation of the progeny that would found the new nation, America's version of this founding myth is complicated by the presence of Pocahontas, where the potential progeny of Smith and the native squaw threaten tribal definition.[40] The American founding myth is invested in distinguishing itself from its European precedents by moving away from the biologically based consummation of the Old World epic tales. It is here that the distinctive role for the poet of the American nation emerges. Where Virgil writes *after* the fact, the dynastic founding of the American epic mode can take place both imaginatively and prospectively. As Whitman contended, 'The theme is creative and has vista'.[41]

---

[38] Reed, *After His Lights*, 50–1.

[39] Ibid.

[40] Gardner's essay takes note of this additional complication to the idea of American citizenship, calling attention to Crane's presentation of a 'halfbreed' in the 'Indiana' section of the poem as the poet's way of following out 'the fatal implications of a traditional biological reading of Pocahontas to a conception of an American race', where the idea of a pure race is impossible to defend on the basis of the nation's traditional founding myth. See Gardner, 'Our Native Clay', 41–3.

[41] Whitman, preface to *Leaves of Grass* (1855), *Complete Verse, Selected Prose*, 573.

The American poets can conjure the moment of the nation's founding as both a prophetic and historical moment simultaneously. As William Carlos Williams has said, 'a new world/is only a new mind' and early twentieth-century poets were beginning to discover that America's history was as much an *imagined* history as it was about the landing of the founding Pilgrim fathers and the Mayflower. It is in these possibilities of imaginative dynastic founding that we can begin to see how America was uniquely 'up for grabs' for the homosexual poet with epic ambitions. The construction of American citizenship allows for the acquisition of national identity: one can *become* American in a way that brings into sharp relief the importance of a non-biological model of citizenship that challenges the epic heritage of the European Old World. Thus, what it means to be American is still up for discussion in a way that, arguably, makes for a more accommodating climate to those otherwise branded as 'alien'.

(v) Queering the epic

My thinking about the ideological assumptions of epic is much indebted to Thomas Yingling's discussion of the cultural authority inherent in the genre and the problems this poses for the would-be homosexual epic poet. Devoting an entire chapter of his study, *Hart Crane and the Homosexual Text* (1990), to a discussion of Crane's epic ambitions, Yingling contends that, 'it is not difficult to imagine how the imperative to national consensus has been wholly incompatible with the projects of homosexual writing'.[42] What needs to be stressed is the extent to which the epic 'genre' here implies the presence of cultural imperatives; as Yingling points out, the epic can be seen to take 'the definition of cultural value as its conscious center'.[43]

Michael Bernstein's discussion of the dominant impulses of the epic voice is also helpful in thinking about the dilemmas facing the homosexual poet. In his analysis of the 'family likeness' to be found in epic verse, Bernstein (writing in 1980) concludes that a 'true' epic must be seen to provide 'models of exemplary conduct':

> The epic presents a narrative of its audience's own cultural, historical, or mythic heritage, providing models of exemplary conduct . . . The dominant voice narrating the poem will . . . not bear the trace of a

---

[42] Yingling, *Hart Crane and the Homosexual Text*, 196.
[43] Ibid., 194.

single sensibility; instead it will function as a spokesman for values generally acknowledged as significant for communal stability and social well-being. Within the fiction of the poem, the dominant, locatable source of narration will not be a particular individual (the poet), but rather the voice of the community's heritage 'telling itself'.[44]

The possibilities for the homosexual poet to speak with the authentic voice of singularity would seem to be overridden by the ideological demands for universality that Bernstein outlines. These criteria immediately withhold epic authority from the poet who does not hold common cultural ground, or who, without such natural 'representability', will not discipline his voice to commonality. This is an aesthetic demand that we might perhaps compare to Eliotic 'impersonality'. However, it is not a matter of suppressing the personality of the poet from the text. Rather, the homosexual poet seeking successfully to tackle the epic form must, under Bernstein's criteria, adopt the mask of the heterosexual norm. However, Crane (to paraphrase his own poem, 'Legend') was not quite so 'ready for repentance' (*CPHC*, 3), and sought instead to authorize his own voice by turning to the example that Whitman had set.

If the ideology underlying the discourse of epic would seem to preclude a homosexual poet from ever successfully ventriloquizing such 'representability', we might then ask what a homosexual epic would look like that bypasses these ideological demands? Might the 'spectacular' or 'important failures'[45] that Jeffrey Walker has spoken of stand as indexes of the power of conventional expectation, where the constraints imposed upon the homosexual poet with epic ambitions by the governing mythologies of his genre predetermine the success of his poetic endeavours? If *The Bridge* is generally conceived of as a failed epic, is this 'failure' imagined purely in generic terms, and, if so, to what extent should we conceive of these generic constraints as a symptom of a residual strain of homophobia in American criticism?

While the argument for Whitman's melding of 'the private confession and the public chant, the lyric voice and the epic vision'[46] has been examined by critics such as James Miller, a deconstruction of the *ideological*

---

[44] Michael Bernstein, *The Tale of the Tribe: Ezra Pound and the Modern Verse Epic* (Princeton, NJ: Princeton University Press, 1980), 14.

[45] Jeffrey Walker, preface to *Bardic Ethos and the American Epic Poem* (Baton Rouge & London: Louisiana State University Press, 1989), xi.

[46] James Miller, *Leaves of Grass: America's Lyric-Epic of Self and Democracy* (New York: Twayne, 1992), 10.

functions behind such genre-bending, and how this kind of move might be seen to make way for the homosexual epic, has yet to be undertaken. Such a critical stance involves a denaturalization of our understanding of the genre of epic. Past attempts to evaluate the history of the American epic have been less than congenial to homosexual readings. Although James Miller has repeatedly advocated reading *The Waste Land* in terms of its buried homosexuality, his evaluation of *The Bridge* does little to account for the relationship between Crane's textual crisis and his own sexual desires.[47]

Approaching *The Bridge* as a textual record of generic innovation, Brian Reed's study of Crane's poetry, *Hart Crane: After His Lights* (2006) revaluates the poet in light of recent developments in literary theory and scholarship. Reed proposes that Crane's 'generic perversity' is the result of a historically specific moment in homosexual history, when the *fin de siècle* mannerisms of aestheticism were no longer a safe haven for a homosexual writer.[48] Seeking to extend the ways in which a queer writer could articulate his desires, Reed sees Crane as simultaneously invoking and undermining the decadent style of those such as Wilde and Swinburne in order to fashion a new mode of queer expression.[49] Advocating an approach to Crane that is 'neither nostalgic nor regressive',[50] *After His Lights* undertakes a thorough rethinking of Crane's legacy, questioning, in turn, his categorization as an 'American', 'Queer' and 'Modernist' – all labels that Reed approaches with caution as groupings that 'obfuscate . . . the origins, character, and aspirations of the poet's work'.[51] While there is no arguing with Reed's contention that Crane's work has been reduced by the various labels imposed upon it, I still believe that placing Crane in the 'Queer' camp is not an obstacle to understanding his ambitions but central to understanding his aspirations as a writer. Similarly, rather than avoiding such labels as 'American', it is the way in which Crane's poems negotiated such categories that is important.

Of all the books devoted to Crane's poetry since the 1960s, Thomas Yingling's *Hart Crane and the Homosexual Text: New Thresholds, New Anatomies*

---

[47] Miller, *T.S. Eliot's Personal Waste Land* (1977) and *T.S. Eliot: The Making of an American Poet* (2005).

[48] Reed, *After His Lights*, 50–1.

[49] Reed uses Crane's first published poem, 'C 33' (with its title a reference to Wilde's cell number at Reading Gaol) as an illustration of Crane's negotiations with a homosexual literary tradition. The title of the poem offers a coded reference to the British decadent style that (Reed argues) its contents inadequately mime. See Reed, 44–7.

[50] Reed, *After His Lights*, 9.

[51] Ibid., 10.

(1990) is the most noteworthy for this study for its lengthy consideration of Crane's negotiation of the epic mode and how it is structured by the tensions between private homosexual knowledge and public poetic performance. However, I can't quite agree with Thomas Yingling's comments on 'how well Crane effaces his homosexuality in *The Bridge*'.[52] Rather than becoming 'the unconscious of the text', I would argue that homosexuality comes to function quite centrally in the poem. The textual implications of the tensions between homosexual subjectivity and national identity are everywhere apparent in *The Bridge* and through his manipulation of contemporary discourses of national identity, Crane insists upon the inscription, rather than encryption, of his sexuality. Furthermore, while *The Bridge* pre-empts the concerns of more recent queer theorists such as Eve Kosofsky Sedgwick, in its attempt to present Crane's sexual identity as something that does not marginalize him, Crane employs the discourse of citizenship available to him at the time to recast the Pocahontas myth as a quasi-Girardian narrative that culminates in the union of red and white man, facilitated through the intermediary female figure of Pocahontas, working to imagine the homosexual male as the ideal American citizen.

Although Crane struggled through what Yingling called a 'long period of nonwriting',[53] the final text of *The Bridge* stands as the record of Crane's challenge to the exclusions of epic's generic requirements. Cultural anthropologist Eric Gans' contention that lyric 'creates a world that permits the imaginary fulfilment [of desire/s] in the context of objective unfufillment',[54] forms a useful framework with which to read Crane's renegotiation of the epic genre. By utilizing a Whitmanian voice that fuses both epic and lyric concerns, *The Bridge* creates a textual space for the reconception of the homosexual in relation to the national body. Reawakening what Gans terms the 'originary' function of the lyric voice,[55] Crane's attempt to *fuse* the lyric voice with the ambitions and the structure of epic situates the poem within a tradition that not only follows the Parian patriotism of Archilochus' lyric foundations, but also continues in the footsteps of Whitman's forging of a new and very American style of epic poem.[56]

---

[52] Yingling, *Hart Crane and the Homosexual Text*, 199.

[53] The poems produced during *The Bridge*'s 'nonwriting' can be seen to bear testament to a crisis of authority. See Yingling, *Hart Crane and the Homosexual Text*, 188.

[54] Personal correspondence with Eric Gans, 31 January 2003.

[55] Gans argues that the lyric was originally used, in the work of Archilochus, to express political resentment. See Gans, *The End of Culture*, 271.

[56] Gans argues that Archilochus promoted the colonial interests of his native island of Paros in a series of verses, one of which elegises a shipwreck that claimed the lives of a number of his fellow citizens. *The End of Culture*, 271.

Gans' framework is part of the recent developments in anthropology that have sought to account for the emergence of literary genres. According to Gans, the birth of the lyric form can be seen to emerge from Archilochus' abandonment of the heroic (and thus epic) ethic, placing himself apart from the pan-hellenism of the Homeric epic form. Greek lyric thus begins, according to Gans, with the 'organized expression of the less fortunate'.[57] While epic gives expression to a universal culture, the 'lyric' subject defines itself through its expression of a tribal cause – in Archilochus' case the cause of his island people. However, this does not distinguish the two forms as clearly as might first appear. As Gans imagines:

> The lyric subject, who expresses an individual desire as significant in itself, can become the spokesman of a political faction – not necessarily a popular one – because, in effect, such a subject is *per se* a 'political' individual, one whose desires are of concern to the community.[58]

While I concur with Yingling's assertion that, at the time Crane was writing, homosexuality was a discourse that stood in direct contradiction to 'the very things the epic is called into being to address',[59] I would argue that Crane's poetics do not ultimately accede to the generic requirements of the European epic tradition. Rather than submerge his homosexuality as those 'signals dispersed in veils' of 'The Harbor Dawn' (*CPHC*, 53), Crane's text works to modify the genre for the expression of what Gans calls 'individual desire', inscribing his sexuality throughout *The Bridge*.

The Bridge was conceived within the context of a 1920s America that was preoccupied with its cultural project of defining its national identity. It answers the call of the dominant culture to 'enunciate a new cultural synthesis of values in terms of our America',[60] while paradoxically issuing from a poet whose authority to create an epic is, historically and ideologically speaking, compromised by his identity as a homosexual. *The Bridge* constitutes an important effort to integrate a range of 'unofficial' American histories into the fabric of the American epic. Pre-dating the 'critical fictions' that Michelle Wallace has spoken of as texts that seek to

---

[57] Gans, *The End of Culture*, 272.
[58] Ibid.
[59] Yingling, *Hart Crane and the Homosexual Text*, 199.
[60] Crane to Otto Kahn, 3 December 1925, *O My Land*, 213.

'remake, demystify, and transform the character of history as the master narrative',[61] the 'new cultural synthesis' that Crane spoke of achieving is, in part, a quasi-reclamatory process that seeks to address the exclusions and omissions of America's national history.

Crane's employment of the Pocahontas myth in 'The Dance' section of *The Bridge* illustrates the more general shift in American culture of the time, away from the inherited Old World cultural economy of Europe and towards the currency of the Native American Indian as a potential symbol of the American nation. As Jared Gardner has noted, Crane's rewriting of this national myth seeks to identify 'the nation's Indian inheritance with a myth of homosexual origins'.[62] This gesture casts Crane at the very centre of America, rather than as a marginal figure of perversion. Through his appropriation of the currency of the Native American, Crane seeks to conjoin America's spiritual inheritance with a myth of homosexual origins, to create 'a pact, new bond/Of living brotherhood!' (*CPHC*, 82) – a manoeuvre that in some ways anticipates Eve Kosofsky Sedgwick's project to recast homosexuality at the very centre of discourse and epistemological endeavour.[63]

(vi) The homosexual epic

O'Hara's poem 'Autobiographia Literaria'[64] points to some of the ideological difficulties of poetic authority for the homosexual poet. The poem's speaker proclaims the irony of the seizing of the authorial voice by his peripheral childhood self, dramatizing the inherent cultural contradictions for the homosexual writer; 'here I am, the/center of all beauty!/writing these poems!/Imagine!'.[65] The unusual confession of a childhood hatred of 'dolls' – we would not expect a male child to 'love

---

[61] However, Wallace's critical fictions do not merely enact a simple process of retrieval. Instead they attempt to both recount and recollect the process of loss and discountment, so that 'we may ultimately make a new kind of history' (Michelle Wallace, *Critical Fictions: The Politics of Imaginative Writing*, ed. Philomena Mariani (Seattle: Bay Press, 1991), 139–42).

[62] Gardner, 'Our Native Clay', 25.

[63] Sedgwick, *Epistemology of the Closet*.

[64] Frank O'Hara, 'Autobiographia Literaria', *The Collected Poems of Frank O'Hara*, ed. Donald Allen (Berkeley, Los Angeles: University of California Press, 1995), 11. Kenneth Koch believes the poem to have been written in 1949 or 1950. It was first published in *Harper's Bazaar*, October 1967.

[65] Ibid.

dolls' – is perhaps an inadvertent signal to the reader of a latent effeminacy associated with the dominant representations of the homosexual
at the time. The young O'Hara is marginalized; imagined as the child
who played 'all alone', shunned by humans and animals alike ('animals
were/not friendly and birds/flew away'). However, the alienated boy
who once played in 'a corner', now seeks to place himself at 'the center',
as writer of 'these poems'.

O'Hara's meditation on the irony of his adult poetic ambitions provides an excellent starting point in framing for us the wider contradictions that would have confronted Crane, some 27 years earlier, as he
sought to write his 'mystical synthesis of America'.[66] At once authorized
by his gender, yet in danger of losing that authority as a homosexual, the
poet now proposes to speak for, and of, a common nation. Crane's own
story is not unlike that of O'Hara's lonely child who cultivates ambitions
to be at the centre of all things. Self-taught, and single-mindedly ambitious, Crane left Cleveland, Ohio, for New York City in 1916 to be at the
centre of the social and cultural changes of the new century,[67] announcing his intention to become a poet. This ambition was forged amidst the
fallout of his parents' divorce, resulting in his changing his name from
Harold to Hart Crane, to incorporate, and thus appease, his 'mother's
side of the house'.[68]

Caught up in the continuing enmity of his parents, Crane's sense of
competing allegiances was repeated in his poetic relationships with Eliot
and Whitman. The warring dynamics of his familial and stylistic affiliations were echoed in the tension between the drive towards comprehen-
sibility and his propensity towards difficulty. Crane's relationship with
Eliot is most notably ambivalent. In 1922, Crane heralded the poet as
'the prime ram of our flock',[69] while the next year figuring him as a
'point of departure toward an almost complete reverse of direction'.[70]
By 1923 Eliot was someone to 'pass through' in order to achieve a
Whitmanian 'universal vision' – a bequest he felt 'still to be realized in

[66] Crane to Gorham Munson, 18 February 1923, *O My Land*, 131
[67] 'It is a great shock, but a good tonic, to come down here'. Crane to his Father, 31
December 1916, *O My Land*, 9.
[68] For an account of Crane's name change (at the suggestion of his mother), see Clive
Fisher, *Hart Crane: A Life*, 49.
[69] Hart Crane, 'Modern Poetry' (1930), *The Complete Poems and Selected Letters and Prose of
Hart Crane*, ed. Brom Weber (Garden City, NY: Doubleday, 1966), 263. Tate later commented that 'a lot of people like Hart had the delusion that Eliot was homosexual'. See
O My Land, 90.
[70] Crane to Gorham Munson, 5 January 1923, *O My Land*, 117.

all its implications'.[71] This 'straddling' of two poetic camps would play an important role in the critical reception of *The Bridge*, especially in its very public rejection by Yvor Winters.

While the closing movement of 'Cape Hatteras' sees Crane's hand in Whitman's, 'never to let go',[72] Crane's poetic dialogue with Whitman was not without its departures. As he wrote to Winters in response to the disparaging review dealt out to *The Bridge* by the critic: 'my acknowledgement of Whitman as an influence and living force . . . apparently . . . discolored the entire poem in your estimation'.[73] Responding to a similar charge from Allen Tate of Whitmanian sentimentality, Crane defended his objective admiration and 'allegiance to the positive and universal tendencies implicit in nearly all [Whitman's] best work', adding, 'you've heard me roar at too many of his lines to doubt that I can spot his worst, I'm sure'.[74] The ongoing construction of Whitman as the national poet during the years Crane was working on *The Bridge* certainly proved to be something of a double-edged sword. Although he offered a distinguished precedent for the ways in which a homosexual might renegotiate the national, Whitman's rising critical favour also necessitated from Crane a distinct departure, if he was to be regarded as anything more than a mere imitator. Following Whitman in his suffusion of the lyric with epic form, however, Crane could imagine a reconciliation of the gay poet with the national, and, in this way, Whitman offered Crane a way of imagining his homosexuality as a source of brotherhood, rather than alienation. However, this poetic brotherhood was subject to disapproval and condemnation from those such as Tate, who could not reconcile Crane's sexuality with the 'right kind of modernism'.[75]

(vii) 'The theme is creative and has vista'

Whitman had begun the redefinition of the American epic project in his 1855 preface to *Leaves of Grass* by proclaiming:

> The American poets are to enclose old and new, for America is the race of races. The expression of the American poet is to be transcendent

---

[71] Crane, 'Modern Poetry' (1930), *The Complete Poems and Selected Letters and Prose of Hart Crane*, 263.

[72] Ibid.

[73] Crane to Winters, 4 June 1930, *O My Land*, 427–30.

[74] Crane to Tate, 13 July 1930, *O My Land*, 433.

[75] Tate to Davidson, 5 February 5 1933, and Tate to Davidson, 16 April 1931. Quoted in Hammer, *Hart Crane & Allen Tate*, xii.

and new. It is to be indirect and not direct or descriptive or epic. Its quality goes through these to much more. Let the age and wars of other nations be chanted, and their eras and characters be illustrated, and that finish the verse. Not so the great psalm of the republic. Here the theme is creative and has vista.[76]

The 'vista' of this new American literature was largely defined by Whitman's own epic, *Leaves of Grass*, that sought to give shape to his notion that 'the United States themselves are essentially the greatest poem'.[77] Through it, Whitman gave expression to these new ideas that would leave behind the 'age and wars of other nations' for a more 'creative' approach to the song of the nation that placed the emphasis upon the seer-poet who is 'complete in himself'.[78] In writing the poems that made up *Leaves of Grass*, Whitman would later say that he had hoped to

articulate and faithfully express in literary or poetic form, and uncompromisingly, my own physical, emotional, moral, intellectual, and aesthetic Personality, in the midst of, and tallying, the momentous spirit and facts of its immediate days, and of current America and to exploit that Personality, identified with place and date, in a far more candid and comprehensive sense than any hitherto poem or book.[79]

In championing the centrality of the poet's 'Personality' to the expression of 'current America', *Leaves of Grass* certainly did much to lyricize the epic for the American tradition, clearing the way for an epic poem that could combine private scope with public purpose. Pursuing this project to 'exploit that Personality' in the 'midst of . . . the momentous spirit' of America, 'By Blue Ontario's Shore' culminates in a final fusion of the self and the nation: 'America isolated yet embodying all, what is it finally except myself?/These States, what are they except myself?'.[80] Whitman thus cleared the way for the 'recorders ages hence',[81] such as Allen Ginsberg, to argue that homosexuality was an appropriate subject

[76] Whitman, preface to the 1855 version of *Leaves of Grass*, *Complete Verse, Selected Prose*, 573.
[77] Ibid., 572.
[78] Whitman clarified this by adding that 'the others are as good as he, only he sees it, and they do not'. Whitman, 1855 preface to *Leaves of Grass*, in *Complete Verse, Selected Prose*, 574.
[79] Whitman, 'A Backward Glance O'er Travel'd Roads' (1888), *Complete Verse, Selected Prose*, 860.
[80] Whitman, 'By Blue Ontario's Shore', *Complete Verse, Selected Prose*, 324.
[81] Whitman, 'Recorders Ages Hence', *Complete Verse, Selected Prose*, 114.

for poetic consideration. He stands as an important precursor for Crane in this sense, for the ways in which he had presented himself in 'a far more candid and comprehensive sense' than any previous 'poem or book'. In this opening up of the epic's discourse of commonality to the realm of the individual or self, Whitman made it possible for Crane to place his 'consciousness' (as Crane recast Whitman's 'Personality') at the centre of the modernist epic poem.

Some 11 years before Crane was born, Whitman had renewed his call for a literature appropriate to America's status as a nation founded upon change, prophesying that America would very soon begin to readjust its 'scope and basic point of view on verse',[82] continuing: 'for all these new and evolutionary facts, meanings, purposes, new poetic messages, new forms and expressions, are inevitable'.[83] However, writing in a short essay of 1930 entitled 'Modern Poetry', Crane claimed that:

> The most typical and valid expression of the American psychosis [is] still found in Whitman . . . but his bequest is still to be realized in all its implications.[84]

The vision of Whitman's last years had not yet been realized, and although Crane was beginning to incorporate his reading into poems such as 'Repose of Rivers' (1926), it would be *The Bridge* that would see him engaging most fully with what he saw as the 'great . . . heritage' left by Whitman to the American poet.[85]

Crane's esteem for Whitman's legacy, however, was accompanied by his own ambition to move beyond his poetic forebear. Crane's correspondence with the novelist and critic Waldo Frank (beginning in 1922) encouraged the poet's first feelings of connection to Whitman,[86] but his admiration was also checked by the ever-present trickle of condemnation that Whitman's poetry still received from some critics and scholars.

---

[82] Whitman, 'A Backward Glance O'er Travel'd Roads' (1888), *Complete Verse, Selected Prose*, 861.

[83] Whitman, *Complete Verse, Selected Prose*, 862.

[84] Crane, 'Modern Poetry' (1930), *The Complete Poems and Selected Letters and Prose of Hart Crane*, 263.

[85] Crane to Wilbur Underwood, 15 December 1925, Warren Herendeen and Donald G. Parker, eds, 'Wind-Blown Flames: Letters of Hart Crane to Wilbur Underwood', *Southern Review* 16.1 (April 1980), 360–2.

[86] 'Since my reading of you [Gorham Munson] and Frank . . . I begin to feel myself directly connected with Whitman'. Letter from Crane to Munson, 2 March 1923, *O My Land, My Friends*, 137.

Writing on Christmas Day, 1925, in the wake of a recent open letter in the *American Collector* that had complained that the author of 'Calamus' was 'abnormal', Crane expressed his surprise at the continuing bigotry present in the reception of Whitman's poetry: 'how he is regarded in some quarters still seems incredible', he wrote to Wilbur Underwood.[87] Crane's curbing of his enthusiasm for the American Bard was no doubt deeply involved with his own anxieties about the incompatibility of homosexuality with literary ambition. However, Whitman's concepts of adhesiveness and 'manly attachments' clearly inform Crane's own sense of the sustaining and redemptive quality of male bonding. This is seen in the 'brother in the half' of Crane's 1924 lyric 'Recitative', as well as in the 'pact, new bound/Of living brotherhood' (*CPHC*, 82) invoked in the most Whitmanian section of *The Bridge*, 'Cape Hatteras'. This second section of 'Cape Hatteras' forms an apostrophe to Whitman, imagining a union of the two poets as Crane himself embarks on a reclamation of Whitman's vision of 'The Open Road', to follow in the 'sure tread' (*CPHC*, 83) of Whitman's example. 'Recitative', however, imagines a more warring relation between brothers:

Twin shadowed halves: the breaking second holds
In each the skin alone, and so it is
I crust a plate of vibrant mercury
Borne cleft to you, and brother in the half.

(*CPHC*, 25)

Langdon Hammer has read these lines as an implicit summons to Crane's friend and fellow poet, Allen Tate.[88] The narrative of Crane's lyric, however, has an altogether more positive conclusion than the fate of the friendship of Tate and Crane was to have in real life. In the poem, the communion with the 'brother in the half' leads to a transcendent moment where the redemptive possibilities of the city are the consequence of the mutually sustaining bond of brotherhood. As 'darkness, like an ape's face falls away,/And gradually white buildings answer day', the city presents the possibility of casting off the 'darkness' that one might read as the shadows of the closet.

The idea of the metropolis as the site of possibility begins to meld with Crane's notion of what Hammer calls 'the special promise of American

[87] Crane to Wilbur Underwood, 15 December 1925, *Southern Review* 16.1 (April 1980), 360–2.
[88] Hammer, preface to *Janus-Faced Modernism*, x.

modernity'. This promise was of a non-hierarchical, democratic community that, echoing Whitman, would be founded upon the mutually sustaining bond between men.[89] This bond is reprised in the handclasp of *The Bridge*'s 'Cape Hatteras'[90] – a passage that caused contemporary critics many problems: Winters, for instance, called it 'desperately sentimental'.[91] However, while Winters' review concluded with its evidence of 'the impossibility of getting anywhere with the Whitmanian inspiration',[92] *The Bridge* evinces just such a breakthrough with regard to both Whitman and Eliot; an ambition to pass through the shadow of Eliot's pessimism in hand with a realization of the Whitmanian bequest that Crane began exploring in his earlier lyric, 'For the Marriage of Faustus and Helen' (1923).[93]

(viii) The road to *The Bridge*

In terms of the themes that would become central to *The Bridge*, the importance of this major preparatory work is clear. By formally 'marrying' the seemingly divergent impulses of his tendency towards high romanticism and his love of modernist difficulty, in 'Faustus and Helen' Crane rehearses the theme of unconventional union that will come to stand at the centre of 'The Dance' section of *The Bridge*. The continuities in Crane's thinking between the completion of 'Faustus and Helen' in 1923 and the conception of *The Bridge* in that same year are not only evident in his poetics but also infiltrate his written correspondence. Crane's dismay at modern society's discarding of the 'superior logic of metaphor in favour of their perfect sums, divisions and subtractions' clearly echoes the 'margins' and 'stacked partitions of the day' seen in the first section of 'Faustus and Helen', populated with 'the memoranda, baseball scores/. . . stock quotations' and 'Numbers' crowding the modern city (*CPHC*, 26). Interestingly, however, Crane's earlier lyric had not provoked the critical divisions so prominent in the reception history of *The Bridge*, its pseudo-Eliotic fragmentation and method seem to have distracted Tate and Winters from its Whitmanian undertones. However, while Eliot's

---

[89] Ibid., xi.
[90] 'My hand/in yours,/Walt Whitman' (Crane, 'Cape Hatteras', *CPHC*, 84).
[91] Yvor Winters, 'The Progress of Hart Crane', *Hart Crane: A Collection of Critical Essays*, ed. Alan Trachtenberg (Englewood Cliffs & London: Prentice Hall, 1982), 23–31.
[92] Winters, 'The Progress of Hart Crane', 108.
[93] Marc Simon dates the composition of the poem from March 1921 to c. late 1923.

'mythical method' emphasized difference, Crane's collage of worlds past and present is centred upon correspondences and continuities. While *The Waste Land* had sought to highlight the sterility of modern culture in contrast to the flourishing, mythic past, Crane's efforts were directed towards 'building a bridge between the classic experience and so many divergent realities of our seething, confused cosmos of today'.[94]

If *The Bridge* was intended to 'continue the tendencies that are evident in "Faustus and Helen"',[95] it is here, in this sense of connection and in the notion of a positive vitality at work among the 'seething, confused cosmos of today', that Crane parted company with Eliot and leant more towards preaching a neo-Whitmanian ideal. Crane worked to reconceptualize the bridge as an emblem of negotiation between the past and future, making it into a symbol that would transcend the personal resonances the actual Brooklyn Bridge held for him. He wanted to use it as the central motif of his expression of the importance of connection and continuity in his myth of America. While Eliot declared he could 'connect/ Nothing with nothing',[96] Crane, as his epic's title aggressively proclaimed, aimed to celebrate an imagination that *could* make manifold connections between America's past and present, and (emotionally) span 'beyond [the] despair' (*CPHC*, 32) that Crane saw as pervading *The Waste Land*.

'For the Marriage of Faustus and Helen' also demonstrates this drive to reconcile or marry contraries and helps us to unravel the politics at work in the critical reception of *The Bridge*. Crane's 'symphonic fusion of antique and modern beauty'[97] in this earlier poem sees him coming closest to the 'mythical method' developed in Joyce's *Ulysses* and Eliot's *The Waste Land*. However, Crane's conception of 'Faustus and Helen' preceded the full publication of both Joyce and Eliot's examples. In May 1922, he had already written to Gorham Munson that he was working on 'a metaphysical attempt of my own – again I mentioned the familiar "Faustus & Helen" affair'.[98] Although five sections of Joyce's text had appeared in 1919 in *The Egoist*,[99] *Ulysses* was not to be published in America

---

[94] Crane, 'General Aims and Theories', 217.
[95] Crane to Gorham Munson, 6 February 1923, *O My Land*, 124.
[96] T. S. Eliot, 'The Waste Land', *Collected Poems 1909–1962* (London: Faber, 1963), 74.
[97] Gorham Munson, 'Hart Crane: Young Titan in the Sacred Wood', *Critical Essays on Hart Crane*, ed. Clark (Boston: G.K. Hall & Co, 1982), 45–6.
[98] Letter to Gorham Munson, 16 May 1922, *O My Land*, 84.
[99] This was followed by its part serialization in *The Little Review* between 1918 and 1920. The magazine was subsequently found guilty of obscenity. Random House published the first full American edition in 1934.

until 1934 and Crane did not receive his smuggled copy from Munson in Paris until July 1922, by which time his own poem was already well under way. Thus, Crane's poem should not be seen so much as merely a minor imitative effort, but rather as an important contemporary contribution to the emergent modernist cause.

It is clear from his own declarations that by the beginning of 1923 'Faustus and Helen' was beginning to emerge as an answer of sorts to Eliot. As he wrote to Munson in January:

> There is no one writing in English who can command so much respect, to my mind, as Eliot. However, I take Eliot as a point of departure toward an almost complete reverse of direction. His pessimism is amply justified, in his own case. But I would apply as much of his erudition and technique as I can absorb and assemble toward a more positive, or . . . ecstatic goal . . . I feel that Eliot ignores certain spiritual events and possibilities as real and powerful now as, say, in the time of Blake.[100]

Allen Tate supports this view of the poem as an answer to the pessimism of the school of Eliot, suggesting that in *White Buildings*, although already present, Crane's vision had not 'yet found a suitable theme';[101] for Tate, *The Bridge* was to be the more complex answer. However, Crane's 'more positive . . . goal' is certainly expressed in his call in the earlier poem's third section to Paris ('O brother-thief of time') to 'Delve upward' for the wine of the new age:

> Delve upward for the new and scattered wine,
> O brother-thief of time, that we recall.
> Laugh out the meager penance of their days
> Who dare not share with us the breath released,
> The substance drilled and spent beyond repair
> For golden, or the shadow of gold hair.
>
> Distinctly praise the years, whose volatile
> Blamed bleeding hands extend and thresh the height
> The imagination spans beyond despair,
> Outpacing bargain, vocable and prayer.
>
> (*CPHC*, 32)

---

[100] Crane to Gorham Munson, 5 January 1923, *O My Land*, 117–18.

[101] Allen Tate, forward to *White Buildings* (1926), reprinted in *Hart Crane: Complete Poems & Selected Letters*, ed. Langdon Hammer (New York: The Library of America, 2006), 795.

Anticipating Crane's melding of images of sacrifice and joy in lyrics
such as 'Lachrymae Christi',[102] the last eight lines of 'Faustus and Helen'
praise a modern spirit that can rise above the 'meager penance of their
days' (*CPHC*, 32). Decrying Eliot's bleak vision, Crane praises the imagination that can span '*beyond* despair' (my emphasis), and imagine the
'spiritual . . . possibilities' he had spoken of to Munson. This transfor-
mative spirit also extends to Crane's use of imagery; the poem's employment of 'shadow' as a positive rather than negative trope prefigures the
similar imagery that would later appear in *The Bridge* as a symbol of hope-
ful desire in the 'cruising' scene below the bridge. The 'shadow of gold
hair' also brings to mind an image of the fine cables of the Brooklyn
Bridge. Perhaps this image was already taking shape in the poet's mind
as a potential symbol for his next major poem, evincing Tate's claim that
'Faustus and Helen' should be read alongside *The Bridge*.

In February 1923, Crane wrote to Waldo Frank describing the Dionysian
attitude of the closing section of his new poem, where 'the last part
begins with catharsis, the acceptance of tragedy through destruction' as
the 'creator and the eternal destroyer dance arm in arm'.[103] If Crane's
correlative system of the 'fusion of our own time with the past' came too
close to Eliot's technique, as manifest in *The Waste Land*, this move away
from the 'pessimism' he spoke of to Munson firmly distinguishes Crane's
vision from that of Eliot's. The contradictory impulses of destruction and
prophecy are key to considering the ways in which Crane's epic vision
departed from *The Waste Land*, and sought instead to realize 'certain
spiritual events and possibilities' intimated by the work of those such as
Blake. For, if Eliot diagnosed the modern condition, Crane, following
Waldo Frank, sought to work towards a healing of the wounded modern consciousness, towards a new synthesis of man's faculties and means
of orientation and knowledge.[104] However, if Frank and Crane were the
would-be attendant physicians to Eliot's recently diagnosed corpse, the
poet felt ill at ease with his own qualifications to attempt such resuscita-
tion. As he wrote to Frank on 4 March 1928: 'At least you have the education and training to hold the scalpel'.[105]

---

[102] Composed c. February 1924–c. April 1925. First published in December 1925.

[103] Crane to Waldo Frank, 7 February 1923, *O My Land*, 126.

[104] For a discussion of Crane's 'queer optimism', see Snediker, 'Hart Crane's Smile',
629–58.

[105] Crane to Waldo Frank, 4 March 1928, *The Letters of Hart Crane 1916–1932*, ed. Brom
Weber (Berkeley & Los Angeles: University of California Press, 1965), 318.

(ix) In the shadow of *The Bridge*

If Whitman's democratic poetics had cleared the way for an epic poem that could combine private scope with public purpose, Crane's negotiation of this relationship was neither swiftly nor confidently won. This is epitomized by his uneasy deployment of Brooklyn Bridge in *The Bridge* as both a universal and personal symbol. As a 'symbol of our constructive future, our unique identity, in which is included also our scientific hopes and achievements of the future',[106] the broader importance of the bridge in the poem as a cipher for the advances of the modern world has already been discussed. Crane clearly hoped, as the title of the poem suggests, that the Brooklyn Bridge would stand at the centre of his poem as a unifying symbol that might cohere his otherwise disparate concerns.

Beginning and ending on the image of the bridge, Crane's poem adheres to the epic model of *nostos* (homecoming), where 'the voyage out is only incidentally a journey of discovery and victory. Primarily it is an ardent quest to return home'.[107] Crane's *nostos*, however, could not be organized around a return to a modern-day Penelope. As Reed notes, *The Bridge* features many archetypal women: the Virgin Mary in 'Ave Maria', Mary Magdalene in 'National Winter Garden' and Eve in 'Southern Cross'. Alongside these women, Crane presents a series of female incarnations of America: Pocahontas in 'The Dance', and the Mayflower pilgrim Priscilla Alden in 'Van Winkle'. However, in the close of the poem, 'Atlantis' (which pre-dates these earlier sections in its composition), Crane had imagined the bridge itself as a figure for the eternal feminine around which his modern epic of *nostos* can be organized: 'Thou Bridge to Thee, O Love./ . . . whitest flower,/ . . . Anemone' (*CPHC*, 107). This 'feminized beloved' came to represent a symbolic 'home' of sorts for the poet, written after Crane came to live with his lover, Emil Opffer, at 110 Columbia Heights, Brooklyn, in the spring of 1924.[108]

In April 1924, Crane had written excitedly to Waldo Frank:

> I am living in the shadow of that bridge . . . There is all the glorious dance of the river directly beyond the back window . . . the ships, the harbour, the skyline of Manhattan . . . it is everything from mountains to the walls of Jerusalem.[109]

---

[106] Crane to Munson, 18 February 1923, *O My Land*, 131.
[107] Reed, *After His Lights*, 153.
[108] Ibid., 163.
[109] Crane to Waldo Frank, 21 April 1924, *O My Land*, 187.

In these short lines, Crane demonstrates his sense that, in this new abode, he had come 'home'. His choice of phrasing echoes many of the titles of the individual poems that would come to make up *The Bridge*: 'The Harbor Dawn', 'The River' and 'The Dance'. The scene from his window evoked the 'changelessness' of the bridge as a symbol that could stay the 'dip and pivot' of his restless life, and come to stand at the very centre of his poem as 'the matchless symbol of America' (*CPHC*, 43).

In the same letter to Frank, Crane reported a breakthrough in his planning for *The Bridge*, as the beginning of his association with Emil signalled a creative outburst in which he completed much of 'Atlantis'. Moving into the Opffer family household, it seems, had been not only a physical relocation but also a creative and emotional one. Crane writes:

> For many days, now, I have gone quite dumb with something for which 'happiness' must be too mild a term . . . I have been able to give freedom and life which was acknowledged in the ecstasy of walking hand in hand across the most beautiful bridge of the world, the cables enclosing us and pulling us upward in such a dance as I have never walked and can never walk with another.[110]

Opffer is an implied presence throughout those sections of *The Bridge* set in view of the harbour, and the private resonances of its location can be seen to bring about a subtle eroticization of its architecture; Crane's choice of the Walker Evans photos for the Black Sun Edition of the poem, for example, depict the arches of the bridge's double towers as suggestively phallic.[111]

The 'shadow' of the bridge that Crane reported in his letter to Frank reappears in the text of the poem itself. It is 'under thy shadow by the piers' that the speaker cruises. This time darkness is transformed into a figure for possibility: if, by daylight, the bridge had become nothing more than 'an economical approach to shorter hours, quicker lunches, behaviorism and toothpicks',[112] then by night it becomes the means to a very different form of exchange. For Yingling, the proem presents the bridge

---

[110] Ibid., 186.

[111] The inclusion of photographs by Walker Evans in the first editions of the poem helped to transform a structure that had opened almost half a century before, in 1883, into a cipher for the 'modern'. Evans' photos emphasized the modernist angularities of the bridge, taking views that highlighted its resemblance to other more aggressively modern examples of architecture, such as the skyscraper. See Edward Brunner, 'Illustrated Editions of *The Bridge*', www.english.uiuc.edu/maps/poets/a_f/crane/bridge_ill.htm.

[112] Crane to Waldo Frank, 20 June 1926, *O My Land*, 259.

as 'a powerful scene of possibility and love . . . not only in providing a
literal cruising place . . . but by offering itself as a symbol for the transfor-
mative structure of homoerotic experience'.[113] This transformation of the
bridge into the 'terrific threshold of the prophet's pledge' is dependent
upon the paradoxical revelation of the 'shadow' (*CPHC*, 44):

> *Under thy shadow by the piers I waited;*
> *Only in darkness is thy shadow clear.*
> *The City's fiery parcels all undone,*
> *Already snow submerges an iron year . . .*

> (*CPHC*, 44)

The metaphysical oxymoron of a darkness that can offer illumination
is coupled with a complaint to the endless cycle of night into morning;
'How many dawns', opens the poet's appeal for respite, speaking of the
incompatibility of the homosexual world of shadows with the daylight
world of 'quicker lunches . . . and toothpicks'.[114]

Crane's orientation towards this architectural icon illustrates the ways
in which he steered an unsteady path between public significance and
personal resonance. Forming a dramatic introduction and invocation to
his central epic image and muse, 'To Brooklyn Bridge' seemed to Crane
an achievement to be proud of: its 'almost the best I've ever written,
there is something steady and uncompromising about it', he wrote to
Waldo Frank in July 1926.[115] And it is precisely this steadiness and stay
of motion that the proem searches for. It explores the implications of
Crane's epigraph from the Book of Job, in particular that of motion: 'the
problem of the modern' is, as Yingling puts it, 'the problem of motion,
the problem for the homosexual who understands himself as displaced,
the fact that nothing "stays" him'.[116] This sense of unrelenting motion is
presented at the root of the central scene of a desperate suicide:

> *Out of some subway scuttle, cell or loft*
> *A bedlamite speeds to thy parapets,*
> *Tilting there momently, shrill shirt ballooning,*
> *A jest falls from the speechless caravan.*

> (*CPHC*, 43)

---

[113] Yingling, *Hart Crane and the Homosexual Text*, 194.
[114] Crane to Waldo Frank, 20 June 1926, *O My Land*, 259.
[115] Crane to Waldo Frank, 24 July 1926, *O My Land*, 264.
[116] Yingling, *Hart Crane and the Homosexual Text*, 191.

It is difficult not to return to Crane's own restless wanderings, and to his ultimate suicide, to appreciate the significance of these lines. The figure of the 'speechless caravan' combines the sense of unrelenting travel with the crushing alienation of the speechless sprawl of the city, while the inevitability of motion is but 'momently' withheld mid-line before resuming its final fall. However, although the bedlamite's 'shrill shirt' offers a desperate reply to the silence that issues from the metropolis, the 'anonymity' bestowed by city-living remains:

> . . . *Accolade thou dost bestow*
> *Of anonymity time cannot raise:*
> *Vibrant reprieve and pardon thou dost show.*

(CPHC, 43–4)

If suicide is presented as the ultimate product of this rootlessness and movement, the bridge does offer some 'reprieve and pardon' from the alienations of the modern city. The 'dip and pivot' of the seagulls' opening flight in the first stanza offers a false vision of liberty that proves to be only apparitional; the bridge enters in the fourth stanza as a true vision that will not 'forsake our eyes'. As a static representation of the seagulls' soaring path, for Crane, the latent power of the bridge lies in the 'motion ever unspent'. Its freedom, paradoxically, resides in its stasis: 'Thy cables breathe the North Atlantic still' (*CPHC*, 43).

(x) Homosexuality in context

As noted in the introductory chapter, Robert Martin was the first critic to offer a fully homoerotic reading of Whitman in *The Homosexual Tradition in American Poetry*. The tradition that Martin delineates, however, is an exclusively Whitmanian one – what he calls 'a gay liberation tradition' that excludes both O'Hara and Merrill for their 'irony and urbanity'.[117] In seeking to understand the ways in which 'the poets used their texts as ways of announcing and defining their homosexuality',[118] Martin's approach concurs with my own reading of *The Bridge* as a textual space that allows Crane to Americanize his homosexuality. However, while Martin's critical treatment of Crane is largely framed with reference

---

[117] Martin, preface to *The Homosexual Tradition in American Poetry*, ix.
[118] Martin, introduction to *The Homosexual Tradition in American Poetry*, xv.

to Whitman, Crane's work also draws on a wider tradition of sexually transgressive writers, such as his contemporary Djuna Barnes.[119] Crane's quest to fashion a national poetry was not only reflective of the examples of Whitman and Emerson but also a reaction against European literary models which stood for effeminacy and indulgence. These were both qualities from which Crane wished to distance himself for fear of being associated with the Victorian scientific models that figured the homosexual as of invert gender.

Rather than risk being associated with the figure of the emasculated homosexual (which was by now integral to the dominant representations of the homosexual), Crane insisted on the masculinity and virility of his sexuality. Crane's appeal to potency chimes with Eliot's use of fertility myths and the quest for the restoration of cultural potency in *The Waste Land*. However, while the sexual sterility of *The Waste Land* is culturally pervasive, in Crane's world, it was the homosexual male who risked being identified as emasculated, impotent and 'inverted'. The gender inversion or 'Third Sex' models of homosexuality proposed by late nineteenth-century sexologists such as Ulrichs, Hirschfeld and Havelock Ellis, however, were soon to be displaced. George Chauncey notes the alienation of homosexuals who did not identify with this feminine model which was, at the time, the 'primary role model available to men forming a gay identity'.[120] However, a new framework for conceiving of homosexuality caused further fragmentations in the emergent subculture. The shift from the definition of homosexuality as the result of some kind of congenital gender inversion[121] to the Freudian emphasis on object choice in the 1920s saw a further split in self-identification for those men engaging in male-to-male sexual practices.

The consequences of the Wilde trial meant that, in the 1920s, the homosexual 'fairy' stood for Old World decadence and the moral degeneracy that America wanted to distance itself from. The homosexual also posed an ideological threat to the heterosexual models on which the nation's economic development would increasingly be founded as the century proceeded. Alongside models of gender inversion, the class aspect of homosexual identity also created contradictions within such models of identity. The attempt to forge a sexual identity removed from gender

---

[119] For a discussion of Crane's work in relation to Barnes, see Reed, *After His Lights*, 40–70.
[120] Chauncey, *Gay New York*, 99.
[121] For an account of the medicalization of homosexuality, see Greenberg, *The Construction of Homosexuality*, 410–14.

was being pioneered among middle-class America, where adopting the stance and style of the fairy was too costly a move.[122] Chauncey quotes Jeb Alexander, a young man living in Washington in the 1920s, as representative of a trend among middle-class homosexuals in the early part of the twentieth century who were beginning to reject the association of effeminacy and homosexuality. Echoing Whitman, these men considered their love for other men as more masculine than love for women: 'The "manly love of comrades" is nobler and sweeter and ought to be sufficient', says Alexander in his diary.[123] However, Whitman had himself drawn on scientific discourse in developing his concepts of 'adhesiveness' and 'manly attachment'.

Pre-dating the German and English sexologists, Franz Joseph Gall (1758–1828) had suggested that excessive attachment to a same-sex friendship was a phrenological matter, rather than one of sexual behaviour. Gall proposed that 'adhesiveness' was the brain function responsible for the friendship instinct, and, if excessively stimulated, could lead to these intense same-sex relationships.[124] Whitman found in Gall's writing the vocabulary through which he could express the comradely love of men upon which he believed that the foundations of a healthy and successful democracy should be built, rejecting the feminine aestheticism of the nineteenth-century homosexual – 'Washes and razors for foofoos – for me freckles and a bristling beard' – in favour of a more masculine tradition.[125]

If sexuality operates in 'Song of Myself' as a counter-narrative to a racial nationality (where race functions as an agent of relatedness for America), Whitman's particular brand of national identity can be seen to make ample provision for the integration of the sexual into the matrix of the national for his poetic inheritors. While the nature of this sexual affiliation is characteristically ambivalent, Whitman does propose a connection between sexuality and the national in his 1876 preface. The 'race of races'[126] of the 1855 edition preface is displaced by a vision of American 'attachment' that is given form by the 'endless stream of living, pulsating love and friendship',[127] which Whitman sees as animating its people. The

[122] Chauncey, *Gay New York*, chapter 4.
[123] Ibid., 104–5.
[124] For an account of Gall and his followers, see Greenberg, *The Construction of Homosexuality*, 405.
[125] Walt Whitman, 'Song of Myself' (1855), *Leaves of Grass* (New York: Grossett & Dunlap, 1976), 29.
[126] Whitman, preface to *Leaves of Grass* (1855), *Complete Verse, Selected Prose*, 573.
[127] Whitman, preface to *Leaves of Grass* (1876), *Complete Verse, Selected Prose*, 734.

power of this intangible 'desire' is such that it brings men into bonds with one another almost at random. This is what makes sexuality, for Whitman, an 'ideal language to describe the nature and substance of US nationality [where] sexuality seems most intensely meaningful to him when it expresses a nearly boundless human capacity for relation to others, for affiliation'.[128]

Crane followed Whitman in discarding the feminine associations of the homosexual. As he wrote to Yvor Winters in May 1927, in defence of his sexuality:

> Your fumigation of the Leonardo legend is a healthy enough reaction, but I don't think your reasons for doubting his intelligence and scope very potent. I've never closely studied the man's attainments or biography, but your argument is certainly weakly enough sustained on the sole prop of his sex – or lack of such. One doesn't have to turn to homosexuals to find instances of missing sensibilities. Of course I'm sick of all this talk about balls and cunts in criticism. It's obvious that balls are needed, and that Leonardo had 'em.[129]

Challenging his conception of the homosexual as castrated, and therefore incapable of artistic production, Crane turns the terms of Winters' attack against him, questioning the potency of Winters' own reasoning, by characterizing it as 'weak' and precariously balanced on a single 'prop'. However, for all his proclaimed impatience with the 'talk about balls and cunts in criticism', Crane had himself, just a few months previously, mocked Hemingway's phallic myth-making, tagging his novel 'the Cock also Rises'.[130] The poet also frequently adopted the feminine as a pejorative term for those who displeased him. For example, the editor Ridgely Torrence was reduced to the moniker, 'Miss T.', when he rejected Crane's poems, and Marianne Moore and others became 'milksops', in a reverse appropriation of homosexual terminology that sought to feminize objects of scorn.[131]

Crane's fear of being engulfed by the cultural construction of the emasculated homosexual male is most powerfully expressed through his

---

[128] Peter Coviello, 'Intimate Nationality: Anonymity and Attachment in Whitman', *American Literature* 73.1 (2001), 111.
[129] Crane to Yvor Winters, 29 May 1927, *O My Land*, 338.
[130] Crane to Susan Jenkins and William Slater Brown, 16 February 1927, *O My Land*, 318.
[131] Crane to Allen Tate, 14 March 1927, *O My Land*, 325.

assertion in *The Bridge* of the phallic potential of the poet. 'The Dance' section of the poem imagines the regeneration of the poetic phallus:

> A distant cloud, a thunder-bud – it grew,
> That blanket of the skies: the padded foot
> Within, – I heard it; 'til its rhythm drew,
> – Siphoned the black pool from the heart's hot root!
>
> (*CPHC*, 63)

Playfully punning on his own name, Crane defends himself against Winters' accusation of homosexual impotence with this aggressive assertion of virile masculinity, even though, as Robert Martin has noted, 'Crane may have not been as total in his adoration of the masculine' as the poetic constructions of his self suggest.[132]

(xi) Contexts of citizenship

To document fully the social and cultural contexts under which *The Bridge* was produced is a project made difficult by the protracted time over which Crane struggled to bring the poem to fruition. From the point of its first conception in 1923, until its completion nearly 6½ years later, the America that Crane had sought to 'gather up' had been dramatically transformed, with significant changes having taken place in the construction of American national identity. The Johnson Immigration Act of 1924, and the Citizenship Act of the same year, both had profound effects on the terms by which a person was able to claim American identity. These are, as Jared Gardner has noted, important contexts for a reading of *The Bridge*, especially in terms of its epic ambitions.

World War I had revealed that the American 'melting pot' had produced fractured racial allegiances that contrasted sharply with the pure patriotism of the Native Indians, who had fought for America in unparalleled numbers.[133] As a consequence, the 1924 Johnson Immigration Act sought to close off access to American citizenship to those whose

---

[132] Martin, *American Modernism across the Arts*, 211–12.

[133] 'Postwar studies estimated that more than ten thousand Indian men served in the United States and Canadian armies during the war, and fully three-fourths of these were volunteers who did not have to enlist because of their noncitizenship status' (Michael L. Tate, 'From Scout to Doughboy: The National Debate over Integrating American Indians into the Military, 1891–1918', *Western Historical Quarterly* 17.4 (October 1986), 430).

European sympathies might prove a threat to the consolidation of an American identity distinct from the European heritage of many of its citizens.[134] While it sought to limit immigrant entrance to America, the American government also opened up the opportunity of citizenship to Native Americans with the Citizenship Act of 1924. Such legislation constituted a radical reconstruction of the idea of American national identity, which was now figured as a common spirit shared by both 'Indian' and American, but alien to immigrant populations.

In imagining a future for America that would sever it from its European biological inheritance, these models of citizenship that arose in the 1920s were founded upon the idea of a bloodless genealogy for the American people. This framework, Jared Gardner has argued, was of crucial significance for Crane in that it opened up a conceptual 'loophole' in the construction of American identity whereby the homosexual could claim a biology-free genealogy that evaded the complications of race.[135] Gardner's reading of *The Bridge* focuses on Crane's manipulation of these contemporary discourses, positing the union between the Native American and the poet in the final section of 'The Dance' as Crane's 'attempt to claim a historical place for the homosexual by inventing a nativist history purified through a marriage between white man and Indian'.[136] Crane presents this ecstatic union in the closing stanza of 'The Dance':

We danced, O Brave, we danced beyond their farms,
In cobalt desert closures made our vows . . .
Now is the strong prayer folded in thine arms,
The serpent with the eagle in the boughs.

(*CPHC*, 65)

After its initial appearance in 'The River', where Crane describes Pocahontas as the embodiment of both America's landscape and history,[137] the motif of the serpent and the eagle reappears as a symbol

---

[134] 'During the years of the war various alien racial groups in the country showed clearly enough that their sympathies were not American but European' (Robert DeC. Ward, 'Our New Immigration Policy' (1924), *Politics of the Nineteen Twenties*, ed. John L. Shover (Waltham: Ginn-Blaisdell, 1970), 127).

[135] 'Only the homosexual can claim a genealogy without biology, and only such a genealogy can truly evade all the complications of race', Gardner, 'Our Native Clay', 26.

[136] Gardner, 'Our Native Clay', 27.

[137] 'I knew her body there,/Time like a serpent down her shoulder, dark,/And space, an eaglet's wing, laid on her hair' (Crane, 'The River', *CPHC*, 59).

that the Native American 'would himself comprehend'.[138] Although Brian Reed suggests that these lines represent the fusion of the American spirit, Crane's image more than likely refers to the feathered or plumed serpent spirit, Quetzalcoatl. This Aztec deity is often represented as the giver of maize, hence Crane's own reference to the cereal in the first stanza of 'The Dance'. Quetzalcoatl was also associated with the resurrection of mankind from the bones of previous races, as he used his own blood (from a wound in his penis) to imbue the bones with new life. This is a resonant myth for a poet attempting to forge an epic partly from his own homoerotic desires. Discarding any attempt at heterosexual imagery, Crane associates this motif with an alternative kind of union that would seem implicitly to sanction his own private behaviours. Undermining the heterosexual bias of the national myth of Pocahontas, this climax sees the fusion of Crane with the Indian, rather than the marriage of John Smith and Pocahontas. As Crane's hope of 'possessing the Indian and his world'[139] is literally manifested, Maquokeeta, figured as a snake, sheds his red skin ('casts his pelt'). He 'lives beyond'[140] by transferring his spirit to the poet who then experiences the sacrificial scene for himself, as Maquokeeta burns to death at the stake in a moment of erotic masochism that recalls Crane's earlier lyrics such as 'Legend'.

The poem's concern with fertility myths or ritual sacrifices, such as that associated with Quetzalcoatl, begins in the opening stanza of 'The Dance'. Crane speaks of the 'winter king' who 'squired the glacier woman down the sky': 'She ran the neighing canyons all the spring;/ She sprouted arms; she rose with maize – to die' (*CPHC*, 62). However, this heterosexual myth of regeneration is never realized. Instead, Crane imagines a union of the homosexual and Native American in an ecstatic dance that will see Crane transformed until he can 'become identified with the Indian'.[141] As Maquokeeta, the Indian chief, 'casts' off his skin in the tribal fertility sacrifice, the poet enters his spirit, becoming a kind of Native incarnation of St Sebastian (with 'arrows' in his 'side'). The poet and Indian chief are then conjoined in an ecstatic marriage of sacrifice.

'For the Marriage of Faustus and Helen' had already seen Crane imagining an unconventional union, and, in this sense, *The Bridge* continues Crane's drive to reconcile contraries: the poet's fantasy marriage seeks

---

[138] Crane to Otto Kahn, 12 September 1927, *O My Land*, 347.
[139] Ibid.
[140] Ibid.
[141] Ibid.

to heal the 'iron dealt cleavage' that divides and separates the white man from the earth and his 'native clay' (*CPHC*, 59). 'The River' juxtaposes the speeding force of 'the 20th Century' with its patent names, 'Overalls ads', and radios in 'EVERY HOME' (*CPHC*, 57) with the restless existence of hoboes wandering 'From pole to pole' (*CPHC*, 59). These hoboes share a privileged, if ignorant, relationship with the body of the land:

> . . . I knew her body there,
> Time like a serpent down her shoulder, dark,
> And space, an eaglet's wing, laid on her hair.
>
> Under the Ozarks, domed by Iron Mountain,
> The old gods of the rain lie wrapped in pools . . .
> Where eyeless fish curvet a sunken fountain
> And re-descend with corn from querulous crows.
> Such pilferings make up their timeless eatage,
> Propitiate them for their timber torn
> By iron, iron – always the iron dealt cleavage!
> They doze now, below axe and powder horn.

(CPHC, 59)

Meditating on the legends of the Native Americans, Crane imagines that the 'old gods' are awaiting revival under the river's surface, 'wrapped in pools', dozing until reawakened by a renewed understanding of the American land. The 'iron dealt cleavage' vividly renders the divorce of modern man from Nature that has been 'dealt' by the industrialization of the twentieth century. The phrase also recalls the 'cleaving' and 'burning' of Crane's early lyric, 'Legend', as a punishment that is 'to be learned' by the homosexual, as an idiom of masochistic sexual sacrifice:

> It is to be learned –
> This cleaving and this burning,
> But only by the one who
> Spends out himself again.

(CPHC, 3)

In 'The River', however, it is the impact of the white man's modern industrial reality that has overwhelmed the native contact with the earth. Like the 'timber torn' down from the clearing of the native wilderness with 'axe and powder horn', 'iron' is a symbol of the threat of separation between the industrialized modern world and the vision of America as a land in which the divine spirit can reveal itself – to 'know a body under the wide rain' (*CPHC*, 59).

At times, Crane lost faith that this balance could any longer be achieved in modern America, despairing of the project that he had from the outset anticipated he might 'have to give up entirely . . . it may be too impossible an ambition'. His doubt was often framed in distinctly Eliotic terms, arising in particular at times when he and Tate were in close association:

> The form of my poem rises out of a past that so overwhelms the pres-ent with its worth and vision that I'm at a loss to explain my delusion that there exist any real links between that past and a future destiny worthy of it . . . The bridge as symbol today has no significance beyond an economical approach to shorter hours, quicker lunches, behavior-ism and toothpicks . . . If only America were half as worthy today to be spoken of as Whitman spoke of it fifty years ago there might be some-thing for me to say.[142]

Crane's answer to this problem of the worthiness of modern America was to turn to the nation's biological origins. Using the figure of the Indian to 'Americanize the homosexual'[143], Crane was not only able to invoke the spiritual legacy of America, but also to implicitly authorize his own epic ambitions. Creating 'a world that permits the imaginary fulfilment' of desire,[144] *The Bridge*'s 'lyric' impetus (in the Gansian sense) creates a textual space akin to what Wolfgang Iser has called 'the Fictive' – a textual mechanism which provides a means of 'overstepping boundaries' and 'specific identity limitations'.[145] In Crane's recasting of the Pocahontas myth, the union of the white and 'red man' becomes the nation's Fictive founding moment; the limitations of homosexual identity are cast off in the textual space created by the joining together of the Native American and the poet. In proffering this homoerotic union, Crane offers a tex-tual 'bridge' between the two non-procreative models of genealogy that contemporary citizenship discourse had polarized as mutually exclusive terms during the war.

---

[142] Crane to Waldo Frank, 20 June 1926, *O My Land*, 259.
[143] Gardner, 'Our Native Clay', 27.
[144] Gans, personal correspondence, 31 January 2003.
[145] Wolfgang Iser, *The Fictive and the Imaginary: Charting Literary Anthropology* (Baltimore & London: Johns Hopkins University Press, 1993), 279.

Implicit in this quest for a non-biological model of American identity is Crane's representation of the failure of the family. This stands at the centre of 'Indiana''s gold trail narrative. Closely following the homoerotic union of the closing scene of 'The Dance', 'Indiana' narrates the disintegration of the family unit: the early death and 'lost bones' of the father in stanza three represent the beginning of this disintegration, with the remaining family winning 'nothing out of fifty-nine' years from the hollow quest for fortune in 'A dream called Eldorado' (*CPHC*, 66). The 'barren tears' of the widow are mirrored by the female homeless squaw's eyes that are 'sharp with pain' (*CPHC*, 67). She also represents a fractured family unit; a 'halfbreed', carrying a 'babe's body' who refuses to enter the heterosexual economy and return the 'gaze' of the white 'silent men', responding only to the widow's presence. 'Mere words could not have brought us nearer' (*CPHC*, 67), the speaker claims, recalling Crane's early poem, 'Episode of Hands', which also brings together two people from different spheres in an episode of homo-erotic tension. If, however, the moment of empathy with the white woman carrying her own child is 'lit with love', it is only a temporary reprieve from the damning report 'Indiana' seems to write for the biological family. As a 'halfbreed', the squaw is no longer representative of the pure spirit of 'our native clay' – the 'gaze/Of all our silent men' bespeaking the lust that has been the ruin and pollution of her native genealogy by the white man.

As Gardner notes, only the return of the prodigal son (which Gardner reads as Crane's own textual incarnation) can restore the ruined patrimony.[146] While Eliot and Pound turned to Europe to invigorate their poetics, Crane, like Williams, must return to American soil to regenerate and work through the national family drama. Asking in 'Quaker Hill', 'Where are my kinsmen and the patriarch race?', Crane understands that he 'must ask slain Iroquois to guide me' (*CPHC*, 93) and return to America's native heritage to access the essence of the nation without recourse to its immigrant histories.

'The Dance' is sandwiched between these two narratives of the failure of family as Crane works to lead the reader 'to the pure savage world, while existing at the same time in the present'.[147] Central to this journey away from the civilized world, and crucial to Crane's re-evaluation of the idea of family, is the introduction of the figure of the hobo-vagabond in 'The River'. The wanderings of the speaker who has 'trod the rumor-ous midnights' (*CPHC*, 59) recall the nights of cruising in 'To Brooklyn Bridge': both hope to 'know a body under the wide rain'. The cruising

---

[146] Gardner, 'Our Native Clay', 43.
[147] Crane to Mrs T. W. Simpson, 4 July 1927, *O My Land*, 341.

figure who waits 'by the piers' under the shadow of the bridge chimes
with this moment recalled from childhood, observing the 'wifeless'
hobos behind his father's factory:

> Behind
> My father's cannery works I used to see
> Rail-squatters ranged in nomad raillery,
> The ancient men – wifeless or runaway
> Hobo-trekkers that forever search
> An empire wilderness of freight and rails.
> Each seemed like a child, like me, on a loose perch,
> Holding onto childhood like some termless play.
> John, Jake or Charley, hopping the slow freight
> – Memphis to Tallahassee. . .

(CPHC, 58–9)

The connection between the young observer and his subject is emphasized by the infantile characterization of these men who, 'like me' are
'Holding onto childhood'. This loose brotherhood of wanderers are, at
first, disconnected from the feminine body of the land, condemned to
'forever search/An empire wilderness of freight and rails' in a wasteland
of modern technology and hollow commerce. If the American landscape
is imagined as the female body of Pocahontas, these 'Hobo-trekkers' are
excluded from its organic fertility, confined instead to a barren and masculine wilderness of modernization, which is composed of a network of
metal 'rails' and 'freight'. Crane's identification of his childhood self
with the aimless play of the hobos' freight-hopping converges with the
homoerotic charge of their 'riding the rods':

> . . . riding the rods,
> Blind fists of nothing, humpty-dumpty clods.

> Yet they touch something like a key perhaps.
> From pole to pole across the hills, the states
> – They know a body under the wide rain;
> Youngsters with eyes like fjords, old reprobates
> With racetrack jargon, – dotting immensity
> They lurk across her, knowing her yonder breast
> Snow-silvered, sumac-stained, or smoky blue-
> Is past the valley-sleepers, south or west.
> – As I have trod the rumorous midnights, too.

(CPHC, 59)

These homosexual connections, however, bring with them a new knowl-edge.[148] Those whose '*addresses are never near*' (*CPHC*, 57–8) now come to know 'yonder breast' of the female body of the landscape that sees the meeting of the industrial with the organic in the rail-tracks that leave the mountain peaks 'snow-silvered, sumac-stained' (*CPHC*, 59). Yet '*knowing her without name*', they are ignorant of the significance of their instinc-tual communion with the mother land, which, Crane imagines, connects these hobos with the Native American, both sharing in the possession of the 'pure' spirit of the American soil.

Crane envisaged the hobos as 'psychological ponies' able to 'carry the reader across the country and back to the Mississippi', functioning as keys to 'unlatch the door to the pure Indian world which opens out in "The Dance"'.[149] However, while 'The River' is a record of the poet's jour-ney through the myths of these wanderers ('Oh I remember watermelon days'), it also reproduces a model of male-to-male relations that prepares the way for the ecstatic union with the Indian chief. By equating these 'wifeless' hobos' unknowing possession of the motherland with the com-munion to be gained from cruising the 'rumorous nights', Crane posits his right not to be excluded in an original knowledge of America, and thus of his, and other homosexuals', right to citizenship. As Pocahontas leads the poet down 'Grimed tributaries to an ancient flow' via the guid-ing current of the 'crescent running' of Pocahontas' hair, the 'Grimed' tales of the rail-squatters give way to the ancient flow of the '*myths of her fathers*' – the Indian heritage of the American nation (*CPHC*, 59–60).

In rewriting the Pocahontas story into his homosexual myth, Crane's Pocahontas becomes a mediating figure in a recasting of the Girardian triangle.[150] She is not only the bridge to the American soil, but also the mediating force that brings together the ecstatic union of the Indian and the poet. As Crane wrote in his exposition of 'The Dance', 'Pocahontas (the continent) is the common basis of our meeting'.[151] However, what Gardner sees as the poem's attempt to claim 'the homosexual as the pure American'[152] was no easy task. The emergence of a national identity defined by the patriotism of the Indian soldier arose concomitantly with

---

[148] 'The prevalence of homosexual relations was so generally assumed to be true among hoboes . . . that whenever a man travels around with a lad he is apt to be labelled a "jocker" or a 'wolf' and the road kid is called his "punk", "preshun", or "lamb"' (Chauncey, *Gay New York*, 90).

[149] Crane to Mrs T. W. Simpson, 4 July 1927, *O My Land*, 341.

[150] Sedgwick has extensively theorized the notion of the 'gender asymmetry and erotic triangles' in her study *Between Men: English Literature and Male Homosocial Desire*, 21–7.

[151] Crane to Otto Kahn, 12 September 1927, *O My Land*, 347.

[152] Gardner, 'Our Native Clay', 26.

the first explicit representations of the homosexual as a threat to that
identity and, as Gardner notes, 'the exclusion of the homosexual from
military service made him the paradigm for decitizenship'.[153] The much-
publicized Newport Scandal of 1919–20 had brought homosexuality into
the public eye and the conceptual 'loophole' created by the new legislation of the time left Crane with the difficult task of convincing his reader
that the union of the white man and the native was not just a homoerotic
debasement of one of America's founding myths.

Literature, however, was on hand to give weight to Crane's formulation. Crane could call on numerous literary precedents for interracial
homoerotic or homosocial relations. In the example of pairings such as
Melville's Ishmael and Queequeg, or Twain's Huck and Jim, or James
Fenimore Cooper's Natty Bumppo and Chingachgook, Crane could
find 'memorable and half-exciting erotic suggestions' for his union.[154]
Such precedents enabled Crane to frame his manoeuvre as a reinvigoration of a long-standing tradition in the American epic of what Leslie
Fiedler has called the 'counter-matrimony' of 'the white refugee . . . and
the dark-skinned primitive' – 'the pure marriage of males – sexless and
holy'.[155]

While Jared Gardner's work on *The Bridge* is illuminating for the ways
in which it employs citizenship discourse for reading Crane's poem, it is
important that these contemporary contexts be read alongside longer-
standing literary motifs and discourses. Crane's symbolic intentions for
the Native American also draw on contemporary primitivist interests,
and in this respect Crane's 'Indian' and 'homosexual' can be seen to
function as textual constructions that reinforce their respective ideological functions in the poem, rather than presenting true historical reflections of these groups. In the same sense, Crane's images of America in
'The Dance' (which he takes from geographically diverse locations),
bespeak an interest in what constitutes 'America', rather than in fash-
ioning his epic from the poetics of local realism, as Williams' *Paterson*
(1946) would go on to do. Following Waldo Frank's claim that 'our root
is in the red men; and our denial of this is a disease within us',[156] Crane
employs Pocahontas, daughter of the chief Powhatan, as a symbol for

---

[153] Ibid., 33.
[154] Crane wrote to Wilbur Underwood on 15 June 1922 of the 'memorable and half-exciting
    erotic suggestions of dear Queequeg' after reading *Moby-Dick*, *O My Land*, 91.
[155] Leslie Fiedler, *Love and Death in the American Novel* (New York: Criterion, 1960), 209.
[156] Waldo Frank, *The Rediscovery of America: An Introduction to the Philosophy of American Life*
    (New York & London: C. Scribner's Sons, 1929, reprinted in Westport, CT, 1982), 230.

'whatever is most real in our little native culture'[157] and as a symbol of
the American earth – 'our native clay' (*CPHC*, 77). In constructing the
Native American in *The Bridge* as a kind of national Id, the recovery of the
Indian also becomes the recovery of America's unconscious and thus an
escape from the 'repressive' forces that Crane felt had been visited upon
himself as a homosexual, as well as the Indian people.

While such constructions are problematic,[158] Crane was tapping into
a post–World War I project that sought to advance the potential of the
Native American as the source of America's spiritual inheritance. As
Gardner notes, by 1930, the notion had gained such currency that Jung
remarked that the 'spirit of the Indian gets at the American within and
without'.[159] This 'spirit' is that which Crane takes possession of in 'The
Dance' as Maquokeeta 'casts his pelt' and the poet becomes identified
with the burning god 'wrapped in that fire':

Dance, Maquokeeta! snake that lives before,
That casts his pelt, and lives beyond! Sprout, horn!
Spark, tooth! Medicine-man, relent, restore –
Lie to us, – dance us back the tribal morn!

Spears and assemblies: black drums thrusting on –
O yelling battlements, – I, too, was liege
To rainbows currying each pulsant bone:
Surpassed the circumstances, danced out the siege!

And buzzard-circleted, screamed from the stake;
I could not pick the arrows from my side.
Wrapped in that fire, I saw more escorts wake –
Flickering, sprint up the hill groins like a tide.

(*CPHC*, 64)

With its evocations of Saint Sebastian, the homoerotic associations of this
transformation are palpable. As the fire is figured in serpentine terms
('red fangs' and 'splay tongues') the poem revisits an image from 'Van

[157] Crane to Winters, *Hart Crane and Yvor Winters: Their Literary Correspondence*, ed. Thomas
Parkinson (Berkeley & London: University of California Press, 1978), 20.
[158] 'In studying primitive societies or inventing versions of them, Westerners pretend to learn
about or to create alternative, less oppressive ways of knowing, all the while establishing mastery and control over those other ways of knowing' (Marianna Torgovnick, *Gone
Primitive: Savage Intellects, Modern Lives* (Chicago, IL: Chicago University Press, 1990), 173).
[159] Carl Jung, 'Your Negroid and Indian Behaviour', *Forum* 83 (1930), 197. Quoted in
Gardner, 'Our Native Clay', 24.

Winkle', where the young Crane stones 'the family of young/Garter snakes' in a symbolic act of refusal of his childhood desires (*CPHC*, 55). This passage, alongside Crane's hymns to Brooklyn Bridge, stands as a symbolic centre of Crane's project, with its scene of homoerotic sacrifice enabling the poet to inhabit the spiritual heart of America as embodied by the Indian chief. Although Crane set out to write a poem that would give expression to the modern industrial age, it is here, in these passages of homoerotic primitivism, that the poet could imagine himself at the very heart of the American myth.

Crane's experience as a homosexual may have been defined by his feelings of rootlessness and restlessness. However, the stasis that the Brooklyn Bridge came to offer, as a symbol of continuity and as the site of his most stable and nurturing relationship, saw the bridge come to stand as a symbol at the very centre of his epic. This urge to be delivered from the endless displacements of homosexual desire resonates throughout his harrowing yet complex lyrics. It was not, however, until the over-throw of New Criticism's ideals of coherence, thematic unity, and purposefulness that *The Bridge* came to be construed as more than just a 'splendid failure' – a fine idea marred by its author's sexuality. With the rise of post-structuralism (and more recently with queer theory), its disconnection and fragmentariness have rightly been recognized as the source of the poem's interest and value. Crane's epic has come to stand as a record of homosexual subjectivity for its times.

Taking its place among an illustrious roll-call of homosexual epics, *The Bridge* is an integral part of the story of how the homosexual poet has tried to write his nation. If the epic form demands the binding of difference into unity and commonality (in Crane's words, 'to bind us throbbing with one voice'), then the homosexual epic responds to this disciplining imperative with some difficulty. *The Bridge*, however, works to imagine the homosexual male as the emblematic figure of America. Manipulating contemporary discourses of citizenship, Crane imagines a union between himself and the Indian chief that evades a biological genealogy and rewrites the homosexual as the true American citizen, rather than as a marginal figure. In this respect, Crane's work signals a new threshold in the expression of gay subjectivity; it embodies an urge to move beyond the 'signals dispersed in veils' (*CPHC*, 53) of 'The Harbor Dawn' towards a fusion of the myth of America with a realized homoeroticism.

Chapter 2

'It occurs to me that I am America':
Ginsberg's Queer Shoulder

(i) Ginsberg's epics

'Why have you come back Allen?' Marc Schleifer asked Ginsberg on
his return to New York from Paris in 1958; 'To save America. I don't
know what from', the poet replied.[1] Ginsberg's half-joke, half-answer suggests an incoherent, if earnest, political objective to one of his many
homecomings, parodying the traditional *nostos* of the epic journey. His
poetry, however, displays a rather more firm idea of what he wishes to
save America from, and it is this that forms the foundations of his epic
ambitions in the two long poems, 'Howl' (1956) and *The Fall of America:
Poems of these States 1965–71* (1972).[2] In the following chapter, I consider
both these poems in terms of their place within a Whitmanian epic genealogy, exploring the ways in which homosexuality functions at the very
centre of Ginsberg's vision for America and in his rethinking of the epic
mode, with sexuality acting as the catalyst for his challenge to traditional
Anglo-American forms.[3]

Although at first it may seem strange to speak of 'Howl' as operating
within the tradition of epic, I propose that Jung's concept of the *nekyia*

---

[1] Allen Ginsberg, Interview by Marc D. Schleifer, *Village Voice*, 15 October 1958, reprinted
in *Spontaneous Mind*, 4.

[2] For the purposes of my discussion, I consider the full text of *The Fall of America* as it is
printed in its reprinted form in Allen Ginsberg, *Collected Poems 1947–1980* (New York:
Harper Row, 1984). At Ginsberg's direction, 'Wichita Vortex Sutra' and 'Iron Horse'
(both originally published separately) now appear as the fourth poem and as the opening poem of section II, respectively. Hereafter, all references to poems appearing in this
collected edition will be abbreviated to *GCP*.

[3] Anne Hartman argues that Ginsberg's poetry evokes the 'confessional mode for counter-
establishment purposes, foregrounding its ability to interpellate an audience and engage
the dialectic between privacy and publicity'. 'Confessional Counterpublics in Frank
O'Hara and Allen Ginsberg'. *Journal of Modern Literature* 28.4 (2005), 42.

can be employed to read 'Howl' 's narrative as an epic-style journey into an underworld that functions as an encounter with the collective unconscious.[4] *The Fall of America*, I will argue, represents Ginsberg's more sustained effort to rethink the epic genre for the modern world by bringing epic significance to the classic cross-country Beat journey, also incorporating the jeremiadical tone that Ginsberg had experimented with in earlier poems such as 'America' (1956).

The conjunction of 'Howl' and *The Fall* serves to illustrate what I perceive as an important shift in Ginsberg's approach to the epic mode. While acting as a poetic barometer for Ginsberg's anxieties about the destruction wrought by the Vietnam War, and as a record of a journey across the nation in search of 'these states',[5] *The Fall* represents a more sustained and meditative exploration of the epic mode. With the questing traveller at its centre, Ginsberg's poetic voyages in *The Fall* constitute a more comprehensive and exhaustive report on the states of America than 'Howl', both metaphysically and geographically. However, while this later poem is more geographically and emotionally extensive than 'Howl', both works share in a desire to record the present moment in American contemporary history and are motivated by the 'here-and-now', rather than by the historical narratives favoured by the European epic tradition.

Just as Crane hoped to incorporate the technological innovations of his age into *The Bridge*, so Ginsberg's poems strive to capture the contemporary spirit of cultural and sexual revolution. In this sense, these are poems that don't observe so much as *participate* in the production and recording of contemporary American history. Their documentation of dialect and speech – a project comparable to that which I observe in my later chapter on John Ashbery's *Flow Chart* – is no less important than the events recorded therein. While 'Howl' stands in part as a record of the Jazz-speak or Beat slang of its time, *The Fall* sees Ginsberg trying to capture what John Bayley identifies in Ashbery's *Flow Chart* as the 'natural noise of the present'.[6] The protest and popular songs heard on the

---

[4] Jung's concept of the *nekyia* (named after the descent to the underworld of the eleventh book of *The Odyssey*) denotes an encounter with the unconscious. See C. J. Jung, *Psychology and Alchemy*, trans. R. F. C Hull, *Collected Works*, Vol. 12 (London: Routledge & Kegan Paul, 1953), 52, n2.

[5] The title of *The Fall*'s opening poem borrows its phrasing from Whitman: 'America isolated yet embodying all, what is it finally except myself?/These States, what are they except myself?', Whitman, 'By Blue Ontario Shore', *Complete Verse, Selected Prose*, 324.

[6] John Bayley, 'Richly Flows Contingency', *New York Review of Books* 38.14, 15 August 1991, 3.

radio newscasts and the newspaper headlines scattered throughout the
text, are a sign of Ginsberg's poem's immanence. It is not an epic in the
spirit of Ezra Pound's encyclopaedia of history, but one that is concerned
to document the present state of American culture, in all its ugliness
and beauty. As William Carlos Williams noted in 1939, 'news offers the
precise incentive to epic poetry'.[7]

As a collection of poems that charts a journey 'Thru the Vortex West
Coast to East 1965–1966' (as the first section of *The Fall* is entitled) and
back again ('Zigzag Back Thru These States 1966–67'), *The Fall of America*
is ordered by both its geography and chronology, with Ginsberg's multi-
vehicled travels across the country bringing an epic significance to the
Beat road journey. Ginsberg's quest, however, is not a search 'for the
Northwest Passage, nor Gold, nor the Prophet/who will save the polluted Nation' (*GCP*, 369). Defining his journey against that of America's
explorers, prospectors, and the pilgrim past, the poem muses instead on
the 'new wanderings to come' and presents Ginsberg himself as a modern day Odysseus (*GCP*, 372).

The Fall illustrates Ginsberg's ambition to redefine the epic as a form
concerned with 'present-day politics'. Speaking in 1965 about his desire
to write an epic, Ginsberg suggested that his approach might be based
upon 'simple free association on political themes' rather than 'narrative
form':

> The epic would be a poem including history, as it's defined [by
> Pound]. So that would be one about present-day politics, using the
> methods of the Blake French Revolution. I got a lot written. Narrative
> was 'Kaddish'. Epic – there has to be totally different organization, it
> might be simple free association on political themes – in fact I think an
> epic poem including history, at this stage. I've got a lot of it written, but
> it would have to be Burroughs' sort of epic – in other words, it would
> have to be *dis*-sociated thought stream which includes politics and his-
> tory. I don't think you could do it in narrative form, I mean what would
> you be narrating, the history of the Korean war or something?[8]

Although in its finished state *The Fall* might be described as narrating
something like 'the history of the Vietnam War', the poem encompasses

---

[7] William Carlos Williams, 'Review of Ezra Pound's *A Draft of XXX Cantos*', quoted in
Mike Weaver, *William Carlos Williams: The American Background* (Cambridge: Cambridge
University Press, 1971), 120.
[8] Ginsberg, 'Interview with Tom Clark', *Spontaneous Mind*, 49–50.

far more than just the 'political themes' first envisaged. Delivering on Ginsberg's plans for a modern epic, with its 'free association' of memory, song, radio crackle, news headlines and invocations of dead poets, the poem creates a sense for the reader of simultaneously inhabiting the world of the poet *and* the consciousness of America, making its 'own music/American mantra' from the juxtaposition of pop culture and literature, radio shows and American landscape (*GCP*, 427). *The Fall of America* fulfils Ginsberg's plans to depart from the traditional 'narrative format' as its trajectory is determined emotionally, as it plots a progressive despair at the state of the nation where 'There's nothing left for this country but doom/There's nothing left for this country but death' (*GCP*, 446). Its questing format thus becomes a futile counter-gesture to a nation in free-fall, doomed to forget the 'lost America of love past' (*GCP*, 136). This nostalgic vision of a lost Whitmanian version of America is at the centre of Ginsberg's journey to America's figural heart and literal heartland, leading him to proclaim himself 'a stranger alone in my country again' (*GCP*, 445), echoing Lowell's conceit of Crane's inalienable outsiderhood as a 'stranger in America'.

(ii) 'Putting my queer shoulder to the wheel'[9]

Both Crane and Ginsberg struggled at times to reconcile with their sexuality. But while Crane saw his sexual desires clash with his literary ambitions, Ginsberg's homosexuality proved to be something of a mobilizing and enabling force for his poetry, acting as a catalyst for his rethinking of poetic traditions and for his formulation of a politically agitative stance on his gay status. By the time he came to write 'Howl', he had incorporated his homosexuality into a coherent poetic strategy that called for frankness, honesty and the celebration of perversity and outsider-hood. In Ginsberg's poetry, same-sex desire functions at the very centre of his vision for America.

If we compare Ginsberg and Crane's incorporation of homosexuality into their epic visions, Ginsberg's frankness might be read as an index of the increasing presence of homosexuality in American public discourse in the 1950s and 1960s. However, while the replacement of Crane's occlusion by bold confessionalism would seem to suggest a more liberal climate, it is important to note that Ginsberg was very much a pioneer

---

[9] Ginsberg, 'America', *GCP*, 148.

of such self-exposure. This was also a move made at great danger to the poet himself. 'Howl' was published at a time when gay liberation was still far from a reality.

Under the shadow of McCarthyism, even the American Civil Liberties Union (ACLU) refused to extend its explicit support to the gay and lesbian community during the Cold War period. In 1957, the ACLU national board of directors claimed that homosexuality was an issue of public health, rather than of personal or sexual freedom, and would only intervene over what it saw as 'unconstitutional' state registration laws for homosexuals. In a policy statement from 1957, issued a year after the publication of *Howl and Other Poems*, the Union directors issued a policy statement stating that 'it is not within the province of the Union to evaluate the social validity of laws aimed at the suppression or elimination of homosexuality'.[10] Going further, the statement emphasized that the ACLU recognized that 'overt acts of homosexuality constituted a common law felony' that some 'states or communities' deemed 'socially necessary or beneficial'.[11] Despite this reluctance to get involved with constitutional issues regarding homosexuality, a more supportive local chapter was happy to take a major role in the defence of *Howl*'s publisher, Lawrence Ferlinghetti, after his arrest for publishing 'obscene material' in April 1957. The ACLU instituted proceedings contesting the legality of the seizure of the second printing of *Howl* (which had been stopped by customs on 25 March 1957). It subsequently posted bail for both Ferlinghetti and bookstore worker Shigeyoshi Murao after they were arrested by the San Francisco police. Although such inconsistencies may be explained by differences between local chapters and the national policy of the ACLU, political pressures during the Cold War made it a risky move for the Union to extend the boundaries of its fight for personal liberties to homosexuals.[12] Conveniently for the ACLU's involvement in the *Howl* trial, Ginsberg was never arrested, as he was out of the country at the time, and the subsequent trial was not focused on the homosexual content of the poem, despite its apparent 'obscenity'.

---

[10] ACLU Union Board of Directors' Policy Statement, 7 January 1957, in *We Are Everywhere: A Historical Sourcebook of Gay and Lesbian Politics*, ed. Mark Blasius and Shane Phelan (New York & London: Routledge, 1997), 274.

[11] Ibid.

[12] In 1967, the ACLU directors reversed its policy after the Supreme Court ruling that affirmed the right to sexual privacy in marriage. See Deborah Nelson, *Pursuing Privacy in Cold War America* (New York: Columbia University Press, 2002), 1–41.

(iii) Ginsberg and the critical field

The public visibility of Allen Ginsberg as a cultural and political icon after the *Howl* trial had a marked effect on the scholarship and literary criticism surrounding the poet. Critical portraits of Ginsberg have, like those of Hart Crane, tended to dwell upon the colourful details of the poet's life. To the detriment of his reputation as a poet, examinations of Ginsberg's literary (as opposed to political) achievements have been greatly outnumbered by what Marjorie Perloff has called the 'journalistic overkill'[13] of biographical material surrounding him and his fellow Beats.

Ginsberg was notorious in the wake of *Howl*'s obscenity trial, and after being ejected from Cuba in January 1965 and deported shortly afterwards from Czechoslovakia (after his controversial election as the *Kraj Majales*), Thomas Merrill was right to observe in 1969 that this particular poet 'makes news wherever he goes'.[14] However, critically speaking, not much of this 'news' related to the poetry itself. As Thomas Merrill notes:

Twenty years ago, a few literary-minded people might have recognized him as a budding young protégé of William Carlos Williams . . . Today, we tend to think of him as the nucleus of a very nebulous attitude that has bloomed across the breadth of the land (and abroad) to which we have given the name Hip.[15]

Excepting Thomas Merrill's book-length appraisal from 1969 of Ginsberg's poetical development (which covers the published collections up to and including *Reality Sandwiches*), much of the early commentary surrounding Ginsberg is, perhaps unsurprisingly, concerned with his reputation as a mischief-maker and his association with what had come to be known as the 'Beat Generation' writers. As Merrill notes in his preface, 'Ginsberg is now recognized more as a phenomenon than a poet',[16] sadly anticipating the reputation that still dominates today.

---

[13] Marjorie Perloff, 'A Lion in Our Living Room: Reading Allen Ginsberg in the Eighties', *Poetic License: Essays on Modernist and Postmodernist Lyric* (Evanston: Northwestern University Press, 1990), 201.
[14] Thomas F. Merrill, preface to *Allen Ginsberg* (Boston: Twayne Publishers, 1969).
[15] Ibid.
[16] Ibid.

The critical tendency to dwell upon what Merrill terms 'the carnival aspects of Ginsberg's career' was not unnoticed by other contemporary critics. Charles Shively joined Thomas Merrill's quiet revolt in 1973, arguing:

> He is not just a cultural phenomenon, not just a prophet, not just a Beatnik, not just a liberator, not just a grand old man for us to play our fantasies on – he is a *poet*.[17]

This misuse of Ginsberg as a receptacle for critical and cultural fantasies persists, to a certain degree. Twenty years after Shively's complaint, Michael Schumacher's *Dharma Lions: A Critical Biography* (1992) would still favour the 'biographical' component over the 'critical' evaluation that its title proposed to undertake, and the market in biographies of the beat writers is as buoyant as ever. Marjorie Perloff's 1986 essay, 'A Lion in Our Living Room: Reading Allen Ginsberg in the Eighties', is one example of a successful attempt by a critic to disentangle the 'poet' Allen Ginsberg from the myth, and to situate him in relation to contemporary poetics. Perloff's essay (revised for the 1990 publication of her collection *Poetic License: Essays on Modernist and Postmodernist Lyric*) reconsiders Ginsberg as a figure caught between tradition and experimentation; between a modernist and romantic lineage that she claims poems such as *Kaddish* and 'Howl' self-consciously engage and revise. Rejecting the received view of Ginsberg's poetry as 'formless' in its 'straight transcription of visionary speech',[18] Perloff's essay examines Ginsberg's use of conventional verse forms and undertakes close readings of his poetic technique, without disregarding the importance of the poet's own mythmaking as a context through which his work demands to be read.

Tony Trigilio's more recent work on the prophetic tradition continues Perloff's project of repositioning Ginsberg within a poetic arena, and provides one of the most interesting contemporary readings of his work. In Allen Ginsberg's *Buddhist Poetics* (2007), he traces the origins of his project to 'a fellow scholar' who had 'derided Allen Ginsberg as a poet of "hysterical loudmouthedness", and another [who] dismissed Ginsberg's poetics as mere "ranting". I felt compelled to reply':[19]

---

[17] Charles Shively, 'Allen Ginsberg: A Prophet on the Electric Networks', *On the Poetry of Allen Ginsberg*, ed. Lewis Hyde (Ann Arbor: University of Michigan Press, 1984), 214.

[18] Perloff, *Poetic License*, 201.

[19] Tony Trigilio, *Allen Ginsberg's Buddhist Poetics* (Carbondale: Southern Illinois University Press, 2007), ix.

It seemed just too easy to dismiss him in this way without at least a glance at how hysteria and loudmouthedness (not to mention the potential value of ranting) could be read as deliberate strategies, as actual crafted prophetic utterance rather than mere spectacle.[20]

Trigilio's earlier consideration of Ginsberg in '*Strange Prophecies Anew*': *Rereading Apocalypse in Blake, H.D., and Ginsberg* (2000) begins this repositioning, looking at the 'complex role *Kaddish* plays in Ginsberg's development of a contemporary poetics of prophecy'[21] and comparing the prophetic strategies of 'Howl''s focus on 'male comradeship' to what he sees as Ginsberg's questioning in *Kaddish* of prophetic authority. Trigilio's project is focused around Ginsberg's statement that, in writing 'Howl', he was trying to restore to American poetry 'the prophetic consciousness it had lost since the conclusion of Hart Crane's *The Bridge*'.[22] For Trigilio, Ginsberg is a religious writer whose poetry attempts to 'fuse the visionary consciousness of Biblical prophecy with what was for him the sacred space of human consciousness'.[23] This spotlight on the revisionary aspect of Ginsberg's poetry is helpful for thinking about the ways in which he was consciously reshaping or rethinking genres in his poetry. In this respect, my approach shares with Trigilio's own work a concern for how Ginsberg's poetic contribution can be seen to lie with his interventions in traditional genres.

Since Ginsberg's death in 1997, little has emerged to resuscitate his reputation as a poet. Jonah Raskin's *American Scream: Allen Ginsberg's 'Howl' and the Making of the Beat Generation* (2004), like Schumacher's earlier study, takes a predominantly biographical approach to its account of 'what it was like for Ginsberg to write "Howl" – how he felt, what he was thinking, why he wrote it, and who influenced him'.[24] Although the importance of the biographical context of Ginsberg's work cannot be denied, it is hard not to feel as though Ginsberg's formal innovations and experiments are still being given short critical shrift. In light of this,

[20] Ibid.
[21] *American Literature* 71.4, December 1999, 773–95. Later revised and collected in Tony Trigilio, '*Strange Prophecies Anew*': *Rereading Apocalypse in Blake, H.D., and Ginsberg* (Madison: Fairleigh Dickinson University Press, 2000).
[22] Allen Ginsberg and Gregory Corso, 'First Reading at the Six Gallery, October 7, 1955', Appendix II, *Howl: Original Draft Facsimile*, 165.
[23] Trigilio, Allen Ginsberg's Buddhist Poetics, ix.
[24] Jonah Raskin, preface to *American Scream: Allen Ginsberg's* 'Howl' *and the Making of the Beat Generation* (Los Angeles & London: University of California Press, 2004), xxii.

and taking cues from Thomas Merrill, Shively and Perloff, this chapter seeks to rectify the critical imbalance surrounding Ginsberg that has sometimes seen his homosexuality as just another misdemeanour in a roll-call of radical postures.[25] Attending to the project of realigning his sexuality with his poetic practice, I hope to bring the public portrait of the poet to bear upon the literary texts, restoring a reciprocal relation between the public and the private aspects that constitute 'Allen Ginsberg' as both a phenomenon and a writer. I argue that Ginsberg's homosexuality constitutes a major catalyst for his challenge to traditional Anglo-American forms, and that his radical political poetics of self-disclosure and confession continue in an alternative tradition that equates progression and liberation with the forging of new formal and thematic traditions.

(iv) A tale of two epics

Let us return to the plans for an epic that Ginsberg outlined in his 1965 interview with Tom Clark for *The Paris Review*. Ginsberg had very different ideas about the method for history's inclusion in a piece of poetry, although he name-checks Pound's dictum that an epic should be 'a poem including history'. Objecting to what he saw as Pound's 'fabricating' the *Cantos* 'out of his reading and out of the museum of literature', Ginsberg thought that the epic should be concerned with recording the 'present-day politics' of the here-and-now.[26] Rather than placing the weight of his poem on the authority of literary history, his thoughts turned to more contemporary methods of drawing on the world around him:

The thing would be to take all of contemporary history, newspaper headlines and all the pop art of Stalinism and Hitler and Johnson and Kennedy and Viet Nam and Congo and Lumumba and the South

---

[25] See Robert Martin, *The Homosexual Tradition*, 164. Ginsberg has defended himself against such charges, contending that, 'the use of sex as a banner to *épater le bourgeois*, to shock, show resentment or to challenge, is not sufficiently interesting to maintain for more than ten minutes; it's not enough to sustain a program that will carry love through to the deathbed or help out Indochina. Or get laid, finally. You have to have something more. You have to relate to people and their problems too' (Ginsberg, '*Gay Sunshine* Interview', reprinted in *Spontaneous Mind*, 336).

[26] Ginsberg, 'Interview with Tom Clark', *Spontaneous Mind*, 49–50.

and Sacco and Vanzetti – whatever floated into one's personal field of consciousness and contact.[27]

Ginsberg posits the Burroughsian 'dissociated thought stream' as the potential means to process such a vast quantity of material, conceiving of the structure and composition of this hypothetical epic poem as 'a basket'. 'Weaving' the poem 'out of those materials', he envisages the logic of the poem's narrative progressing 'by a process of association'.[28]

While James Miller has noted that these poetic methods are not far removed from Pound's own notion that 'the modern world/Needs such a rag-bag to stuff all its thoughts in',[29] Ginsberg's explicit refusal of literature as a source for his epic clearly marks where the younger poet wishes to dissociate himself from his predecessor and the high modernist epic tradition.[30] Unlike Pound or James Merrill, Ginsberg does not build his poems upon a canon of literature and intertextual references. Although both Merrill and Ginsberg make frequent references to their friends and artistic associates in their work, Ginsberg's frame of connoisseurial reference is more subcultural. Merrill's frame of reference is distinctly classical, while Ginsberg's poetry inhabits a world that is a million miles away from Merrill's elite existence of inherited money, the European milieu and political insouciance; 'I rarely buy a newspaper, or vote', Merrill confesses in 'The Broken Home'.[31]

Drawing on the world around him in the newspapers, newscasts, political protests and pop songs that populate *The Fall*, Ginsberg turns to the epic not only to explode and rethink the very myth of 'America' itself, but also as a way of bringing himself inside of a culture that had ideologically excluded him as a homosexual, Jew, and as an alleged former communist. His reworkings of the epic mode in both 'Howl' and *The Fall of America* are at once a gesture towards belonging, as well as defiant reminders of his outsider-hood and alienation. For example, while Ginsberg repeatedly casts himself as a prophetic figure – the 'lone man from the void' (*GCP*, 394) or 'the lone One singing to

---

[27] Ginsberg, *Spontaneous Mind*, 50.

[28] Ibid.

[29] Ezra Pound, *Selected Cantos* (New York: New Directions, 1970), 1.

[30] Miller, The American Quest, 287.

[31] James Merrill, 'The Broken Home', *Collected Poems*, ed. J. D. McClatchy and Stephen Yenser (New York: Alfred J. Knopf, 2001), 199.

myself' (*GCP*, 397), it is also this loneliness that *connects* him to the
nation at large:

> I'm an old man now, and a lonesome man in Kansas
>> but not afraid
>>> to speak of my lonesomeness in a car,
>>> because not only my lonesomeness
>>>> it's Ours, all over America,

(*GCP*, 405)

It is between these two positions that the poet seems perpetually torn,
and this situation is echoed in Ginsberg's approach to the epic mode.
Both 'Howl' and *The Fall* deviate from the traditional or classical epic
narrative format, and despite Ginsberg's recorded musings on his potential epic ambitions, it could not be said that either of the poems constitutes a premeditated effort to set out and write an epic poem of America
in the way that, say, Crane conceived of *The Bridge*.

In 'Howl''s *nekyiac* construction, however, and in *The Fall*'s recasting
of the jeremiad-as-epic, what these poems do is enable us to observe
the ways in which the epic traditions can be cannibalized, hybridized
and reborn. Casting himself as the nation's countercultural epic hero,
Ginsberg presents himself as longing to connect with a utopian idea of
America. At the same time that they illustrate Ginsberg's role as a countercultural icon through their political content, both 'Howl' and *The Fall*
hark back to older traditions of religion and poetry, using the language
of Biblical prophesy and deifying long-dead poets. For example, the title
of *The Fall of America* immediately invokes an epic tradition of Biblical
proportions, and its journeying format draws palpably on the traditions
of the Homeric epic voyage.

However, if Milton's epic account of the fall of man in *Paradise Lost* was
concerned 'to justify the ways of God to men', Ginsberg's poem is one
preoccupied with prophesying the consequences of the ways of man himself. It is a fulfilment of Whitman's prophecy of America as the nation
of the 'fabled damned' that the poem imagines.[32] Ginsberg denounces
any redemptive intentions for his poem, refusing to offer a Prophet 'who
will save the polluted Nation' (*GCP*, 369); the value of its journey lies
not with the revelation of a solution or saviour, but in the journey itself.

---

[32] Whitman, 'Democratic Vistas', *Complete Verse, Selected Prose*, 720.

Travelling towards the central 'vortex' of 'Wichita Vortex Sutra' (and to the emotional vortex of the 'Elegies for Neal Cassady') the poem goes in search of the heart of both America's goodness and of the roots of its destruction. This desperate pursuit of the source of America's madness, as exemplified by Wichita's contribution to the manufacturing war effort, shapes both the structure and rhythm of the poems' frenzied sifting of the personal and national consciousness.

Alongside his documentation of the physical landscape that he passes through, Ginsberg acts as a witness to the cultural and political landscapes of the time. By incorporating these signs of contemporary history, the tone of *The Fall* modulates rapidly from the telegraphic to the prophetic, as Ginsberg speaks about 'The Eve of Destruction' when 'my man world will blow up' (*GCP*, 372). Shifting from the casual diction of the song lyrics that are introduced as a refrain in *The Fall*'s first poem, 'Beginning of a Poem of these States', to the confessional rush of the poet's diaristic anecdote in 'Iron Horse' where Ginsberg recalls masturbating aboard a train, the poem takes in a wide variety of voices and tones as it makes its way across America.

Conversely, the structure of 'Howl' is dictated by a journey of the spirit, rather than of an earthly body. The poem charts a passage through an apocalyptic underworld populated by a generation that Ginsberg perceived as betrayed by a nation bent upon eradicating individuality. By virtue of its shorter length, its structure is more rigidly defined than *The Fall*, which is characterized by its unfolding composition. 'The poem is really built like a brick shithouse',[33] Ginsberg wrote to Richard Eberhart in 1956, as he attempted to defend 'Howl' against charges of formlessness. With its returning chorus of 'I am with you in Rockland', the third segment of 'Howl' constitutes a balancing return from the hellish brink of the poem's initial nightmare descent into an underworld of insanity, suicide and despair, and illustrates the symmetrical structure of the poem. The rage, horror and defiance of the opening sections of the poem give way to the expression of sympathy and affection for the poem's dedicatee, Carl Solomon.[34]

Ginsberg was clearly still thinking of 'Howl' as he began writing the poems that would make up *The Fall of America*. In 'A Methedrine Vision in Hollywood', written in the Christmas of 1965, he muses on his past

---

[33] Ginsberg, letter to Richard Eberhart, 18 May 1956, 'Appendix I: Contemporaneous Correspondence & Poetic Reactions', *Howl: Original Draft Facsimile*, 152.
[34] Ibid.

missives. The shift from confessional to national concerns is emphasized by the solitary, floating 'Americans' that stands almost as a corrective afterthought:

> Here at the atomic Crack-end of Time XX Century
> History swifting past horse chariot earth wheel
> So I in mid-age, finished with half desire
> Tranquil in my hairy body, familiar beard face,
>> Same fingers to pen
>> as twenty years ago began
> scribbled Confession to fellow Beings
> Americans –

(GCP, 380)

The focus has shifted from 'Howl''s anxious confessions of desire to the state of the nation at the apocalyptic 'Crack-end of time'. This change is emphasized by the line break, where Ginsberg almost corrects his younger self that was so preoccupied with the notion of the angelic potential of human beings that he forgot their citizenship. As 'Americans' they must listen now, as Ginsberg now performs the confession of the nation itself. The poem also shares a concern with the passing of time: 'Where did it all *go?*' the 'old Jew in the Hospital' asks (*GCP*, 381). But as the 'swifting' change of history passes, so it must also impinge upon the now 'mid-age' poet, 'finished with half desire', serene where once he was 'starving, hysterical, naked'. Ginsberg describes himself as now 'tranquil in my hairy body', his hirsute image now 'familiar' to a generation, as well as to himself.

(v) 'Wichita Vortex Sutra': Black magic language

'Howl' presents the malevolent forces of the world embodied as one in the figure of Moloch, however, *The Fall of America* is much more specific in its attack upon the modern world. Ginsberg's incessant raking of popular culture in *The Fall* is concerned with wrenching the control of language back from its cheap manipulation for the purposes of war:

> The war is language,
>> language abused
>>> for Advertisement,

language used
like magic for power on the planet:
Black Magic language,
        formulas for reality –
            Communism is a 9 letter word
                used by inferior magicians with
the wrong alchemical formula for transforming earth into gold
            – funky warlocks operating on guesswork,
                handmedown mandrake terminology

                                                        (*GCP*, 401)

The politicians have hijacked the words of the people to create a new reality controlled by war production and propaganda. Ginsberg turns back to the Whitmanian project of reclaiming the American tongue for the people: 'how many in their solitude weep aloud like me –/On the bridge over Republican River/almost in tears to know/how to speak the right language', he asks (*GCP*, 405). The corruption of language stands at the centre of Ginsberg's jeremiad tirade in 'Wichita Vortex Sutra'. Politicians decline to 'speak public language', vaunting aloud their own versions of events after a 'bad guess . . ./that's lasted a whole decade' (*GCP*, 401):

Generals faces flashing on and off screen
                            mouthing language
State Secretary speaking nothing but language
McNamara declining to speak public language
        The President talking language,
                Senators reinterpreting language

                                                        (*GCP*, 402)

In *The Fall*, the radio, the 'Soul of the nation', is the source of the true language of the people (*GCP*, 369). It is also the symbol through which Ginsberg can express the existence of the epic wanderer-prophet (himself) as simultaneously isolated from, and connected to, the America he is trying to awaken from the nightmare of war. The radio waves that carry the voice of Bob Dylan in the opening scene of *The Fall* are the counter-voice to the US Military Spokesmen, establishing the potential of the radio as a conduit for the political protest that is at the heart of the poem's message. As a 'mass machine-made folksong of one soul', Ginsberg is naming both the contradictions of the radio as a medium for government communications of casualty numbers and economic growth, while acknowledging its dissident potential. If the State Secretary and President can only inadequately mime a performance of real communication, the radio can speak directly *to* and *from* the 'public language' of the people themselves. Reaching for words that cannot be manipulated and polluted by the politicians, this 'Mantra of American Language' that the poem seeks is finally spoken by Ginsberg. Like a priestly radio announcer he lifts his 'voice aloud':

> make Mantra of American language now,
>   I here declare the end of the War !
>   Ancient day's Illusion !–
>   and pronounce the beginning of my own millennium.
> Let the States tremble,
>   let the Nation weep,
>   let Congress legislate its own delight
>   let the President execute his own desire –
> this Act done by my own voice,
>
> (*GCP*, 407)

In a world where words are nothing but 'formulas for reality', abused by Generals and Senators, Ginsberg's poem attempts to construct his reality, ending the war in a prophetic declaration. In Ginsberg's new millennium, the government will exist to legislate only pleasure and Presidents can deliver orders only to pursue their own gratification. If language has the power to alter reality as a tool for war-time propaganda (Ginsberg's logic reasons), why can it not be summoned to end the fighting? Assuming the role of mystical prophet, Ginsberg's schema creates a world of 'inferior magicians' and 'Sorcerer's Apprentices who lost control/of the simplest broomstick in the world:/Language' (*GCP*, 401). Turning the 'Black Magic Language' against these incompetent 'errand-boys', Ginsberg summons his own mantra, and so re-enters the 'youthful voice' of Dylan's 'soft prayer on the airwaves' as 'Language language' that might counter the 'vortex of hatred' (*GCP*, 409–10). As we shall see, this concern with language is central also to Ginsberg's sexual politics.

(vi) The American *nekyia*

In *The Fall*, Ginsberg never fails to offer the reader moments of hope. 'Howl', however, presents a much more unrelenting vision of a nightmare world gone to ruin, leading many of its readers to conclude that the poem offers nothing more than a sustained journey through hell. However, as a way of looking more closely at Ginsberg's engagement with an epic tradition, I propose that Jung's concept of the *nekyia* (as an encounter with the unconscious) can be employed to read the narrative of 'Howl' as an epic-style descent into an underworld that fuses the horrors of contemporary America with Ginsberg's own personal psychodrama.

Jung suggested the term *nekyia* in *Psychology and Alchemy* (1944) as 'an apt designation for the "journey to Hades"'[35] (after the title of the eleventh book of Homer's *Odyssey*), employing it to denote the descent into the unconscious, with the night-journey constituting its archetypal mythological incarnation:

> The night sea journey is a kind of *descensus ad infernos* – a descent into Hades and a journey to the land of ghosts somewhere beyond this world, beyond consciousness, hence an immersion in the unconscious.[36]

The descent to the underworld as a rite of passage is a classic epic motif that runs from Homer, through Virgil, and the prophetic tradition of Blake.[37] Its presence in a modern epic poem by a poet such as Ginsberg (who was more than familiar with psychoanalytic discourse through both his own reading and therapy) cannot be discussed without reference to Jung's extrapolation of 'the unconscious [as corresponding] to the mythic land of the dead, the land of the ancestors'.[38] While *Kaddish* takes its form and tone from the Jewish prayer for the dead, both 'Howl' and *The Fall* can be seen to draw on the classical and American epic traditions for their journeying format and depiction of heroic trials and ordeals.

For Dorothy Van Ghent (writing in 1959), the 'night journey or journey underground' was integral to what she saw as the Beat Generation's 'distinguishing myth', cohering their otherwise disparate work.[39] She identifies this recurring motif as one that 'follows authentic archaic lines', where the hero-quester 'has received a mysterious call – to the

---

35] Jung, 'The Psychology of the Transference', *Collected Works*, Vol. 16, 455.
[36] Ibid.
[37] The *nekyia* or night-journey also recurs as a motif in one of the most important examples of the modern American prose epic, *Moby-Dick*. Critics such as Edward Edinger have approached the novel as the record of a spiritual journey or symbolic record of the nation's unconscious. See Edward F. Edinger, *Melville's Moby-Dick: A Jungian Commentary: An American Nekyia* (New York: New Directions, 1978).
[38] Jung, *Psychology and Alchemy*, 52.
[39] Dorothy Van Ghent, 'Comment', *Wagner Literary Magazine* (Spring 1959), 27.

road, the freights, the jazz-dens, the "negro streets" . . . Where he goes is hell, the realm of death, ruled by the H- or Hades-Bomb'.[40] The epic flavour of Van Ghent's description continues in her anatomy of the Beat hero who is 'differentiated from the mass of the population of hell by his angelic awareness: he knows where he is'. Undergoing the 'heroic ordeals of myth' followed by a 'paean of ascent' (to accompany the 'return to the Kingdom'),[41] Van Ghent casts the archetypal Beat hero in the same mould as the epic adventurer.

It is easy to see that Van Ghent's model draws most heavily from the narrative presented by 'Howl', which, along with *On the Road*, was the most prominent example of Beat literature at the time of her writing (1959). The descent into the nightmarish world of the 'negro streets' by the angelic hero who eventually ascends into a joyful refrain of comradeship and empathy with Carl Soloman ('I am with you in Rockland') clearly resonates with Van Ghent's model. However, this movement from descent to ascent is also one that is revisited in the centripetal-centrifugal thrust of *The Fall of America*, where we journey with Ginsberg to the centre of the maelstrom in Wichita – America's heartland, where the national trauma can most fully be felt. In this respect, Van Ghent's model becomes a useful framework for thinking about the influence of epic on Ginsberg's narrative in his long poems.

'Howl''s vision of a collective hell of tortured and alienated minds updates the classical representation of Hades (or the land of the dead). These individuals are spiritually dead, inverting the original implications of the term 'beat' – connoting 'beatific'[42] – and psychologically stranded in a world that provides no respite from the demands of Moloch. However, Ginsberg does not use the descent to the underworld to paint a picture of despair without hope. This immersion in the collective unconscious of America is utilized in order to restore the nation, transforming the solitary nature of the Jungian *nekyia* into a journey that has a public impact. As the following passage reveals, Jung was clear about the productive and restorative role of the *nekyia*:

The Nekyia is no aimless and purely destructive fall into the abyss, but a meaningful *katabasis eis antron*, a descent into the cave of initiation and secret knowledge. The journey through the psychic history of

[40] Ibid.
[41] Ibid.
[42] Ann Charters, introduction to *Beat Down Your Soul: What Was the Beat Generation* (London: Penguin, 2001), xxiii.

mankind has as its object the restoration of the whole man, by awakening the memories in the blood. The descent to the Mothers enabled Faust to raise up the sinfully whole human being – Paris united with Helen – that *homo totus* who was forgotten when contemporary man lost himself in one-sidedness.[43]

In the same way, 'Howl' should not be read as an 'aimless and purely destructive' vision but as a restorative journey, as Ginsberg himself argued in a letter to Richard Eberhart.[44] In this sense, the therapeutic function of the *nekyia* shares much ground with the jeremiad. In both the jeremiad and the *nekyia* the mechanism is dependent upon the symbiosis of the individual and the collective and Ginsberg's nekyiac journey in 'Howl' rests upon the conflation of the personal and the public, where one man's infernal descent becomes an encounter with modern America's unconscious and the nation's psychic history (as encapsulated by the terrors of Moloch's influence).

As a purposeful confrontation with the self that seeks to 'raise up' the fallen soul through a descent into the inner 'abyss', the *nekyia* serves many of the functions of the jeremiad. However, where the *nekyia* usually operates on an individual basis (both in the Jungian and mythological examples), the jeremiad works to restore an entire nation or community.

(vii) Ginsberg's 'America': Rethinking the jeremiad

With its angry, yet comic, call for the renewal of the nation, 'America' (1956) stands not only as an important thematic precursor text to *The Fall* but also exemplifies Ginsberg's renegotiation of the jeremiad mode. Making use of comic juxtapositions and wry humour, as well as powerful and controversial rhetoric, 'America' provides a rehearsal for Ginsberg's later, sustained efforts in rethinking the jeremiad for *The Fall*.

In his 2001 book-length study of the religious visions of the Beat writers, *The Bop Apocalypse*, John Lardis talks about the jeremiad as the 'art form used to bring the sins of the nation to bear on the individual conscience'.[45]

---

[43] C. G. Jung, 'On Picasso' (1932), *The Spirit in Man, Art, and Literature, Collected Works,* Vol. 15 (London: Routledge & Kegan Paul, 1953), 135–41.

[44] Ginsberg, letter to Richard Eberhart, 18 May 1956, 'Appendix I: Contemporaneous Correspondence & Poetic Reactions', *Howl: Original Draft Facsimile*, 152.

[45] John Lardis, *The Bop Apocalypse: The Religious Visions of Kerouac, Ginsberg, and Burroughs* (Urbana & Chicago: University of Illinois Press, 2001), 36.

Ginsberg's Queer Shoulder 95

Lardis' definition is helpful here for thinking about how we might see Ginsberg's re-imagining of the modern epic poem as incorporating the punitive or didactic element of the traditional jeremiad. In *The American Jeremiad* (1978), Sacvan Bercovitch defined the mode as a sermon or other oral or written work that sought to unify a people by creating tension between ideal social life and its real manifestation.[46] Bercovitch emphasizes the mode, which originated in the European pulpit, as a 'ritual designed to join social criticism to spiritual renewal, public to private identity, the shifting "signs of the times" to certain traditional metaphors, themes, and symbols'.[47] For Bercovitch, the jeremiad's function is rooted in the way in which it seeks to account for the misfortunes of an era by heralding them as a divine penalty for social or moral degeneracy – their rhetorical formula is designed to incite contrition and a renewal of piety and good behaviour.

Bercovitch's definition is pertinent to our discussion for the importance it places upon the interdependency of the individual and his or her community, where the jeremiad sustains a paradoxical rhetoric of hope and fear – a tension between the ideal and the real. Interestingly, Bercovitch attributes this paradoxical element to the American jeremiad only. Its European predecessor, according to Bercovitch, conforms to a more 'static' model that describes an inevitable decline of civilization from its mythic or ideal beginnings. Ginsberg's approach to the mode in both 'Howl' and *The Fall of America* certainly echoes Bercovitch's definition of the American jeremiad as a ritual designed to join social criticism to spiritual renewal. The modulation of the poetic voice from ecstatic reverie to apocalyptic despair at the state of America conjoins the 'public to private identity' and presents contemporary signs alongside Bercovitch's 'traditional metaphors'. However, the tendency towards pessimism in *The Fall* (which invokes Whitman's fear of America's decline) sees Ginsberg's jeremiad poetics fitting more closely with Bercovitch's European model.

Whitman's essay, 'Democratic Vistas', is crucial to Ginsberg's thinking about the fate of the American nation and also pertinent to the pervasive sense in both 'Howl' and *The Fall* that America is a country gone to spiritual ruin. Specifically, in 'Democratic Vistas' Whitman warned that

---

[46] Sacvan Bercovitch, *The American Jeremiad* (Madison, WI: University of Wisconsin Press, 1979).
[47] Bercovitch, preface to *The American Jeremiad*, xi.

America might become the 'fabled damned among nations' if it did not counter its current 'materialistic bearings':

> I say of all this tremendous and dominant play of solely materialistic bearings upon current life in the United States, with the results as already seen accumulating, and reaching far into the future, that they must either be confronted and met by at least an equally and tremendous force-infusion for purpose of spiritualization, for the pure conscience, for genuine esthetics, and for absolute and primal manliness and womanliness – or else our modern civilization, with all its improvements, is in vain, and we are on the road to a destiny, a status, equivalent, in its real world, to that of the fabled damned.[48]

Both 'Howl' and *The Fall* are greatly indebted to what Ginsberg would call the 'Prophecy of the Good Gray Poet' (*GCP*, 400) for their representations of a nation in decline. Writing in 1986, Ginsberg claimed that 'in publishing "Howl", I was curious to leave behind after my generation an emotional time bomb that would continue exploding in U.S. consciousness in case our military-industrial-nationalist complex solidified in a repressive police bureaucracy'.[49] As a poetic talisman against the threat of 'authoritarian strong-arming',[50] Ginsberg repositions his poem 30 years on in similar terms to those used in *The Fall of America*. Framing these poems as following in Whitman's footsteps in using the power of the word to arm against the future decline of America, both 'Howl' and *The Fall* use the force of their poetry to construct a Whitmanian 'force-infusion for purpose of spiritualization'.[51]

While Ginsberg makes extensive use of 'Democratic Vistas' in *The Fall* (in particular in 'Wichita Vortex Sutra'), 'Howl' makes no explicit reference to Whitman's text. However, in its vision of Moloch's 'Filth! Ugliness!' and 'unobtainable dollars!' (*GCP*, 131), 'Howl' echoes Whitman's vision of a world ruled by the 'dominant play of solely materialistic bearings'.[52] Echoing the symbolic function of usury in Pound's *Cantos*, money and materialism form the core characteristics of Moloch's hold upon the modern nation and are the enemies of 'Visions! Omens!

[48] Whitman, 'Democratic Vistas', *Complete Verse, Selected Prose*, 720.
[49] Ginsberg, 'Author's Preface', *Howl: Original Draft Facsimile*, xii.
[50] Ibid.
[51] Whitman, 'Democratic Vistas', *Complete Verse, Selected Prose*, 720.
[52] Ibid.

hallucinations! miracles! ecstasies!' and 'the whole boatload of sensitive bullshit' venerated by the poet and his circle (*GCP*, 132).

'Paterson', from 1949 (often read as a rehearsal for 'Howl') is similarly concerned with the misplaced values of materialism: 'What do I want in these rooms papered with visions of money?', the poem asks:

> How much can I make by cutting my hair? If I put new heels on my shoes,
> bathe my body reeking of masturbation and sweat, layer upon layer of
>   excrement
> dried in employment bureaus, magazine hallways, statistical cubicles,
>   factory stairways,
> cloakrooms of the smiling gods of psychiatry;
> if in antechambers I face the presumption of department store supervisory
>   employees,
> old clerks in their asylums of fat,
>
> (*GCP*, 40)

The acquisition of money is equated with the shedding of the bohemian trappings of long hair and days spent in masturbatory ecstasy in exchange for the surrendering of the self to the establishment and the institution's spaces of employment. These are all characterized as confined spaces – 'hallways', 'cubicles', 'stairways', 'cloakrooms'; verbally equated with the enclosure of the asylum (Ginsberg was residing at the New York Psychiatric Institute at the time of writing the poem). Figuring a life enslaved to materialism as a less preferable option than to 'go mad' (*GCP*, 40), Ginsberg reprises these images of enclosure in Part I of 'Howl', moving towards the vision of a poetry that conforms, not to the demands of the tedium of the nine-to-five routine, but 'to the rhythm of thought in his/naked and endless head' (*GCP*, 131).

Although such poems evince Ginsberg's early concern with Whitman's counter-quest 'for the pure conscience' and 'genuine esthetics', it was only after years of returning time and again to Whitman's work that the poet would make his most direct evocations of Whitman's essay and insist on its resonance for modern America. Late in 1958, Ginsberg wrote a lengthy letter to John Hollander, including in it his reassertion of the importance of Whitman's drive for 'Bardic frankness prophecy':

> . . . what Whitman called for in American poets – them to take over
> from Priests – lest materialism & mass-production of emotion drown

America (which it has) & we become what he called the Fabled Damned among nations which we have.[53]

Ginsberg's first use of the phrase 'fabled damned' occurs in his 1957 poem, 'Death to Van Gogh's Ear!'; 'Whitman warned against this "fabled Damned of nations"' (*GCP*, 169). Its sentiment, however, is prefigured in the closing stanza of 'A Supermarket in California' (written in 1955, 3 years before Ginsberg's letter to Hollander):

> Will we walk all night through solitary streets? The trees add shade to shade, lights out in the houses, we'll both be lonely.
> Will we stroll dreaming of the lost America of love past blue automobiles in driveways, home to our silent cottage?
> Ah, dear father, graybeard, lonely old courage-teacher, what America did you have when Charon quit poling his ferry and you got out on a smoking bank and stood watching the boat disappear on the black waters of Lethe?
>
> (*GCP*, 136)

Here, Ginsberg maps the Greek underworld onto the modern-day streets of Berkeley: the 'shades' of the dead souls of Hades are conjured by the trees on the sidewalk that add the literal 'shade' to the 'shade' of the lonely souls (and in the case of the dead Whitman – literally a 'shade') passing outside in the darkness through 'solitary streets'. Although Ginsberg erroneously relocates Charon from the River Styx to the amnesia-inducing Lethe, the mythological ferryman is an apposite figure for the poet who wrote 'Crossing Brooklyn Ferry', and perhaps gives us some insight into the unconscious parallels Ginsberg was drawing between the mythic underworld and the modern-day metropolis of 'Filth! Ugliness! Ashcans and unobtainable dollars!' (*GCP*, 131).

Ginsberg's most direct evocation of Whitman's essay, however, was not to appear until 1966. Affirming the links between his own work and Whitman's words of nine decades earlier, the phrase 'fabled damned' reappears in 'Wichita Vortex Sutra' (1966):

> nine decades after Democratic Vistas
> and the Prophecy of the Good Gray Poet
> Our nation 'of the fabled damned'
>
> (*GCP*, 400)

---

[53] Ginsberg to John Hollander, in Kramer, *Allen Ginsberg in America*, 174.

Prophesying a terrible destiny for the nation if it did not veer from its current path, Ginsberg makes use of techniques that are clearly jeremiadical: 'Let the States tremble,/Let the Nation weep', he demands as he catalogues the sins of America and 'prophes[ies] blood violence' (*GCP*, 385).

If we return to Ginsberg's earliest experiments with the jeremiad in 'America' (1956), it is clear to see that by the time Ginsberg came to write *The Fall*, the time for infusing the sermon with humour has passed. In this earlier example, however, the poet recasts the rhetoric and form of its traditional incarnation to fashion an imagined conversation with his own country through a litany of reprimands and questions. 'I'm addressing you', Ginsberg reminds both the reader and America, as he reels off a state-of-the-nation catalogue of cultural crisis:

Asia is rising against me.
I haven't got a chinaman's chance.
I'd better consider my national resources.
My national resources consist of two joints of marijuana millions of genitals
    an unpublishable private literature that jetplanes 1400 miles an hour
    and twentyfive-thousand mental institutions.
I say nothing about my prisons nor the millions of underprivileged who live
    in my flowerpots under the light of five hundred suns.

(*GCP*, 147)

In order for the jeremiad to be effective, the strength of the bond between the nation and the individual must be firmly established. The gravity of this relationship between the speaker and his country is evident in the opening line of the poem: 'America I've given you all and now I'm nothing' (*GCP*, 146). The body politic has sucked dry the body of the poet, both emotionally and economically. In the passage quoted above, the 'national resources' of the nation are syntactically conflated with those of the poet. Ginsberg's drug 'stash' and the Whitmanian 'millions of genitals' get equal billing with America's planes, asylums, and prisons, as the jeremiadical rhetoric binds the individual and the nation to such an extent that they become confused and indistinguishable from one another. Likening the American people to marijuana plants grown in 'flowerpots' under the heatlamps of 'five hundred suns', Ginsberg evokes the recent memory of Hiroshima's atomic explosion to comment upon the stupefied state of the nation. Transforming the effects of the atomic bomb into a nourishing force, Ginsberg seems to suggest that Hiroshima allowed post-war America to 'grow' into something that could, like the marijuana plants, artificially numb the world and dull the pain of memory, through the explosion of consumption and production.

Playing with the absurdity of rhetorical conjunctions, 'America' juxtaposes serious political intent with a playful delight in the bizarre:

> America when will you be angelic?
> When will you take off your clothes?
> When will you look at yourself through the grave?
> When will you be worthy of your million Trotskyites?
> America why are your libraries full of tears?
>
> (*GCP*, 146)

Ginsberg calls for the nation to be honest – to be naked in front of its people and to adopt the 'Bardic frankness' preached by the poet.[54] Utilizing the same anaphoric techniques as he calls upon in 'Howl', the Biblical tones of 'America' are buried under the Dadaist absurdity of the poem's comic personifications. 'How can I write a holy litany in your silly mood?' Ginsberg writes, drawing attention not only to his own absurdist technique but also to the inhospitable climate of the times, where automobile production is more important than the writing of poetry, imagining selling 'strophes $2500 apiece $500 down on your old strophe' (*GCP*, 147).

'America' picks up the theme of subverting economic exchange from 'A Supermarket in California' (1955), where Ginsberg imagines the transformation of poetry into a quasi-consumerist act: 'shopping for images' (*GCP*, 136). In 'America', Ginsberg asks, 'When can I go into the supermarket and buy what I need with my good looks?' echoing the free-for-all sensual feast of 'A Supermarket in California' where Ginsberg imagines 'possessing every frozen delicacy, and never passing the cashier' (*GCP*, 136). This fantasy of bypassing or corrupting the process of capitalist exchange is at the heart of Ginsberg's comic conflation of Ford automobiles with lines of poetry. However, the utopia that 'America' imagines is neither 'the next world' nor the 'city on the hill' coveted by the

---

[54] 'This kind of Bardic frankness prophecy is what Whitman called for in American poets – them to take over from Priests.' Ginsberg, letter to John Hollander, in Jane Kramer, *Allen Ginsberg in America* (New York: Random House, 1970), 174.

Puritan jeremiad, but the imminent here-and-now of 'you and I' (*GCP*, 146). The poem calls for the recognition of the potential of alternative ways to both protect and represent the nation: 'It occurs to me that I am America' (*GCP*, 147), he confesses at the poem's mid-point, claiming representative status and refusing to be marginalized as Jew, homosexual and former Communist. Closing the poem on a reprise of these senti- ments – 'America, I'm putting my queer shoulder to the wheel' (*GCP*, 148), Ginsberg's confrontational promise to his country (to protect and defend the values of his nation by being his queer self), follows his admis- sion of unsuitability to serve his country in the traditional sense:

> It's true I don't want to join the Army or turn lathes in precision parts Factories, I'm nearsighted and psychopathic anyway.
>
> (*GCP*, 148)

In juxtaposing his thoughts in this way, Ginsberg seems to pose an implicit challenge to the exclusion of homosexuals from the military, conflating the mechanical ('the wheel') and the sexual (queer) in an archetypal Ginsbergian image.

If the nation can throw off the 'machinery' and its 'insane demands' generated by the paranoia of Cold War politics, it might be able to retrieve the 'angelic' America that Ginsberg bathetically represents by his 'sentimental' memories of 'the Wobblies'. In this respect, 'A Supermarket in California' and 'America' could be read together as poems that both dream of 'the lost America of love past' and imagine responses or solutions to the nation's current dislocation from such val- ues. However, whereas 'A Supermarket . . .' sees Ginsberg take refuge in his Whitmanian influences, 'America' confronts the 'national resources' of the present to conjure a dialogue that might produce some solutions to the unanswered question on which 'A Supermarket . . .' closes: 'What America did you have . . .?' (*GCP*, 136).

As Ginsberg's most direct evocation of the nation prior to *The Fall*, 'America' is significant for its appearance alongside 'Howl' in Ginsberg's first published volume. As a poem that speaks through a melding of the public and the private, it offers a more humorous and condensed politici- zation of the concerns voiced more obliquely in 'Howl' (written around 5 months prior to 'America'). The opening of 'America' ('I've given you all and now I'm nothing') resonates strongly with 'Howl' 's sense of the sanity of a generation held to ransom by the nation ('I saw the best minds of my generation . . .'). Although 'Howl' is generally conceived of as an example of hyperbolic lyric,[55] in these ways it speaks to the issues of belonging and outsider-hood that make it feasible to think of Ginsberg's first foray into the long poem as engaging quite purposefully with the ideas of representing and speaking about a nation.

The conflation of the personal and the political upon which 'America' turns is a trope that Ginsberg returns to again and again in his writing, with its rhetoric reflecting a crucial shift in political ideology. By the 1960s, the rallying cry of 'the personal is the political' echoed well beyond the realms of its feminist originators, resonating throughout the gay and lesbian movements that were beginning to emerge and break free of the pathological labels associated with homosexuality. Emerging as a consequence of the 1944 G.I. Bill of Rights (which had denied the benefits of the Bill to any soldier with an undesirable or 'blue discharge' issued because of 'homosexual acts or tendencies'),[56] the intersection of same-sex desire with political loci (such as citizenship or national identity) became an explicit preoccupation of the McCarthy era. As Deborah Nelson has observed, these Cold War era anxieties serve to illustrate the ease with which 'questions of national security [turn] into questions about normative gender and sexuality',[57] where sexual and political deviance become different incarnations of the same crime – namely threatening the 'American way of life'. In this way, so-called private behaviour (sex) acquired distinct political (and therefore public) significance during this period, and hence Ginsberg is able to make a statement of intent to serve his country ('I'm putting my queer shoulder to the wheel') sound like a statement of subversive intent.

However, as Michael Rogin has noted, the extension of Cold War surveillance into the domestic sphere of sexual expression was paradoxical. The defence of the private domain is only accomplished by the 'takeover of the private by the falsely private':[58]

They politicize privacy in the name of protecting it and thereby wipe it out. Domestic and cold war ideologies not only dissolve the private

[55] Ginsberg, 'Interview with Tom Clark', *Spontaneous Mind*, 49.

[56] For an account of the heteronormative bias of the G.I. Bill, see Margot Canaday, 'Building a Straight State: Sexuality and Social Citizenship under the 1944 G.I. Bill', *The Journal of American History* 90.3, December 2003, 935–55.

[57] Nelson, *Pursuing Privacy*, 12.

[58] Michael Paul Rogin, *Ronald Regan, the Movie and Other Episodes in Political Demonology* (Berkeley, Los Angeles & London: University of California Press, 1987), 245.

into the public; they also do the reverse. They depoliticize politics by blaming subversion on personal influence.[59]

This negotiation is clearly a two-way street, making plain the problem with conceiving of the relationship between the public and the private as a dichotomy. If we unpack Rogin's analysis of the increasing inter-penetration of the public and private realms, we can begin to see the mechanisms of their erosion. By 'blaming subversion on personal influ-ence', the fantasy of the security of the compliant community can be maintained through the spectacle of the ejection, conversion or punish-ment of those individual 'subversives'. In 'America', this is parodied in the absurd personification of Russia as a 'power mad' harpy who 'wants to take/our cars from out our garages/ . . . Her needs a Red *Reader's Digest*' (*GCP*, 147–8).

Let us put these lines in context with the historical moment being con-sidered here: The highly publicized hearings of the House Un-American Activities Committee in the fifties provided the necessary spectacle not only for reinforcing the consequences for those who engaged in 'Un-American' activities (the committee did not take a Whitmanian approach to homosexuality) but also served to present a picture of a proactive government that was aggressively shown to be seeking to main-tain the domestic security of its citizens.[60] Ginsberg mocks this suspi-cion of communists by challenging their stereotypical representation in 'America''s nostalgically benign vision of the Party meetings he attended with his mother as a child: 'the speeches were free everybody was angelic . . . it was all so sincere you have no idea what a good thing the party was in 1835 . . . Everybody must have been a spy' (*GCP*, 147). Mocking the notion of 'the- communist-in-our-midst', Ginsberg confesses, 'I used to be a communist when I was a kid' (*GCP*, 146). Following his sentimental vision with the farcical repetition of 1950s' American stereotypes of 'them bad Russians' and 'them China men', the poem tries to mitigate the hos-tility and paranoia of the contemporary climate by exposing the ridicu-lous nature of a situation which would brand a child a national traitor. Later, in 'Wichita Vortex Sutra', Ginsberg seeks to avenge his mother's death from 'communist anticommunist psychosis', describing his recol-lections of his mother's 'complaining about wires of masscommunication

---

[59] Ibid.
[60] See David K. Johnson, The Lavender Scare: The Cold War Persecution of Gays and Lesbians in the Federal Government (Chicago: University of Chicago Press, 2006).

in her head/and phantom political voices in the air/besmirching her girlish character' (*GCP*, 410). Here, Ginsberg associates his mother's actual psychosis with the national mood, exposing the illness manifest in the rhetoric of 'protecting' American citizens (whereas the rhetoric claims to refer to an illness implicitly separate). Such spectacles of intolerance to the 'other' are resonant with interpretations of the function of typical scapegoat rituals, which theorize the re-establishment of community boundaries through the ritualized ejection or sacrifice of a symbolic 'other'. With its role in delineating boundaries between alien and kin, the conceptual power of sacrifice makes it a key mediator at moments of cultural change;[61] a mechanism more recently at work in the 1980s and 1990s representations of HIV and AIDS as the 'gay plague' (as discussed in the introductory chapter). Speaking of AIDS as a 'cold war redux', Deborah Nelson makes clear the ideological and rhetorical overlap between these two historically disparate moments:

> The disease and its victims were cast as the internal weakness that made America vulnerable to internal decay, and perhaps, even worse, drained the United States of its will to combat the ideological enemy.[62]

In 1965, the Secret Service designated Ginsberg as just such an 'ideological enemy'. With a photograph of the poet 'pictured in an indecent pose' placed in the Federal narcotics files and copied to the FBI, the poet was listed as 'potentially dangerous' and a 'subversive' with 'evidence of emotional instability (including unfixed residence and employment record) or irrational or suicidal behaviour' who had made 'expressions of strong or violent anti U.S. sentiment', and had 'a propensity for violence and antipathy toward good order and government'.[63] Ginsberg's 'critical sentiment' was of course part of his programme to recover the true America: he was concerned to explore the 'internal decay' at the heart of the nation. Perceiving a sickness at the very centre of American consciousness, Ginsberg proposed that this national disease could only be cured by the awakening of the 'individual'.

---

[61] See Susan L. Mizruchi, *The Science of Sacrifice American Literature and Modern Social Theory* (Princeton: Princeton University Press, 1998).
[62] Nelson, *Pursuing Privacy*, 25.
[63] Herbert Mitgang, 'Allen Ginsberg FBI Files', *American Poets Online Resource*, www.english.uiuc.edu/maps/poets/g_l/ginsberg/fbi.htm, extracted from *Dangerous Dossiers: Exposing the Secret War against America's Greatest Authors* (New York: D.I. Fine, 1988), site visited on 7 September 2011.

Writing his 'Independence Day Manifesto' in 1959 (a post-'Howl' tirade against the censorship of the poet and individual), the poet speaks of 'a crack in the mass consciousness of America': 'America is having a nervous breakdown', he declares.[64] Equating the state of the nation with his own (and his mother's) personal history of mental instability, the poet is at once symptom and saviour of America; victim and cure:

> There is a crack in the mass consciousness of America [. . .] Poetry is the record of individual insights into the secret soul of the individual and because all individuals are one in the eyes of their creator, into the soul of the world. The world has a soul. America is having a nervous breakdown.[65]

As a vision of a nation on the brink of self-destruction, Ginsberg draws upon biblical and spiritual discourses to illuminate what he sees as the 'the suppression of contemplative individuality'. The 'conspiracy' to 'impose one level of mechanical consciousness on mankind' draws on the same language of industrialization that we see in part II of 'Howl'. Ginsberg casts the response to his poem as a symptom of a national crisis; a 'sexless and soulless America' is trying to 'determine our mode of consciousness, our sexual enjoyments, our different labours and our loves', the poet laments. Censorship, he implies, is a symptom of a government that persecutes those who seek the path to enlightenment: 'To be a junky in America is like having been a Jew in Nazi Germany'.[66]

The Fall of America does nothing to break with this sense of a conflation or confusion of the personal and the national. As James Miller has noted, the persistent theme of the poems is of 'national nightmare [and] personal ecstasy';[67] 'the political report comes in the form of a personal vision or nightmare; the personal report is placed in the context of the national hallucination'.[68] The political landscape is reported through snippets of overheard radio newscasts, juxtaposed alongside the sexual overtones of popular song lyrics, with no recognizable hierarchy between these fragments:

---

[64] Allen Ginsberg, 'Poetry, Violence, and the Trembling Lambs or Independence Day Manifesto', first published in *San Francisco Chronicle*, 26 July 1959, reprinted in *Deliberate Prose: Selected Essays 1952–1995*, ed. Bill Morgan (London: Penguin Books, 2000), 3.
[65] Ibid.
[66] Ginsberg, *Deliberate Prose*, 4.
[67] Miller, *The American Quest*, 288–9.
[68] Ibid., 290.

'. . . Korean troops killed 35 Viet Cong near Coastal highway Number One.'

> "For he's oh so Good
> and he's oh so fine
> and he's oh so healthy
> in his body and his mind"
>   The Kinks on car radio
>
>   (*GCP*, 382)

If the radio is (as Ginsberg proposes) the 'soul of America' (*GCP*, 369), then the sins of the nation, and the means for its salvation, are broadcast simultaneously by *The Fall*, across the airwaves of radio. The songs of sexual celebration, by evoking the 'fine' and 'healthy' bodies of the young men being sacrificed in the cause of War, highlight the relative health and sickness of the body politic. Just as he had imagined America as undergoing a 'nervous breakdown' in 1959, Ginsberg now saw America as being irrevocably alienated from the utopian visions of Crane and Whitman; 'What'll happen to that?' he asks in 'Iron Horse' (*GCP*, 452).

(viii) Tracing Whitman's influence

Whitman's confusion of the personal and the public realms provided Ginsberg with an important poetic precedent to justify his frankness about homosexuality. Of all the poets considered in this study, Ginsberg is certainly the most indebted to Whitman, with the 'barbaric yawp' of the 'Good Gray Poet' (*GCP*, 400) not only providing the verbal cue for 'Howl',[69] but also constituting the conceptual catalyst for much of Ginsberg's ideological framework concerning comradeship, mysticism and the role of the poet in the American nation.[70] As James Miller has remarked in his essay considering the relationship between the two poets,[71] Ginsberg's relation to Whitman is 'constant and continuous'.[72] Throughout his interviews and essays, Ginsberg cites Whitman as providing the precedent for pushing his poetic subjectivity to the outer limits. For Ginsberg, this is the

---

[69] Or, as Kerouac sardonically renamed it, 'Wail'.
[70] 'I sound my barbaric yawp over the roofs of the world', Whitman, *Complete Verse, Selected Prose*, 85.
[71] Miller, *The American Quest*, 276–317.
[72] Ibid., 278.

important legacy of *Leaves of Grass*, as the scene of Whitman's life-long project to articulate an 'outline of his own mind', and to push forth the boundaries of what Ginsberg called 'Bardic frankness'.[73]

In his 1980 essay, 'On Walt Whitman, Composed on the Tongue or Taking a Walk Through Leaves of Grass', Ginsberg places poetic 'honesty' at the very heart of his portrait of the poet:

> There was a man, Walt Whitman, who lived in the nineteenth century, in America, who began to define his own person, who began to tell his own secrets, who outlined his own body, and made an outline of his own mind, so other people could see it. He was sort of the prophet of American democracy . . . because he was so honest and so truthful and at the same time so enormous-voiced and bombastic . . .[74]

In Ginsberg's account of the legacy left by Whitman for American poetry, the confessional voice fuses with that belonging to the epic or public project, as the interior world that belongs to the expression of the 'outline of his own mind' is externalized and projected ('so other people could see it'). For Ginsberg, Whitman's revolutionary gesture was to make the personal become the subject for public articulation, expanding 'the area[s] of poetic experience'[75] into the quotidian and the domestic:

> He began announcing himself, and announcing his person, with a big capital P, Person, self, or one's own nature, one's own original nature, what you're really thinking when you're alone in bed, after everybody's gone home from the party or when you're looking in the mirror, shaving . . . or you're just walking down the street, looking at people full of longing.[76]

For Miller too, this is the locus of Whitman's legacy to the poets of the twentieth century. In his narrative of Whitman's pivotal role in the development of modern American poetry, Miller cites Ginsberg's 'Howl' as providing the catalyst for Robert Lowell to break free from the traditional tenets he had followed for a decade, produce *Life Studies* (1959) and

---

[73] 'This kind of Bardic frankness prophecy is what Whitman called for in American poets – them to take over from Priests' (Ginsberg to John Hollander, quoted in Jane Kramer, *Allen Ginsberg in America*, 174).

[74] Ginsberg, *Deliberate Prose*, 285

[75] Ginsberg, Letter to John Hollander, quoted in Kramer, *Allen Ginsberg in America*, 174.

[76] Ginsberg, *Deliberate Prose*, 285

kick-start the 'confessional' strain that was to dominate poetry in the latter half of the century.[77] Miller argues convincingly that Whitman should take credit for laying the foundations of a confessional subjectivity that could serve as an escape from the strictures of Eliotic 'impersonality'.[78] Indeed, in Miller's narrative, Whitman forms the connective tissue between all of the great American poets.

However, unlike Eliot's, Whitman's influence is not so much a question of formal or thematic imitation, as one of encouraging difference – 'the *personal* of Whitman could not be the genuinely *personal* of any other poet'.[79] Even those who reject his legacy cannot escape his influence, according to Miller: 'every American poet must come to terms with [Whitman's] presence and is influenced as deeply in rejecting as in accepting him'.[80] So with Ginsberg, it is in the very *terms* of his acceptance of Whitman that we find the importance of his influence for the younger poet, and also begin to see the crucial differences in their visions of nationhood.

In his delineation of the dynamic between the public and the private in Whitman's poetry, Ginsberg locates an active dialogue between the private realm of the 'Self' or individual mind, and the expansive sphere of the 'World' or universe, that leaves an indelible mark on his own life-long quest to speak for, and of, America. Ginsberg opens his essay on Whitman, quoting from the opening of the final edition of *Leaves of Grass*:

One's-Self I sing, a simple separate person,
Yet utter the word Democratic, the word En-Masse.[81]

The private–public dialectic is at the foreground of this passage that Ginsberg chooses as his first illustration of Whitman's poetry; the lyric impulse of the 'simple separate person', inextricable from the epic project of the articulation of the 'word En-Masse'. Despite all his emphasis

---

[77] 'I was in San Francisco, the era and setting of Allen Ginsberg . . . I became sorely aware of how few poems I had written . . . I began to paraphrase my Latin quotations, and to add extra syllables to a line to make it clearer and more colloquial . . . When I returned home, I began writing lines in a new style . . . When I began writing "Skunk Hour", I felt that most of what I knew about writing was a hindrance' (Robert Lowell, 'On "Skunk Hour"', quoted in Miller, *The American Quest*, 4–5).
[78] Miller, *The American Quest*, 3–10.
[79] Miller, preface to *The American Quest*, xi.
[80] Miller, *The American Quest*, 13.
[81] Ginsberg, 'Walt Whitman, Composed on the Tongue', *Deliberate Prose*, 285.

on the personal, however, Whitman's individualism is always tied to a sense of the nation as a utopian, ideal space. This sense of connection and belonging is one that Ginsberg continuously covets in his poetry.

However, Allen Grossman has argued that this battle for connection is one that is doomed to failure for a Jewish poet: 'Ginsberg's attempt to trace his particular form of transcendental ambition to Whitman is, in all but the grossest sense, absurd'.[82] Grossman argues that the naturalization of Ginsberg's transcendentalism is (in contrast to Whitman's) an uphill struggle against the inherently 'international culture' of Ginsberg's poetry which cannot escape its Jewish roots. If the national image in Whitman is 'a stable symbol of an ideal form of the self', Ginsberg's references to America constitute, for Grossman, an effort to naturalize 'a fundamentally alien consciousness'.[83] As a Jew, a homosexual *and* the son of a communist, Ginsberg is certainly writing from the position of an outsider, where Whitman had (arguably) only to conceal his non-normative desires when challenged, and comfortably and proudly incorporated them into his notion of good American citizenship. Grossman, however, argues that in Ginsberg's case, 'the poetic identity must supersede the ethnic identity if the poet is to survive'.[84] For him, Ginsberg can only inadequately hover between the position of being a national and an ethnic poet, condemned to be never fully resident in either the realm of the native or that of the Jewish alien.

While (excepting its obvious importance to the composition of 'Kaddish') ethnicity seems less pivotal to Ginsberg's poetry than Grossman's thesis allows, what is important about Grossman's argument is that he posits Ginsberg's Jewishness as an alienating factor without once mentioning his homosexuality as another minority grouping which renders the poet 'alien'. Grossman's comments about the necessity of superseding Jewishness might equally be applied to Ginsberg's homosexuality. When Ginsberg talks about national identity, sexuality is always an implicit issue; his pervasive agenda is the reclamation of America for the 'queer shoulder' that he first envisaged in 'America'. Whitman assists Ginsberg in this cause, for his prior challenge to 'official' narratives of citizenship in *Leaves of Grass* provides a weighty literary precedent for representing the full warp of American life.

---

[82] Allen Grossman, 'Allen Ginsberg: The Jew as American Poet', *On the Poetry of Allen Ginsberg*, ed. Lewis Hyde (Ann Arbor: University of Michigan Press, 1984), 106.
[83] Ibid.
[84] Ibid.

In his 1992 essay on 'Whitman's Influence: A Mountain Too Vast to be Seen', Ginsberg figures Whitman's revolution in the 'imaginative conception of the individual' in terms of a shift away from nationalistic discourse:

> Whitman's breakthrough from official conventional nationalist identity to personal self, to subject, subjectivity, to candour of person, sacredness of the unique eccentric curious solitary personal consciousness changed written imaginative conception of the individual around the whole world.[85]

Ginsberg figures Whitman's 'breakthrough' to a new mode of poetry in terms of its privileging of the individual in the narrative of the nation, locating the heart of his achievement in the epic realm. This is the Whitman who championed the 'man living well the practical life . . . as ordinary farmer, sea-farer, mechanic, clerk, laborer, or driver' as a 'flight loftier than any of Homer's or Shakespeare's – broader than all poems and bibles – namely, Nature's'.[86] In this democratization of the poetic and epic subject Ginsberg found his precedent to celebrate the junkies and lunatics of America in 'Howl', and to elevate the cross-country American road trip of *The Fall* into a State-of-the-Union poetic sermon that would form his own 'long survey of America' (as he called Whitman's 'Song of Myself').[87]

If Ginsberg's portrait of Whitman is coloured by his own concerns, it is also no accident that he locates Whitman's lasting contribution in his celebration of 'candour of person' and 'the unique eccentric curious solitary personal consciousness'. Whitman's own personal candour is manifest in his extended eulogy on the centrality of 'intense and loving comradeship' to the democracy of America. In this respect, the Whitmanian nation is inextricably tied up with the homoerotics of 'manly attachments' and 'adhesiveness' and it is in this convergence that Ginsberg is most invested:

> Whitman said that unless there was an infusion of feeling, of tenderness, of fearlessness, of spirituality, of natural sexuality of natural

[85] Ginsberg, 'Whitman's Influence: A Mountain Too Vast to be Seen', *Deliberate Prose*, 332.
[86] Whitman, preface to Centennial edition of *Leaves of Grass*, in *Complete Verse, Selected Prose*, 733–4.
[87] Ginsberg, 'On Walt Whitman, Composed on the Tongue', *Deliberate Prose*, 296.

delight in each others' bodies, into the hardened materialistic, cynical, life denying, clearly competitive, afraid, scared, armored bodies, there would be no chance for spiritual democracy to take root in America – and he defined that tenderness between the citizens as in his words, an 'Adhesiveness', a natural tenderness, flowing between all citizens, not only men and women, but also a tenderness between men and men as part of our democratic heritage, part of the Adhesiveness which would make the democracy function: that men could work together not as competitive beasts but as tender lovers and fellows. So he projected from his own desire and from his own unconscious a sexual urge which he felt was normal to the unconscious of most people, though forbidden for the most part.[88]

For Ginsberg, Whitman's 'Calamus' had prophesied the 'gay liberation for American and World literatures',[89] imagining a 'democracy . . . that hangs together using the force of Eros'.[90] Ginsberg's sense of homoerotic community (frequently reiterated in accounts of the close-knit associations and sexual relations within the group of writers that came to be known as the Beats) is openly acknowledged to be indebted to Whitman's vision of an American democracy bound together by comradeship:

The idea of the buddy is just a thin, label, vulgarisation of it. The tradition of comradeship, of companionship, spoken of in the Bible . . . between David and Jonathan . . . all the way up to the body of relationships as we know them.[91]

In positing a biblical precedent, Ginsberg attempts to grant further authority to his own homosexual genealogy, from David and Jonathan, to Whitman, through to his own love for Neal Cassady and Jack Kerouac. In 'Howl', Ginsberg updates Whitman's manifesto for 'adhesiveness', presenting such tenderness as the antidote to Moloch's 'hardened, materialistic, cynical, life denying' force. This 'natural tenderness' infuses the third section of 'Howl''s uplifting mantra, giving new life to Whitman's

---

[88] Ginsberg, in testimony before Judge Hoffman at the 'Chicago Seven' trial. In reply to a question by prosecutor Foran on the religious significance of 'Love Poem on Theme by Whitman'. (Cited in Brian Docherty, 'Allen Ginsberg', *American Poetry: The Modernist Ideal*, ed. Clive Bloom and Brian Docherty (New York: St. Martin's Press, 1995)).

[89] Ginsberg, 'Whitman's Influence: A Mountain Too Vast to be Seen', *Deliberate Prose*, 332.

[90] Ginsberg, 'On Walt Whitman, Composed on the Tongue', *Deliberate Prose*, 304.

[91] Ginsberg, '*Gay Sunshine* Interview', *Spontaneous Mind*, 311.

notion that only through such attachments could America's spiritual democracy be realized.

In form, as well as in content, Whitman pointed the way for Ginsberg's approach to the incorporation of his sexuality into his poetry. Ginsberg frames his initial public disclosure of his homosexuality[92] in terms that strongly echo Robert Creeley's characterization of the Whitmanian legacy as centred on the conflation of the public and the private:

> Homosexuality has been for me like a koan – a Zen riddle – for me . . . Is it something public? Anything that common is public; anything that happens to us is as good or bad as anything else as a subject for poetry. It's actual. So I can write naturally about my own homosexuality. The poems get misinterpreted as promotion of homosexuality. Actually, it's more like a promotion of frankness, about any subject.[93]

While Ginsberg may claim that his confessional approach to his sexuality is part of a broader programmatic 'frankness', his status as a gay poet in 1950s Cold War America should not go unremarked as merely a symptom of Whitmanian influence. Ginsberg's sexuality can be seen to constitute a major catalyst for the challenge that his poetics pose to the inherited forms of the New Critical tradition as he moves towards 'the discovery of new appropriate forms',[94] seeking to distance himself from what he calls the 'literary aesthetic hangovers from stupid education experiences'.[95]

Unlike Crane's discriminating praise for Whitman (which rejects his more mawkish moments), Ginsberg's acceptance is continuously enthusiastic and imaginative. Whitman serves as a male muse, or guardian guide: 'dear father, graybeard, lonely old courage-teacher':

> What thoughts I have of you tonight, Walt Whitman, for I walked down the sidestreets under the trees with a headache self-conscious looking at the full moon.

---

[92] As already noted, Ginsberg thought of 'Howl' as his literary 'coming out'.

[93] Ginsberg, 'Playboy Interview', *Spontaneous Mind*, 167. Woods echoes this sentiment in his own study of Ginsberg's poetry: 'The argument that one's homosexuality is entirely her or his own affair, a private matter to be lapped in secrecy, cannot honestly be upheld. Sexual orientation has as much to do with social life and politics . . . as with internal emotion and the gymnastics of the boudoir' (Woods, *Articulate Flesh*, 195).

[94] Ginsberg, letter to John Hollander, quoted in Kramer, *Allen Ginsberg in America*, 174.

[95] Ibid.

In my hungry fatigue, and shopping for images, I went into the neon
fruit supermarket, dreaming of your enumerations!

(GCP, 136)

In Ginsberg's hands, Whitman's 'enumerations' are transported to the
modern supermarket: 'Aisles full of husbands! Wives in the avocados,
babies in the tomatoes!' The characteristic variety of the Whitmanian
accumulation is ripe for its transposition to the consumer paradise of the
modern supermarket. Poetic inspiration becomes an act of shopping for
images, as the two poets freely taste 'every frozen delicacy' – the fruits
suggestive of the corporeal feast, both sensual and visual, on offer from
the grocery boys:

> I saw you, Walt Whitman, childless, lonely old grubber, poking
> among the meats in the refrigerator and eyeing the grocery boys.
> I heard you asking questions of each: Who killed the pork chops?
> What price bananas? Are you my Angel?
> I wandered in and out of the brilliant stacks of cans following you,
> and followed in my imagination by the store detective.

(GCP, 136)

The spectre of McCarthyism hovers in Ginsberg's paranoid conjuring of
the watchful eye of the 'store detective' that doubles his own surveillance
of Whitman through the 'open corridors' and aisles. However, the wry
pun on 'poking/Among the meats' keeps the focus of the poem firmly
upon the sensual delicacies of bodily pleasures. 'Are you my Angel?'
he enquires of a seraphic grocery boy, as Ginsberg's vocabulary of sex-
uality-as-religious-encounter finds its way into the mouth of Whitman.
The policing of sexuality remains a suggestive presence that gestures
towards the 'lost America of love past'[96] – the imagined Whitmanian idyll
where 'manly attachments' might be expressed without restriction (or
certainly without a summons before the House Un-American Activities
Committee). However, it would be reductive to talk of the Whitmanian
tendencies in Ginsberg's work as possessing only a nostalgic thrust.
Ginsberg's own evolution of the Whitmanian vision is often obscured
under the heavy debt of reference and imitation. The young poet's

---

[96] The line can be read both as 'dreaming of the lost America of love [,] past blue automobiles' and 'the lost America of love past[,] blue automobiles'.

absorption of Whitman's notions of 'frankness' and 'manly attachment' give way to a more radical foregrounding of the physical body than we witness anywhere in 'Calamus'. The overt sexuality of poems in *The Fall* such as 'Please Master' extends Whitman's poetic frankness to new extremes. However, while pushing the boundaries of 'personal candour', the opening scene of a poem such as 'Iron Horse' retains Whitman as a trace presence:

> This is the creature I am!
>   Sittin in little roomette Sante Fe train
>   naked abed, bright afternoon sun light
>   leaking below closed window-blind
> White hair at chest, ridge
>   where curls old Jewish lock
> Belly bulged outward, breathing as a baby
>   old appendix scar
>   creased where the belt went
> detumescent cannon on two balls soft pillowed
> Soft stirring shoots thru breast to belly –
> What romance planned by the body unconscious?
>   What can I shove up my ass?
>   Masturbation in America!
>
> (*GCP*, 432)

Opening on this description of the poet masturbating aboard a train full of soldiers returning from Vietnam, Ginsberg catalogues his body in all its gross detail. The poem emphasizes the ravages of age and life – the greying hair on the chest, 'appendix scar' and creases on the skin left by the tourniquet of a belt against the bulging flesh of his middle-aged belly. Eschewing an image of virile machismo, in contrast to the implied youth of the soldiers with their 'Cambodia gossip', Ginsberg presents his genitalia in farcical martial terms as a half-erect cannon-penis, then 'baton' and 'flagpole' (*GCP*, 423).

Fantasizing that the soldiers might come in and join him in his plea-sure, the moment of climax evokes Whitman's 'body electric' as the 'flash came thru body/And the Sphincter-spasm spoke/backward to the soldiers in the observation car' (*GCP*, 433). Achieving a parodic moment of Whitmanian 'manly attachment' in the 'conversation' between ass-hole and soldier, Ginsberg moves further towards establishing a poetic genealogy for himself in comparing his 'little spasm delight' to Crane's visionary revelations of 1922:

Hart Crane, under
    Laughing Gas in the Dentist's Chair 1922 saw
        Seventh Heaven
    said Nebraska scholar.
On thy train O Crane I had a small death too.

(*GCP*, 433)

This new incarnation of the 'body electric' was, of course, apposite for the emerging sexual revolution that 'Howl' would in some ways both embody and pre-empt.[97] However, if Ginsberg's poem seemed radical in the immediate fall-out of the obscenity trial in 1956, its courageous aesthetics of frankness were, as James Miller has noted, imagined by a Whitman a century earlier:

Through me forbidden voices,
Voices of sexes and lusts, voices veil'd and I remove the veil,
Voices indecent by me clarified and transfigur'd.[98]

Ginsberg's poetry offers in some sense 'a fulfilment of these lines', as Whitman's 'Bardic frankness' is given new and obscene force by the voices of the Beat writers. Alongside Burroughs and Kerouac, Ginsberg pulled back the 'veil' of propriety to reveal the underbelly (both literally and psychically speaking) of America, giving full reign to the 'forbidden voices' of homosexuality and madness for, arguably, the first time in the history of American Literature. While these overt professions of same-sex desire have often been conceived of as part of the broader beat or 'hippy' project to 'undermine American society and its pretensions to respectability',[99] Ginsberg's tales of sodomizing 'saintly motorcylists' and fellating 'human seraphim' are part of a distinctly personal, and private, mythology, where the sexual encounter is a

---

[97] Diane DiPrima heralds the publication of *Howl* as a landmark in America's rediscovery of its sexuality. See DiPrima, *Memoirs of a Beatnik* (New York: Traveller's Companion, 1969).
[98] Whitman, 'Song of Myself', *Complete Verse, Selected Prose*, 49.
[99] Martin, *The Homosexual Tradition*, 165.

quasi-religious or 'mystical' experience, as epitomized by the 'human seraphim' of 'Howl':

> who bit detectives in the neck and shrieked with delight
>   in policecars for committing no crime but their
>   own wild cooking pederasty and intoxication,
> who howled on their knees in the subway and were
>   dragged off the roof waving genitals and manuscripts,
> who let themselves be fucked in the ass by saintly
>   motorcylists, and screamed with joy,
> who blew and were blown by those human seraphim,
>   the sailors, caresses of Atlantic and Caribbean
>   love,

(GCP, 127–8)

The Whitmanian democratic vision of sexuality is reprised here in the reciprocal phallic energy of those 'who blew and were blown'. The repetitious subordinate clause beginning 'who' is also distinctly Whitmanian in flavour,[100] demonstrating the 'breath line'.[101] For Ginsberg, formal progression is the means by which to explore homosexual subjectivity: new traditions must be forged for the expression of these new lifestyles and modes of being, and this is the distinctive vision accounting for the centrality of Ginsberg's homosexuality to his poetry.

(ix) 'The culture of my generation, cocksucking and tears'[102]

While Ginsberg was certainly not the only contemporary poet striving to integrate his homosexuality with his poetic voice, he is notable for the ways in which his sexuality became an integral part of both his public persona and his poetry.[103] Ginsberg's poetics create an intimate relationship

---

[100] 'I depend on the word "who" to keep the beat, a base to keep measure, return to and take off again onto another streak of invention' (Ginsberg, 'Notes Written on Finally Recording "Howl"', *On the Poetry of Allen Ginsberg*, ed. Lewis Hyde, 80).

[101] 'Ideally each line of "Howl" is a single breath unit . . . My breath is long – that's the measure, one physical and mental inspiration of thought contained in the elastic of a breath' (Ginsberg, 'Notes Written on Finally Recording "Howl"', *On the Poetry of Allen Ginsberg*, ed. Lewis Hyde, 81).

[102] Ginsberg, *Spontaneous Mind*, 312.

[103] By 1957, however, Ginsberg was already beginning to regret his political fervency: 'and poets should stay out of politics or become monsters/ I have become monstrous with politics', 'Death to Van Gogh's Ear!', *GCP*, 169.

between self-disclosure and the liberation of the sexual self from the
shackles of traditional poetic forms, and he repeatedly placed himself
at the forefront of gay activism, proclaiming the Whitmanian precedent
for celebrating the 'self confidence of . . . knowing that [your] existence
is just as good as any other subject matter'.[104] At the centre of this self-
celebratory agenda is sexual expression, and Ginsberg's poetry revels in
the physical detail of the body in the sexual act. 'Please Master' (1968)
unfolds a litany of requests to the beloved:

Please master can I touch your cheek
please master can I kneel at your feet
please master can I loosen your blue pants
please master can I gaze at your golden haired belly
please master can I gently take down your shorts
please master can I have your thigh bare to my eyes
please master can I take off my clothes below your chair
please master can I kiss your ankles and soul
please master can I touch lips to your hard muscle hairless thigh
please master can I lay my ear pressed to your stomach
please master can I wrap my arms around your white ass
please master can I lick your groin curled with blond soft fur
please master can I touch my tongue to your rosy asshole.

(*GCP*, 494)

Tantalizingly revealing the scene before our eyes, Ginsberg shifts after the
first two lines from the admiring gaze of the traditional love lyric mode
to the paradoxical position of the submissive slave imploring his lover.
Requesting permission to act, the narrator asks, 'can I kiss your ankles and
soul', as if to emphasize the importance of the spiritual quest of the encounter before launching into the explicit physicality of the sex that follows:

please master push me up, my feet on chairs, til my hole feels the
    breath of your spit and your thumb stroke
please master make me say Please Master Fuck me now Please
Master grease my balls and hairmouth with sweet vaselines
please master stroke your shaft with white creams
please master touch your cock head to my wrinkled self-hole

[104] Ginsberg, 'Interview with Tom Clark', *Spontaneous Mind*, 24.

please master push it in gently, your elbows enwrapped round my
    breast
your arms passing down my belly, my penis you touch w / your fingers
please master shove it in a little, a little, a little,
please master sing your droor thing down my behind

(GCP, 494)

As the sexual frenzy of the scene mounts, the pulses of its opening litany begin to break down. The 'rhythm thrill-plunge & pull-back-bounce' (*GCP*, 495) of their activity takes over, as the refrain of 'please master' is stretched out across line-endings, enjambed and forced to fracture and reproduce itself ('please please master') to an ecstatic release.

   This poem appears as part of the 'Elegies for Neal Cassady' section of *The Fall of America*, perhaps as an antidote to the encroaching reminders of mortality that make up this suite of poems. Ginsberg follows 'Please Master' with 'A Prophecy', a poem which invokes Whitman's 'poets and orators to come' and Crane's 'recorders ages hence' in its call to 'O Future bards' to 'Vocalize all chords', once the poet has himself died, leaving his 'body/in a thin motel' (*GCP*, 496). Although both 'Howl' and *The Fall of America* are loaded with these reminders of death and apocalyptic visions, like 'Please Master', these poems also share a sense of the redemptive potential of sexual expression as a counter to the spiritual bankruptcy of modern America:

Common Sense, Common law, common tenderness
                & common tranquillity
our means in America to control the money munching
                war machine,

(GCP, 460)

The 'Elegies for Neal Cassady' bear witness to a more enduring sense of salvation than that offered by the brief sexual-religious ecstasy offered by 'saintly motorcyclists' in 'Howl', intimating a maturity and mellowing of the poet's approach to sex as a utopian experience. Although the poems meditate on the past bodily pleasures of 'Ribs I touched . . ./mouth my tongue touched' (*GCP*, 505), the poet ends by asking forgiveness for his 'phantom body's demands' (*GCP*, 489). If Ginsberg had begun his redefinition of the holy with 'Howl' 's search for transcendence through sexual communion with 'angelheaded hipsters', his 'Elegies for Neal Cassady' retreat somewhat from the hedonistic desire for religious enlightenment through sexual ecstasy. Displaying both anxiety and courage simultane-ously in his professions of same-sex desire, Ginsberg's early and mid-period work draws upon shamanistic rituals and the prophetic tradition of the poet-as-visionary to figure the sexual encounter as a religious or mystical experience where the 'Poet is Priest' (*GCP*, 167).

In 'Howl', it might be argued, Ginsberg performed the priestly function of baptizing his flock in the hellish waters of the American subcultural underground. As a literary 'coming out' of the closet, 'Howl' constituted the breakthrough for Ginsberg as a homosexual poet. He called it 'a public statement of feelings and emotions and attitudes that I would not have wanted my father or my family to see, and I even hesitated to make public'.[105] Such reticence should be read in the context of the scandalous potential of allegations of homosexuality for a family who also had past links to the communist party and the fact that, during the 1940s, homosex-uality was still primarily thought of as a mental illness. For a time, Ginsberg himself concurred with this perception of his sexuality, seeing his 'main psychic difficulty' as the result of 'the usual oedipal entanglement'.[106] The poem 'Don't Grow Old' (1978) recalls Ginsberg's half-confession to his father, Louis, of his 'sickness' and wish to be 'cured':

> Twenty-eight years before on the living room couch he'd stared at me,
>   I said
> 'I want to see a psychiatrist – I have sexual difficulties – homosexuality'
> I'd come home from troubled years as a student. This was the weekend I
>   would talk with him.
> A look startled his face, 'You mean you like to take men's penises in your
>   mouth?'
> Equally startled, 'No, no,' I lied, 'that isn't what it means.'
>
> (*GCP*, 710)

Renouncing to his father the primacy of the sexual within the psychopa-thology of the homosexual, the younger Ginsberg's words try to distance his sexual identity from the acts of fellatio and sodomy (which in 1950 was still a felony).

It was not until 1973 that the Board of Trustees of the American Psychiatric Association (APA) decided to remove homosexuality from the *Diagnostic and Statistical Manual of Psychiatric Disorders*, its official list

---

[105] Ginsberg, 'Gay Sunshine Interview', *Spontaneous Mind*, 313.
[106] Allen Ginsberg, quoted in Michael Schumacher, *Dharma Lion: A Critical Biography of Allen Ginsberg* (New York: St Martin's Press, 1992), 89.

of mental diseases, with private and consensual homosexual acts subsequently being decriminalized in approximately half of American states in the 1970s.[107] For the young Ginsberg, however, his sexual orientation still put him at risk of prosecution, and before he returned to university in 1948, after his 8-month stretch at the Columbian Presbyterian Psychiatric Institute, he had announced his renunciation of homosexuality in a letter to Jack Kerouac. Speaking of his hopes for the future, he wrote: 'I wish I could meet a really gone sweet girl who could love me',[108] and seemed to be determined to put his sexual 'misdemeanours' behind him.

On his return to Columbia, he continued (unsuccessfully) to consult an analyst, still conceiving of his homosexuality as being at the root of his depression. He embarked upon his first heterosexual relationship (with Helen Parker), and questioned the homosexuality of his past, considering it 'camp, unnecessary, [and] morbid, so lacking in completion and sharing of love as to be almost as bad as impotence and celibacy'.[109] This was a view that Ginsberg would return to in his 1961 poem, 'This Form of Life Needs Sex', where he laments that homosexuality is 'no more answer to life/than the muscular statue':

> I felt up its marbles
> envying Beauty's immortality in the
>   museum of Yore –
> You can fuck a statue but you can't
>   have children
> You can joy man to man but the Sperm
>   comes back in a trickle at dawn
> in a toilet on the 45th Floor –
> & Can't make continuous mystery out of that
>   finished performance
>   & ghastly thrill
> that ends as began,
>   stupid reptile squeak
> denied life by Fairy Creator

(*GCP*, 285)

---

[107] In 1961, the new Illinois Model Penal Code led the way for a number of states to decriminalize male homosexual relations between consenting adults, in private.

[108] Ginsberg to Kerouac, quoted in Schumacher, *Dharma Lion*, 128.

[109] Schumacher, *Dharma Lion*, 128.

As we will observe in the next chapter, in Merrill's *The Changing Light at Sandover,* the childless status of the homosexual male is a potent theme for the gay poet trying to establish his place in the world. Here, Ginsberg wrestles with his repulsion at the female body – 'Not the Muse but living meat-phantom' – and contemplates turning to 'ignorant fuckery' in order to reproduce. 'I will have to accept women/if I want to continue the race', he laments: gay sex is figured as a wasted excretion that has no destination but the men's room, ending 'as it began' rather than in the conception of a new life. Ginsberg envies the immortality granted to the classical statue, although it remains, paradoxically, lifeless.[110]

In November 1954, however, Ginsberg granted himself a new life of sorts, and renounced the pathologization of his sexuality – the beginning of a sexually liberated lifestyle that he maintained until his death. It was Dr Phillip Hicks of the Langely Porter Institute who was to provide a breakthrough for the poet with his suggestion that Ginsberg might live just as he wanted to; 'find an apartment, live with Peter [Orlovsky], quit working, and write poems':

> I asked him what the American Psychoanalytic Association would say about that, and he said, 'There's no party line, no red book on how people are supposed to live. If that is what you really feel would please you, what in the world is stopping you from doing it?'[111]

However, in 1954 there was still plenty in the world to stop Ginsberg from doing just that. The anti-homosexual narratives of the McCarthy era made clear the 'party line' for those whose lives were seen to pose a 'threat' to national security. During the 1940s and early 1950s, the House Un-American Activities Committee had sought to oust 'homosexuals' from the federal government, claiming their 'susceptibility to blackmail' (due to what was deemed a pathological 'emotional instability') as a security risk, equal to that posed by communist infiltrations.[112]

---

[110] In his 1969 *Playboy* Interview Ginsberg still located the 'disadvantages' of homosexuality in the same areas saying, 'it keeps you from reproducing your own image, if that's biologically important anymore; and it shits me off from full relations with women', *Spontaneous Mind*, 168.

[111] Ginsberg, quoted in Schumacher, *Dharma Lion*, 193.

[112] In fact, 'more homosexuals and lesbians were expelled from the federal government during the 1950s than were suspected Communists and fellow travellers' (Robert J. Corber, *In the Name of National Security: Hitchcock, Homophobia and the Political Construction of Gender in Postwar America* (Durham: Duke University Press, 1993), 8).

While the expulsion of this 'internal weakness' from the government arose as the domestic component of America's Cold War politics, the broader impact of such ideas persisted beyond the McCarthy years,[113] and homosexuality was still widely conceived of as 'anti-American' by the public at large.

Nevertheless, the 1950s also saw the emergence of the first American homophile organizations: The Mattachine Society, the Daughters of Bilitis and ONE, being the most notable.[114] Not to be confused with post-Stonewall activism, these organizations emphasized assimilation and discreetness. Members of the Mattachine Society and the Daughters of Bilitis were encouraged to dress 'appropriately' for public meetings, and would certainly not have approved of Ginsberg's hirsute appearance. However, these moderate organizations played a crucial role in bringing homosexuality into the political arena, and although Ginsberg was exceptional in his candour, his increasing politicization of his sexual orientation was in keeping with the climate of slow social reform. In the wake of the 1948 Kinsey report, and the growing rebellion against the McCarthyist tendencies of mid-fifties American politics, a significant number of Americans were beginning to put sex back on the political agenda.

Robert Duncan's essay of 1944, 'The Homosexual in Society', pre-empted many subsequent developments in gay politics of the latter half of the twentieth century, most crucially in its rallying cry for the 'struggle toward self-recognition' for the homosexual in the public domain.[115] Duncan's essay stands alone, not only as a pioneering statement of the complexities of homosexual identity, but also in its refusal of ghettoization for the homosexual, rejecting the formation of homosexual subcultures and proposing instead the reformation of all human rights. Duncan certainly would have admired Ginsberg's interpretation of his call for the homosexual to 'take in his own persecution a battlefront toward human freedom'.[116] However, but while Duncan advocates the exchange of the camp closet for the politicization of sexual identity (a kind of proto- 'coming out') he believed that 'one must disown all the special

---

[113] After the McCarthy hearings were broadcast on television in 1954, the Senator's influence waned, as he began to be perceived as a bully by the majority of Americans. See Raskin, *American Scream: Allen Ginsberg's Howl and the Making of the Beat Generation*.

[114] For a detailed account of the rise of the Homophile movement in the 1950s and 1960s see, *We Are Everywhere*, ed. M. Blasius and S. Phelan, (London & New York: Routledge, 1997), 283–379.

[115] Robert Duncan, 'The Homosexual in Society' (1944), reprinted in *We Are Everywhere*, 230.

[116] Duncan, 'The Homosexual in Society', 231.

groups' to achieve true 'human freedom',[117] a warning that certainly has resonance in terms of the critical caricatures that Ginsberg's writing has subsequently endured as a result of his political activities.

The logic of Cold War discourse encouraged what Eric Keenaghan calls 'closed communities' or 'bounded interests',[118] staking safety in recognizable social groupings and a clearly bounded sense of what constituted 'American identity'. What Duncan and Ginsberg both share is this concern to question and disrupt such mechanisms, which necessarily exclude and reject difference. If American politics in the 1950s and 1960s was concerned with the preservation of boundaries (both geographical and ideological), Ginsberg's poetics work to disrupt the logic of containment that dominated Cold War politics and Vietnam rhetoric, breaking the physical boundaries of the line unit with his 'breath-line', and confounding identity limitations.

(x) 'Let the crooked flower bespeak its purpose'[119]

In terms of his formulation of the breath-line and his expansive poetics, Ginsberg looked both to Whitman and to Crane as exemplars. In Crane, Ginsberg found the model for a poetic line that spoke from the spirit rather than from the constraints of formal tradition:

> His blank verse builds an ecstatic postulation of spirit similar to Shelley's abandon. Crane provides an American benchmark of spiritual breath, updated with industrial landscape and futurist vision.[120]

Providing him with a model for speaking with 'spiritual breath', Crane becomes a mentoring presence in Ginsberg's work. 'Kansas City to Saint Louis' (1966) forms an ode of sorts, with Ginsberg addressing the poet in a manner similar to that in which Crane had addressed Whitman in *The Bridge*. Reclaiming this vision of America, just as Crane had attempted to reclaim Whitman's before him, Ginsberg evokes the poet's journeying in 'Powhatan's Daughter':

---

[117] Ibid., 233.

[118] Eric Keenaghan, 'Vulnerable Households: Cold War Containment and Robert Duncan's Queered Nation', *Journal of Modern Literature* 28.4 (Summer 2005), 59 and 60.

[119] Ginsberg, 'Playboy Interview', in *Spontaneous Mind*, 171.

[120] Ginsberg, 'Appendix IV, Model Texts: Inspirations Precursor to "Howl"', *Howl: Original Draft Facsimile*, 175.

Crane all's well, the wanderer returns
        from the west with his Powers,
   the Shaman with his beard
        in full strength,
   the longhaired Crank with subtle humorous voice
           enters city after city
      to kiss the eyes of your high school sailors
      and make laughing Blessing
           for a new Age in America
spaced with concrete but Souled by yourself
      with Desire,
   or like yourself of perfect Heart, adorable
           and adoring its own millioned population
           one by one self-wakened
      under the radiant signs
           of Power stations stacked above the river
highway spanning highway,
           bridged from suburb to suburb.

                                                    (*GCP*, 417–18)

Caricaturing himself as the 'longhaired Crank', 'the Shaman with his beard', Ginsberg revisits the image of himself as a wandering 'Poet-Priest', delivering blessings 'one by one' to enlighten individuals with a new vision of America that could reconcile the concrete materialism of the modern age while reclaiming a place for 'desire' and for the 'soul'. Envisioning a new kind of prophecy, 'without death as consequence' (*GCP*, 168), and melding the political sermon of the jeremiad with the 'humorous voice' of his trickster-fool persona, Ginsberg looks to Crane – the 'perfect H[e]art' – to fashion his own bridge of communication to 'self waken' the people. Turning to the American jeremiad (distinctive from its European predecessor for what Bercovitch calls 'its unshakable optimism'),[121] Ginsberg comes in the end to share in this vision, making 'laughing blessing' alongside his lament at the sins of the nation, ultimately leaving the reader of *The Fall* with the hope of salvation.

Whitman had asked in 'Song of Myself', '[w]hat living and burned speech is always vibrating here, what howls restrained by decorum'.[122]

---

[121] Bercovitch, *The American Jeremiad*, 7.
[122] Whitman, 'Song of Myself', *Complete Verse, Selected Prose*, 34.

Ginsberg responded to this call with his refusal to be restrained in his poetry by decorum, tradition or social expectation. Preaching his mantra of sexual inclusiveness to one and all, Ginsberg's castigations are always instinct with an unshakable faith in the love of mankind for one another. His poetry envisions a better world for all, where empathy and tolerance are in full supply and the 'crooked flower' can 'bespeak its purpose in crookedness, to seek the light'.[123]

---

[123] Ginsberg, 'Playboy Interview', *Spontaneous Mind*, 171.

Chapter 3

'Narcissus bent/Above the gene pool': James Merrill's Epic of Childlessness

(i) A child of tradition

There will be no wife;
The little feet that patter here are metrical.[1]

KEEP IN MIND THE CHILDLESSNESS WE SHARE THIS TURNS US
OUTWARD TO THE LESSONS & THE MYSTERIES[2]

I WONT BE
WHITE WONT BE A POET WONT BE QUEER
CAN U CONCEIVE OF LIFE WITHOUT THOSE 3???[3]

With its polyvocal and encyclopaedic account of the afterlife, James
Merrill's trilogy, *The Changing Light at Sandover*, is epic in both tone and
scope. Comprising 'The Book of Ephraim' (1976), *Mirabell: Books of
Number* (1978) and *Scripts for the Pageant* (1980), *The Changing Light at
Sandover* was published with its coda, 'The Higher Keys', in 1982.[4] Taking
in a cast of characters from W. H. Auden and the Archangel Gabriel, to
Hitler and Homer, Psyche and Proust, this trilogy of long poems sets out
to explicate the structures of the universe from revelations which Merrill

---

[1] James Merrill, 'The Emerald' (1972), *Collected Poems*, ed. J. D. McClatchy and Stephen
Yenser (New York: Alfred J. Knopf, 2001), 342.

[2] James Merrill, *The Changing Light at Sandover: Including the Whole of the Book of Ephraim,
Mirabell: Books of Number, Scripts for the Pageant and a New Coda, the Higher Keys*, 3rd edn
(New York: Alfred J. Knopf, 2003), 216. For ease of discussion, I have abbreviated the full
title of the poem to *Sandover*. Hereafter, all references refer to the 2003 edition.

[3] Merrill, *Sandover*, 184.

[4] Hereafter, all references to the individual sections of the poem are abbreviated to
Ephraim, *Mirabell* and *Scripts*.

claims were dictated to him and his partner, David Jackson, by 'spirit guides' speaking through a Ouija board.

While it eschews the overt confessionalism of Ginsberg's poetry, *Sandover* is explicit about homosexuality in ways that *The Bridge* could not be. The poem is important in this history of the homosexual epic for its consideration of childlessness, as well as for its foundations on a gay relationship between its 'authors' that lasted 25 years. The trilogy develops a sustained meditation on the problems of both an artistic and a genetic legacy for the homosexual artist, with its apocalyptic preoccupations resulting, in part, from this sense of mortal finality. My focus in the second half of this chapter will be on the ways in which 'childlessness' can be read as one of the 'generative complex[es]' behind the poem, and will suggest that *Sandover* can be read as a 'surrogate child' or textual substitute for procreative fulfilment.[5]

Merrill's poem is certainly no Whitmanian exposition of the American dream. Nor does *Sandover* invoke the 'barbaric yawp' of Whitmanian polemic. The democratic nationalism that resounds in Ginsberg's jeremiad wail and Crane's hymn to a modern America is replaced here with the sophisticated domestic interiors of Merrill's homes in America and Greece. While Ginsberg's homosexuality is a major catalyst for his challenge to Anglo-American New Critical forms, *Sandover* looks to ways of exploring homosexual subjectivity without jettisoning prosodic and lyric traditions. However, Merrill's poetry is, in its own way, as radical, challenging and existentially valuable as Ginsberg's overtly queer and politically charged poetry.

Thematics aside, whereas Ginsberg follows Pound in breaking the pentameter, Merrill rejects the idea that formal experimentation in the form of avant-garde poetics is the only path to liberation for the expression of homosexual subjectivity. Rather than renouncing tradition, Merrill finds his voice by appropriating a range of traditional modes. His poetics embrace the Anglo-American lyric of the 1940s, as practised by Auden and the acolytes of Eliot; his work can also be situated in a tradition that includes figures such as Marcel Proust, Henry James and Elizabeth Bishop. Merrill's civilized and subtle tone has more in common with what we might call the 'Horatian' aspects of epic,[6] where

---

[5] As suggested by C. A. Buckley to Merrill, 'Exploring the Changing Light at Sandover: An Interview with James Merrill', *Twentieth Century Literature* 38.4 (Winter 1992), 418. For a discussion of the relationship between childlessness and homosexuality, see Woods, 'Childless Fathers', *Articulate Flesh*, 81–121.

[6] Here, I distinguish between the Virgilian tradition of epic and the Horatian mode, while Virgil's epic was concerned with the heroic founding of a nation, Horace participates more subtly in the act of nation-building by emphasizing the virtues of what Ashbery calls 'civic pride'. See 'The One Thing That Can Save America', *Self-Portrait in a Convex Mirror* (Harmondsworth: Penguin Books, 1976), 44.

the dignifying of civic pride and obligation constitutes an act of nation-building, which is very different from the Virgilian epic's concern with nation-founding. It is here that *Sandover* makes its contribution to a genealogy of homosexual epics. As an education in connoisseurship, Merrill's trilogy recasts on an epic scale Henry James' injunction to 'try to be one of those on whom nothing is lost', transforming the clichés of 'homotextuality' by harnessing the power of the *double-entendre* to ambitious epic ends.

By demonstrating American society's capacity for sophistication, in the example that Merrill's elite coterie presents, *Sandover*'s connoisseurial codes recast what might have been written off in Merrill's early lyrics as a camp preoccupation with 'the surfaces of things'.[7] His taste for fine porcelain and chinoiserie takes on new significance within the trilogy's elaborate mythology.[8] The 'Age . . . of the Wrong Wall-paper'[9] turns out to be 'No Accident' of interior décor. Rather, the choice of furnishings in Merrill's house is shown to have symbolic resonance with the 'DARK SHAPE' of the sinister bat-angels that reveal themselves in the opening sections of *Mirabell*:

DO YOU IMAGINE YOU CHOSE THAT CARPET THAT WALLPAPER

Our bats! The gargoyle faces, the umbrella

Wings – of course, *of course* that's how you look![10]

The 'watermelon' walls of the Stonington dining room, and the Victorian mirror that sets the scene for the exchanges with the spirits, replace Crane's eroticized Brooklyn Bridge or Ginsberg's nightmare metropolis. This is a poem that both diminishes the epic scale (here with echoes of Pope's 'The Rape of the Lock'), while simultaneously maintaining a Dantesque enormity, in terms of the cosmology of the afterlife that the poems envision.

It is not so much that the epic stakes of nationhood have disappeared. Rather, for Merrill and his wall-paper, the impulse to map the New World has dissipated to allow the poet to accommodate the two

---

[7] Martin, *The Homosexual Tradition in American Poetry*, 202.

[8] Richard Saéz calls *Sandover*, 'a masterpiece of sustained camp', while rightly noting the 'seriousness' of Merrill's project. See Saéz, 'At the Salon Level', *James Merrill: Essays in Criticism*, ed. David Lehman and Charles Berger (Ithaca & London: Cornell University Press, 1983), 212.

[9] Merrill, *Sandover*, 97.

[10] Ibid., 116.

extremes of locale between which the trilogy oscillates: the domestic and the universal. In place of an explicit exposition of the myth of America, Merrill chooses to foreground the anxieties of subjectivity that I propose were always implicit in the American epic project (most notably in the Thoreauvian concept of self-fashioning in the wilderness). Merrill follows both Whitman and Wordsworth by interrogating the self, and modifies this tradition by doing so through the polyphonous voices that make up the fabric of the poem's Ouija voices.

Sandover expands upon Merrill's lyric meditations on the contingencies of subjectivity and the provisionality of the self by utilizing an array of voices that Helen Vendler has identified as 'recognizably [Merrill's] own but bearing a different name'.[11] Within the trilogy, these anxieties manifest themselves as issues of authorship: 'Here I go again', he jests, 'a vehicle/In this cosmic carpool'.[12] Merrill laments the lack of his 'own words' amid the *dictées* from the other world, before the voice of Auden reminds him of the 'MINOR/PART THE SELF PLAYS IN A WORK OF ART/COMPARED TO THOSE GREAT GIVENS'[13] of form and tradition.[14] However, such disaggrandisement of the self (or, as Bloom puts it, 'the overcoming of solipsism'[15]) is not just implicit in his attempt to rise to the challenge that the genre of epic presents to a predominantly lyric poet such as Merrill. Rather, the trilogy must be read as part of the slow evolution of Merrill's lyric voice in his 'CHRONICLES OF LOVE AND LOSS',[16] towards 'self and the eclipse thereof'.[17] As Charles Molesworth suggests:

An epic is an attempt to avoid the burdens of the self. A cosmology, or even a national epic, Whitman notwithstanding, would give the poet a chance to escape the ephemeral losses and misgivings of the 'confessional self'.[18]

[11] Helen Vendler, *Part of Nature, Part of Us* (Cambridge: Harvard University Press, 1980), 212.
[12] Merrill, *Sandover*, 262.
[13] Ibid.
[14] The Ouija transcriptions are denoted by capitals throughout the poem.
[15] Harold Bloom, review of *Divine Comedies*, from *New Republic*, 20 November 1976. Reprinted in *A Reader's Guide to James Merrill's A Changing Light at Sandover*, ed. Robert Polito (Ann Arbor: University of Michigan Press, 1994), 133.
[16] Merrill, *Sandover*, 176.
[17] Merrill, 'A Room at the Heart of Things' (1988), *Collected Poems*, 508.
[18] Charles Molesworth, review of *Scripts for the Pageant, A Reader's Guide*, ed. Polito, 173.

Molesworth's conception of the dichotomous relation between the confessional and the epic requires some modification.[19] If we return to Robert Creeley's contention that the overriding achievement of *Leaves of Grass* is the combination of private scope with public purpose, clearly, the divide between the confessional and the epic self that Molesworth discerns is not present in America's foremost epic poem. However, in his analysis of Merrill's approach to the epic, Molesworth is rather closer to the mark in identifying an attempt to avoid the 'burdens of the self'. Although Merrill's dramatization on an epic scale of his coterie life-style means that *Sandover* is intimately concerned with himself, 'JM', as Merrill's avatar in the poem, is a self-effacing and dispersed presence. Despite acting as a ringmaster to the increasingly chaotic occult circus, Merrill refuses the demiurgic pretensions of Whitman, eschewing 'the intellectual's machismo' to be, instead, one of the 'docile takers-in of seed'.[20] Whereas Whitman is the central focus of his epic poem, Merrill creates a paradoxical presence for himself in *Sandover* – at once pivotal in his role as medium while contracting his poetic ego to the avatar 'JM'.

The compendium-like form of *Sandover* also provides an escape from the self (in the sense that Molesworth outlines) into a dazzling display of Protean forms and metres, that stretch the poet's lyric skills to new lengths in the course of a narrative that exceeds 17,000 lines. However, it is the modifications of the poem's central consciousness that constitute the most interesting of these 'escapes' in relation to a homosexual tradition of epic poetry. As Merrill himself has said; 'It's not so much a visionary poem as a revisionary one'.[21] I propose that the fragments and reflections throughout the trilogy of the poet's avatar substantially revise the myth of Narcissus most commonly associated with the homo-sexual psyche.[22] As JM and DJ break the mirror in the closing sections of *Sandover* to release Auden and Maria Mitsotàki to their new 'lives', Narcissus' reflection is shattered into innumerable shards, creating an apt metaphor for *Sandover*'s central poetic conscience, which depends on doublings of characters and refractions of Merrill's own personae. This constitutes a substantial modification of the bardic voice of epic, which is

---

[19] For example, Wordsworth's *The Prelude* could not be said to employ the epic form to 'avoid the burdens of the self'.
[20] Merrill, *Sandover*, 154.
[21] James Merrill, 'An Interview with Fred Bornhauser', *Recitative: Prose by James Merrill*, ed. J. D. McClatchy (San Francisco: North Point Press, 1986), 56.
[22] For a discussion of the relationship between the Narcissus myth and homosexuality see Woods, *Articulate Flesh*, 18–22.

traditionally monolithic and singular. Even where Whitman's voice conjoins the lyric and the epic, the multitudes that Whitman's poem contains are subsumed in the poet's distinctive voice, whereas the central tenet of Merrill's trilogy relies on the poet maintaining a dispersed presence.

The dialogue between the lyric and epic voices is one that is dramatized within the pages of *Sandover*. For instance, Merrill's worries that the poem is 'all by someone else!'[23] suggest an enactment *in extremis* of the disciplining impetus of the epic 'to bind us throbbing with one voice',[24] in Crane's words. The anxieties of being 'outed' had greatly dissipated by the time Merrill came to begin his trilogy, post-Stonewall, in the mid-1970s. Nevertheless, the idea of binding remains central, in a more formal sense, to Merrill's task, where, as poet-medium, he must translate the polyphonous ramblings of the Ouija board into a coherent fabric of narrative and rhyme, in order to deliver the 'POEMS OF SCIENCE' that are demanded by the spirits.[25]

(ii) Issues of authorship

Sandover opens by announcing itself as the product of 'a Thousand and One Evenings Spent/With David Jackson at the Ouija Board'.[26] The authorship of the trilogy, however, is less clear than the dust jacket may at first suggest. As Merrill records in a later poem, 'Clearing the Title' (1985): '*Our* poem now. It's signed JM, but grew/From Life together, grain by coral grain'.[27] As Thom Gunn suggests in his 1979 review of the first two sections of the trilogy, Merrill's indirect portrayal of the 'gay marriage' or 'FORTUNATE CONJUNCTION'[28] between himself and David Jackson is no minor 'triumph' of its time.[29] It is this 25-year union that makes the poem possible, as Richard Sáez has noted:

> An unmentioned but essential premise of Merrill's trilogy is that its revelation – because of the nature of the Ouija board – can only come to a pair who have shared a lifetime.[30]

---

[23] Merrill, *Sandover*, 261.
[24] Crane, *CPHC*, 83.
[25] Merrill, *Sandover*, 113.
[26] Ibid., 4.
[27] Merrill, 'Clearing the Title' (1985), *Collected Poems*, 408.
[28] Merrill, *Sandover*, 15.
[29] Thom Gunn, 'A Heroic Enterprise', *San Francisco Review of Books*, August 1979. Reprinted in *A Reader's Guide*, ed. Polito, 157.
[30] Sáez, *James Merrill: Essays in Criticism*, ed. Lehman and Berger, 212.

An early review of Merrill's poem by Irvin Ehrenpreis suggested that JM and DJ's acts of 'communing' with a series of successive spirit-guides might be seen to correspond to a promiscuity then associated with the homosexual lifestyle.[31] In fact, as JM and DJ celebrate their twenty-fifth anniversary during *Scripts for the Pageant, Sandover* might be seen to have more to say about the continuities of domestic life than the ephemeral pleasures of cruising.

Ehrenpreis' account of the homosexual content of Merrill's poem constitutes a serious misreading of the importance of same-sex desire to the poem's mythology. Conversely, Edmund White's short account of 'Homosexuality as a Theme' (1983) in Merrill's trilogy begins the important project of understanding the role of the poet's sexuality to the construction of *Sandover*'s elaborate cosmology. Highlighting the 'gay aspects' of the poem as a 'tale . . . a bit like Proust's, in which virtually everyone turns out to be queer', White praises Merrill's references to both the 'social and linguistic resources of contemporary gay experience'.[32]

The more recent additions to the body of criticism surrounding the trilogy have not always paid close attention to the homosexual content of *Sandover*. For example, Devin Johnston's essay (from 2000) on the relation between the poem's 'experiential claims' and its occult origins talks about Merrill's dispersed subjectivity without reference to how such divisions of the self may relate to the psychosexual experience of homosexual subjectivity.[33] However, Peter Nickowitz's *Rhetoric and Sexuality: The Poetry of Hart Crane, Elizabeth Bishop and Hart Crane* (2006) closely links Merrill's self-representation with his sexuality. Nickowitz suggests that 'Merrill's craft is often engaged in creating the illusion of direct self-representation',[34] citing his work as an example of the ways in which 'poetic language serves simultaneously to reveal and conceal a dramatization of the poet's sexual, personal and artistic identity'.[35] Piotr K. Gwiazda's *James Merrill and W.H. Auden: Homosexuality and Poetic*

---

[31] Irvin Ehrenpreis, 'Otherworldly Goods', *New York Review of Books*, 22 January 1981, 47–51.

[32] Edmund White, 'The Inverted Type: Homosexuality as a Theme in James Merrill's Prophetic Books', *Literary Visions of Homosexuality* (New York: Haworth Press, 1983), 47–52.

[33] Devin Johnston, 'Resistance to the Message: James Merrill's Occult Epic', *Contemporary Literature* 4.1 (Spring 2000), 87–116.

[34] Peter Nickowitz, *Rhetoric and Sexuality: The Poetry of Hart Crane, Elizabeth Bishop and Hart Crane* (New York & Basingstoke: Palgrave Macmillan, 2006), 2.

[35] Nickowitz, *Rhetoric and Sexuality*, 8.

Influence (2007) also pays close attention, as its title suggests, to the role
of homosexuality in Merrill's composition of the trilogy, seeing its chief
innovation as its 'epic-scale celebration of same sex desire', going on to
consider portions of *Sandover* as a response to Lee Edelman's 'ideology
of "reproductive futurism"'.[36]

Timothy Materer's *James Merrill's Apocalypse* (2000) challenges the view
that *Sandover* is something of an anomaly in Merrill's oeuvre. Taking
Sandover as its central focus, Materer's book re-reads the entirety of
Merrill's oeuvre through the lens of 'apocalypse', tracing the genesis of
the poet's preoccupation with apocalyptic themes back to his early novels,
The Seraglio (1958) and *The (Diblos) Notebook* (1965). For Materer, 'reading Merrill backwards' from *Sandover,* reveals the 'coherent imaginative
world [that] is the mark of a major writer',[37] and he argues for the importance of the imminent threat of nuclear holocaust in Cold War America
as an important context for reading Merrill's work, with *Sandover* constituting an 'extended warning about the nature of the nuclear age'.[38]
Materer suggests that *Sandover* is unique among apocalyptic literature
in that not only does it present apocalyptic themes but is also, formally
speaking, an apocalypse, with its narrative performing an 'unveiling'.[39]
This concern with revelation, Materer maintains, is a preoccupation that
can be traced throughout Merrill's writing.

Looking at the recurrence of apocalyptic motifs in Merrill's poetry,
Materer argues for Merrill as a poet 'not only of personal "love and loss"
but also of a world in a perpetual state of loss'.[40] Materer emphasizes the
importance of the apocalyptic climate of the 1950s and 1960s to Merrill's
poetics, and stresses this sense of the connection between personal and
global catastrophe; *Sandover* is shown to provide the form in which
Merrill could finally express this long-held anxiety.

As the first critical study to make extensive use of the Merrill archives
at Washington University in St Louis, Materer's book makes a strong case
for Merrill as a poet in the visionary tradition by revisiting many of his
earliest writings. However, despite the many fruitful continuities that can
be traced in this way, *Sandover* threatens to collapse under the weight

[36] Piotr K. Gwiazda, *James Merrill and W.H. Auden: Homosexuality and Poetic Influence* (New York & Basingstoke: Palgrave Macmillan, 2007), 4.
[37] Timothy Materer, *James Merrill's Apocalypse* (Ithaca & New York: Cornell University Press, 2000), ix.
[38] Materer, *James Merrill's Apocalypse*, 103.
[39] Ibid., 16.
[40] Ibid., xi.

of importance that Materer wishes to place upon it in his reading. In championing the poem as the work that can provide coherence to the poet's entire oeuvre, Materer's study threatens to homogenize Merrill's voluminous output. Furthermore, he does not address the ways in which Merrill's apocalyptic obsession might be seen to resonate with *Sandover's* preoccupation with childlessness – the 'end of the world' being nowhere more present than in the prospect of one's own genetic mortality. As Helen Caldicott has written:

> To contemplate nuclear war is to entertain the concept of the end of immortality, not just the idea of death. We need to feel that we leave a part of ourselves behind when we die – our children, a great work, books, buildings, paintings – or that we live on in the spiritual or organic life cycle. Nuclear war obliterates these possibilities.[41]

Merrill's apocalyptic vision is partly derived from the fact of his child-lessness and the sense of a lack of a future that this brings with it. If a future beyond the self is usually predicated upon one's genetic legacy, Merrill persuasively argues for a continuation of the self after death through non-procreative means.[42] However, despite such complex argu-mentation for the purposefulness and privilege of the childless, the optimistic and progressive social visions of Whitman and Crane's epics are nowhere to be seen amidst Merrill's anxieties about the imminent destruction of the world, with Whitman's democratic vision replaced by an uneasy lack of sympathy for the 'human average'.[43] Although Materer argues that the poem recovers the 'millennial hopefulness' of the nine-teenth-century American apocalyptic tradition, he doesn't address the particular resonance of apocalypse for the homosexual writer. Materer comments so briefly on Merrill's anxieties about 'his failure to continue the family line' and his 'feelings that he may be emotionally as well as physically barren',[44] that one cannot help but feel this is a major over-sight of the study.

---

[41] Helen Caldicott, *Missile Envy: The Arms Race and Nuclear War* (New York: William Morrav, 1984), 14.

[42] The true horror of nuclear holocaust in Sandover is revealed as the total destruction of human souls, and not just physical matter: 'NO SOULS CAME FROM HIROSHIMA U KNOW/. . . SMASHED ATOMS OF THE DEAD' (Merrill, *Sandover*, 55).

[43] Materer unsuccessfully argues that Merrill's elitism is 'an inevitable feature of apoca-lyptic thinking . . . one draws together with a small group who share one's values and reactions' (*James Merrill's Apocalypse*, 99).

[44] Materer, *James Merrill's Apocalypse*, 49.

(iii) Going by the board: Structuring the trilogy

I'm rather shaky as to genres and modes, but it does seem to be a romance in certain ways – and perhaps a mock-romance in others? . . . Actually, I suspect the trilogy touches on a variety of modes, and the one thing that holds it all together, if anything does, is that it all truly happened to us, came to us in these various ways.[45]

If the dual-authorship of *Sandover* registers the demands of supernatural communication, so do the component parts of the trilogy. Each of the poems is organized around a particular aspect of the architecture of the standard Ouija board design. Their precise structural schema not only relates to but also modifies Dante's architecture of Hell and Yeats' Pythagorean representations of eternity in *A Vision* (1937). Merrill rethinks Dante's hierarchical, spiral model, figuring the universe as a circular structure that mirrors the atomic charges:

When we suppose that history's great worm
Turns and turns as it does because of twin
Forces balanced and alert within
Any least atom, are we getting warm?[46]

Unlike Dante's, Merrill's design requires no great imaginative leap – it literally goes 'by the board'. The 26 sections of *Ephraim* take in 'the letters A to Z/Spread in an arc', the board's Arabic numerals organise *Mirabell*, while 'YES & NO' provide the outline for *Scripts*, or, as Auden describes it, '2 GOLDEN TRAYS OF 'YES' & 'NO' WITH '&'/AS BRIDGE OR BALANCE').[47] The *Scripts'* 25 lessons also parody the didactic component of the traditional epic form, as well as providing a second tier to the organizing conceit of the board's design.

Sandover is largely composed of 'transcripts' of conversations between the living and the dead who, alongside the poet's own interpolations, draw together a circle of friend, relatives and historical figures. In this way, Merrill's epic might also be thought of as an elegy writ large.[48]

---

[45] Merrill, *Recitative*, 60–1.

[46] Merrill, *Sandover*, 478.

[47] Ibid., 328.

[48] However, subsequent publications of the original Ouija transcripts have shown the extent to which Merrill edited the content of the conversations, as well as the metrical shaping palpable in the text. See David Jackson, 'Lending a Hand', *James Merrill: Essays in Criticism*, ed. Lehman and Berger, 298–305.

'YR DEAD' are 'THE SURROUND OF THE LIVING', Ephraim tells his
scribes in 'Q'; 'ALL CONNECTED TO EACH OTHER DEAD OR ALIVE
NOW DO YOU UNDERSTAND WHAT HEAVEN IS'.[49] However, despite
the poem's persistently elegiac tone, much of the criticism surrounding
Sandover has concerned itself with the extent to which Merrill's trilogy
follows within the tradition of epic poetry.[50] Helen Vendler, for one,
suggests that we read the poem in terms of its redefinition of the epic
field:

> The whole of Merrill's trilogy can be seen as a substitution of the vir-
> tues of mind and heart – culminating in music and poetry – for the
> civic and familial and martial virtues usually espoused by epic.[51]

While Vendler identifies a displacement of 'the civic and familial', I contend that Merrill's trilogy places these virtues at the very centre of its
vision. In its consideration of 'the virtues of mind and heart' (particularly in relation to homosexuality), the poem explores many layers of
anxiety regarding the childlessness of Merrill and his extended 'family'.
Part of Merrill's 'family' is also made up of the influences appropriated
from literary history with whom he feels some spiritual or intellectual
kinship.

The publication history of *Sandover* situates the poem within a tradition of other epic poems that have emerged over time or undergone
progressive revision such as *Leaves of Grass* or *Paterson*. The trilogy's com-
pendium format also shares ground with the encyclopaedic 'rag bag'
of Pound's *Cantos*. However, Merrill's most overt dialogue with the epic
tradition occurs in *Sandover*'s many references to Dante's *Divine Comedy*.
Rachel Jacoff explores this relationship by employing a Bloomian
model of anxious influence: 'if', she argues, 'Dante provides Merrill
with certain privileged rhyme schemes and verse forms, images, and
a precedent of poetic authority, he also suggests a challenge'.[52] The
initial appearance of 'The Book of Ephraim' in the collection *Divine
Comedies* announces the nature of Merrill's dialogue as a playful revision

---

[49] Merrill, *Sandover*, 59.
[50] For a consideration of the trilogy as an elegy, see Peter Sacks, 'The Divine Translation:
Elegiac Aspects of *The Changing Light at Sandover*', *James Merrill: Essays in Criticism*, ed.
Lehman and Berger, 159–85.
[51] Helen Vendler, 'Mirabell: Books of Number', *A Reader's Guide*, ed. Polito, 164.
[52] Rachel Jacoff, 'Merrill and Dante', *James Merrill: Essays in Criticism*, ed. Lehman and
Berger, 153.

of the Italian master in the pluralism of the poet's impish title. Merrill is neither wholly dismissive of the importance of *The Divine Comedy* as a blueprint for his own 'guidebook' to the afterlife, nor lacking in reverence for Dante's epic authority: 'We'd long since slept through our last talk on Thomist/Structures in Dante',[53] JM quips upon intimating that Ephraim (their first spirit guide) wants the poet to try where Yeats had failed with *A Vision*:

. . . POOR OLD YEATS

STILL SIMPLIFYING

But if someone up there thought *we* would edit
The New Enlarged Edition,
That maze of inner logic, dogma, dates –
Ephraim, forget it.[54]

While *Sandover* shares much with its epic precursors, the crucial issue for my discussion of the trilogy's place in the American homosexual epic tradition is the ways in which Merrill's vision diverges from Yeats' and Dante's examples, and the centrality of Merrill's homosexuality to such a move. The trilogy draws on prior cosmologies and mythologies, I argue, only to re-create and re-envision an alternative structure for its universe that can make normal the sexuality of its author(s). Re-inscribing homosexuality within both secular (i.e. dominant, heteronormative) and esoteric traditions, Merrill's poem places the gay poet at the centre of a cosmic design that drives towards the production of 'V WORK', that is to say, divinely inspired works of arts or scientific breakthroughs.[55]

In positing *Sandover* as a 'homosexual epic', my discussion focuses on the poem's meditations on 'childlessness'. The trilogy's major female protagonist, Maria Mitsotáki (or MM as she is acronymically known through the board), is 'insouciantly childless', Merrill tells us.[56] But is the poem itself so free of anxiety about its paucity of progenitors, or does the role of the unconscious in the poem betray something else?

---

[53] Merrill, *Sandover*, 14. See also *Sandover*, 45: 'This dream, he blandly adds, is a low budget/Remake – imagine – of the *Paradiso*'.

[54] Merrill, *Sandover*, 14.

[55] V work is the term applied to a 'SCIENTIFIC OR ARTISTIC BREAKTHRU' or work 'GUIDED BY HIGHER COLLABORATION'. See *Sandover*, 108 and 162.

[56] Merrill, *Sandover*, 102.

(iv) The role of the unconscious

Merrill begins with a certain reluctance about his epically styled task, 'to speak to multitudes and make it matter'.[57] However, *Sandover* absorbs these internal conflicts as part of the record of its own making, with its self-reflexivity culminating in a reading of the poem *within the poem* to an audience including both the living and the dead. The trilogy becomes a Joycean *ourobouros* – a 'snake that swallows its own tail',[58] closing with what had been its opening refrain, as an elegiac 'dance of slow acceptance' of loss and grief.[59] Despite this structural precision, *Sandover* opens with an anxious flourish, announcing its own failure in appearing in 'its present form'. Plunging *in medias res*, into an account of the history of the poem's composition, Merrill recapitulates the struggles of its conception:

> Admittedly I err by undertaking
> This in its present form. The baldest prose
> Reportage was called for, that would reach
> The widest public in the shortest time.[60]

Although he claims to aim to 'reach/The widest public in the shortest time', Merrill clearly never envisioned reaching a truly 'popular' audience, and of course the poem has not had the wider cultural impact of 'Howl'. Comparing the two poems, it seems that Ginsberg's poem allegorizes the nekyiac journey through the unconscious; *Sandover*'s framing device is a mechanism whereby the unconscious is literally given voice.

This interest in the repressed seems to be crucial to Merrill's modification of the homosexual tradition. Merrill plays with the idea that the whole enterprise of *Sandover* may be nothing more than an elaborate nekyiac journey – a ruse to 'shuffle off the blame/For how we live', having not 'sired a child'.[61] 'WE ARE U YOU ARE WE EACH OTHERS DREAM', Mirabell explains in Book I.[62] Merrill's assemblage of quotations in section 'Q' of 'The Book of Ephraim' also supports this. He cites Peter Quennell (on Pope's grotto), suggesting a parallel between his own poem and Pope's construction of 'a private underworld . . . encrusted . . .

---

[57] Ibid., 82.
[58] Ibid., 83.
[59] Ibid., 335.
[60] Ibid., 1.
[61] Ibid., 30.
[62] Ibid., 117.

with a rough mosaic of luminous mineral bodies . . . Pope intended . . .
that the visitor, when at length he emerged, should feel that he had been
reborn into a new existence'.[63] A few pages later, Merrill adds his own
meditation on Wallace Stevens' contention that the imagination and
God are 'as one':

> Stevens imagined the imagination
> And God as one; the imagination, also,
> As that which presses back, in parlous times,
> Against 'the pressure of reality'.
> Scholia discordant (who could say?)
> Yet coursing with heart's-blood the moment read.
> Whatever E imagined – my novel didn't
> Press back enough, or pressed back against him –
> He showed his hand, he nipped it in the bud.[64]

Recalling the 'lost novel' that Merrill had intended to fashion from his
supernatural adventures (its disappearance in the back of a Georgia taxi
is documented in Merrill's short poem, 'The Will'),[65] the poet goes on to
present the reader with what amounts to a 'false start'. Merrill recounts the
planning of character and setting with a self-reflexivity that comes to be
central to the fabric of *Sandover*'s entwined narratives and time frames:

> Best after all to do it as a novel?
> Looking about me, I found characters
> Human and otherwise (if the distinction
> Meant anything in fiction). Saw my way
> To a plot, or as much as one still allowed
> For surprise and pleasure in its working-out.
> Knew my setting; and had, from the start, a theme
> Whose steady light shone back, it seemed, from every
> Least detail exposed to it. I came
> To see it as an old, exalted one:
> The incarnation and withdrawal of
> A god.[66]

---

[63] Ibid., 61.
[64] Ibid., 66
[65] Merrill, *Collected Poems*, 392.
[66] Merrill, *Sandover*, 3.

Merrill places us here on 'old, exalted' territory. Eliot's attempt to find
and resurrect a deity that might rejuvenate the wasteland of modern
culture resounds in *Sandover*'s 'incarnation and withdrawal of/A god'.
This epic theme cuts through Merrill's narrative as a 'steady light', whose
reflection also shapes the poet's stylistic hopes:

> . . . Fed
> Up so long and variously by
> Our age's fancy narrative concoctions,
> I yearned for the kind of unseasoned telling found
> In legends, fairy tales, a tone licked clean
> Over the centuries by mild old tongues,
> Grandam to cub, serene, anonymous.[67]

Merrill's hopes for the age-refined song of Homer, 'licked clean/Over
the centuries', are echoed in the 'twenty/Years in a cool dark place
that *Ephraim* took/In order to be palatable wine'.[68] These stylistic hopes
become framed in bodily terms; Merrill talks of a 'tone licked clean'
to serene anonymity – a ritualized process of self-effacement where
the tone is 'bald', hairless and 'unseasoned'. Extending this metaphor
throughout his account of the poem's birth, Merrill frames his shortcomings as a novelist in terms of finding the 'shoe of prose' to be a
poor fit:[69]

> The more I struggled to be plain, the more
> Mannerism hobbled me. What for?
> Since it had never truly fit, why wear
> The shoe of prose? In verse the feet went bare.
> Measures, furthermore, had been defined
> As what emergency required.[70]

Here, we can see Merrill struggling with his feelings about prose, as a
form that hinders the expression of his own personal interests. Finding
he prefers the 'bare' feet of verse – both bodily and metrical 'feet'
are implied here – Merrill discovers that poetry can provide just the

---

[67] Ibid.
[68] Merrill, *Sandover*, 261
[69] Ibid., 136.
[70] Ibid., 4.

emergency 'measures' that are required, although he doubts the value of 'all this/warmed up Milton, Dante, Genesis'.

(v) The influence of Whitman

Leaving aside these other influences, which are beyond the purview of this book, Merrill's relation to Whitman is rather subtler than Ginsberg's palpable debt of both tone and form. Although Robert Martin includes a small section on Merrill in *The Homosexual Tradition in American Poetry*, his account makes no reference to the two sections of the trilogy that Merrill had already published by this time.[71] Instead, Merrill's place among the homosexual tradition is illustrated by what Martin calls the 'gay sensibility' of his lyrics.[72] Leaning heavily on his most Cranean poems, 'In Nine Sleep Valley' and 'To My Greek', Martin concludes that, 'Merrill returns to Whitman's view that only in the rediscovery of the warp of American life, only in adhesive love, can the American democratic dream be realized'.[73]

In *Sandover*, Merrill makes only two brief references to the 'good gray poet'. There is a pun on 'the body electric' in a discussion on the role of salt:

IN MAN SALT IS THE SWITCH IN US, THE BASIC RADIUM
Salt – imagine! Fuel and stabilizer
Of the body electric (thank you, Walt);[74]

His second appearance is among a roll-call of dead poets who have failed to bridge the 'GENERATION GAP IN HEAVEN', alongside the nineteenth-century English poets who are 'VEXED TO HAVE FOUND NO HARPS'.

'WHITMAN MINED HALF WITLESS STAYS AT 6', Maria tells JM and DJ.[75] 'MINED' illustrates here the degenerative effect of the Research Lab's culling of percentages of Whitman's cloned soul to be reborn in new forms. This results in the failure of the American Bard to ascend to

---

[71] Martin's study appeared in 1979, a year before *Scripts for the Pageant* – the final component of the trilogy – was published.
[72] Martin, *The Homosexual Tradition in American Poetry*, 208.
[73] Ibid.
[74] Merrill, *Sandover*, 140–1.
[75] Ibid., 527.

the top of the nine stages of the after-world. Perhaps such vignettes can be attributed to Merrill's own literary tastes; Merrill's literary affiliations certainly lie more with Proust, as illustrated by his claim that 'psychological action' has dethroned the epic.[76] However, in conceiving of the relationship of *Sandover* to what he calls the 'long, "impossible" poem', Merrill does express a sense of his belonging to an 'American phenomenon' of sorts.[77] His notion of this tradition, however, is undercut by his struggle with a sense of estrangement:

> I feel American in Europe and exotic at home – and haven't we our own 'expatriate' tradition for that? I was about to suggest . . . that the long, 'impossible' poem was an American phenomenon in our day. The thought didn't comfort me. How many of us get out of our cars when we hit the badlands in the *Cantos*, or take a detour through downtown *Paterson*? In such context, 'foreignness' would be the storyteller's rather than the missionary's concern for his reader's soul.[78]

Merrill characterizes these poets' disregard for the reader's comprehension as alienating, expressing his frustration at the obliqueness of American epic poems such as Ezra Pound's *Cantos* or Williams' *Paterson*. Speaking of his own sense of 'foreignness', Merrill claims to take on the role of the exotic outsider, whether in America or Europe. The poet is both 'stranger in America' and expatriate abroad; there is no sense of belonging, except in that felt as difference. These feelings of foreignness, mapped on to non-normative sexuality, strongly recall the fascination of Elizabeth Bishop (one of Merrill's favourite poets) with 'Questions of Travel', where Bishop's preoccupation with questions of home and peculiarity were also intimately bound up with 'that world inverted'.[79]

To return to Robert Martin's seemingly erroneous identification of a strong Whitmanian flavour to Merrill's vision, it is perhaps the 'democratic' in Whitman's 'vista' that strikes a chord in Merrill's writing – the *otherness* within the whole. Hence, in an interview with J. D. McClatchy, Merrill claims that, 'I like the idea of nations, actually, and even more those

---

[76] 'Everybody has agreed that psychological action is more than interesting than epic. One mainly wants a form where one thing leads to another.' 'An Interview with Ashley Brown', *Recitative*, 46.

[77] 'An Interview with Helen Vendler', *Recitative*, 52.

[78] Ibid.

[79] Elizabeth Bishop, 'Insomnia', *Complete Poems* (London: Chatto & Windus, 1991), 70.

pockets of genuine strangeness within nations'.[80] However, whereas the epics of Whitman and Crane are full of vagrants and hoboes, *Sandover's* 'outsider' manifests himself in the elite coterie of Merrill's friends, from the pinnacle of which the poem conducts its business. Merrill does not share the Whitmanian impulse to document the whole spectrum of American life, preferring to focus on a metonymic other – the homosexual coterie – an alternative family of the kind that Robert Duncan railed against in 1944 in 'The Homosexual in Society'.[81] This impulse is perhaps paralleled in 'Howl''s grotesque catalogue of the American underbelly. However, unlike Ginsberg, Merrill repeatedly expresses his lack of interest in politics and what he calls 'public life':

> The lobbies? The candidates' rhetoric – our 'commitments abroad'? The Shah as Helen of Troy launching a thousand missile carriers? One whiff of all that, and I turn purple and start kicking my cradle.[82]

Merrill's seeming aversion to the political, epitomized by his confession that 'I rarely buy a newspaper, or vote',[83] places him in sharp contrast to Ginsberg's highly politicized and contextually aware poetics. Speaking on the power of social or political poetry, Merrill emphasizes the aesthetic qualities of language:

> These immensely real concerns do not produce *poetry*. But of course one responds. A word-cluster like *napalm-baby-burn* stimulates the juices infallibly as the high C of a Donizetti mad scene. Both audiences have been prepared for what they get and are strongly moved. The trouble with overtly political or social writing is that when the tide of feeling goes out, the language begins to stink.[84]

One of the few poems written by Merrill to make an explicit political reference is 'In Nine Sleep Valley' (1972). Here, the deaths of Martin Luther King and Robert Kennedy form the backdrop to a meditation on his own citizenship of 'the botched country/Where shots attain the eagle'.[85] However, Merrill's concern in the poem remains with the preservation of

---

[80] Merrill, 'An Interview with J. D. McClatchy', *Recitative*, 71.
[81] Duncan, 'The Homosexual in Society', 232–3.
[82] Merrill, 'An Interview with J. D. McClatchy', *Recitative*, 71.
[83] Merrill, 'The Broken Home' (1966), *Collected Poems*, 199.
[84] Merrill, 'An Interview with Joan Boatwright and Enrique Ucelay DaCal', *Recitative*, 38.
[85] Merrill, 'In Nine Sleep Valley' (1972), *Collected Poems*, 323.

something more precious than the political moment. 'The beauty I meant
to press fading/Between these lines is yours', he concludes, wanting to
preserve the 'day when beauty, death, and love/Were coiled together in
one crowning glory',[86] in lines that recall Crane's 'Voyages'.[87]

(vi) Voicing the Other

As Samuel Schulman has noted, Merrill's dispersal of himself among the
many voices of *Sandover*'s cast sees the concept of reincarnation displace
the Whitmanian empathetic technique as the means by which the poet
can take on a plethora of identities and voices in the epic poem.[88] Where
Whitman moves in and out of a series of ever-shifting identifications with
the lives of other Americans in *Leaves of Grass*, Merrill literalizes the idea
of the epic poet as a 'medium' by using the Ouija board as the prime
organizing principle around which *Sandover* is constructed. Merrill's trilogy takes the traditional poet–muse relationship of the epic to a new
level, even by comparison with the nightly visitations of Milton's *Paradise
Lost.* Merrill's homosexual modification of the traditional invocation of
the female muse arrives in the form of their first spirit guide, Ephraim,
'A Greek Jew/Born AD 8 at XANTHOS', and a lover of Caligula.[89]

In this sense, it could be argued that Merrill's myth of reincarnation
brings to American poetry a new metaphor to defamiliarize the concept
of a metaphysical union and diffusion of the self that Whitman made his
own. The penultimate section of Ephraim sees the poet meditating on
just such an issue, framing it in terms of Keatsian negative capability:

> Young chameleon, I used to
> Ask how on earth one got sufficiently
> Imbued with otherness. And now I see.[90]

But if Merrill imbues himself with this 'otherness', via the mechanism
of the Ouija board, the implications of the poet's choice to overcome

---

[86] Ibid.
[87] 'Hasten, while they are true, – sleep, death, desire,/Close round one instant in one floating flower' (Crane, 'Voyages II', *CPHC*, 35).
[88] Samuel E. Schulman, 'Lyric Knowledge in the Fire Screen and Braving the Elements',
James Merrill: Essays in Criticism, ed. Lehman and Berger, 98.
[89] Merrill, *Sandover*, 8.
[90] Ibid., 89.

solipsism by means of an 'occult journey' (as Harold Bloom has seen it), is intimately bound-up with the poet's sexuality.[91] Thom Gunn recast this continuum between living and dead in the early nineties, speaking of 'my dear, my everpresent dead'[92] in his tragic metaphor for the 'community of the carnal heart'[93] that the AIDS pandemic created within the gay community in the 1980s and early 1990s. The homosexual fraternity expressed within the pages of *Sandover* foreshadows this, prefiguring what would become an all too frequent poetic trope only a decade on from *Sandover's* publication. As Helen Vendler has noted:

> *Mirabell* is a poem about the dead in part because it is a poem of the single life and childlessness; since there is no question of posterity, life is composed of oneself and one's friends, the dead as much as the living.[94]

Although Vendler proposes that 'there is no question of posterity', Merrill's trilogy does suggest a continuity for JM and DJ beyond the confines of their earthly life. If, traditionally, the creation of a child is the culmination of the love between two people, the trilogy itself might be seen as a textual substitute for Merrill and Jackson. Ortega y Gasset's description of the child as 'neither the father's nor the mother's' but as 'the personified union of the two . . . a striving for perfection modelled after flesh and soul'[95] might be equally applied to a poem grown 'From Life together, grain by coral grain'.[96]

(vii) Childlessness

THE TYPE YOU SET JM, INVERTED & BACKWARD,

IS YET READ RIGHTSIDE UP ON THE BIOLOGICAL PAGE.[97]

Sandover's cosmology explicates the homosexual negotiation between erotic and biological urges. Merrill's lyric, 'Childlessness' (1962)

---

[91] Bloom, 'Review of *Divine Comedies*', *New Republic*, 20 November 1976. Reprinted in *A Reader's Guide*, 133.

[92] Thom Gunn, 'Postscript: The Panel', *Boss Cupid* (London: Faber, 2000), 17.

[93] Gunn, 'Saturday Night', *Boss Cupid*, 46.

[94] Vendler, *A Reader's Guide*, ed. Polito, 163.

[95] Ortega and Gasset, *On Love . . . Aspects of a Single Theme* (London, 1967), 33–4. Quoted in Woods, *Articulate Flesh*, 81.

[96] Merrill, 'Clearing the Title' (1985), *Collected Poems*, 408.

[97] Merrill, *Sandover*, 216.

demonstrates an earlier working-through of the anxieties that come to stand at the centre of the trilogy's account of the structures of the universe. This earlier poem displays a rather more ambivalent attitude towards the exclusion of the homosexual from the reproductive realm, where Merrill's epic expresses a more distinct stance on the spiritual 'pay-off' of childlessness for the homosexual artist. The title of the poem announces itself as a meditation on barrenness. It moves quickly in the opening stanza to contrast its speaker's lack of progeny to the abundant natural forces at work in the raging storm:

> The weather of this winter night, my dream-wife
> Ranting and raining, wakes me. Her cloak blown back
> To show the lining's dull lead foil
> Sweeps along asphalt. Houses
> Look blindly on; one glimmers through a blind.
> Outside, I hear her tricklings
> Arraign my little plot:
> Had it or not agreed
> To transplantation for the common good
> Of certain rare growths yielding guaranteed
> Gold pollen, gender of suns, large, hardy,
> Enviable blooms? But in my garden
> Nothing is planted. Neither
> Is that glimmering window mine.[98]

The identity of this 'dream-wife' remains ambiguous; does she stand for Nature and its reproductive imperative? In this case she can only be an imagined, and is therefore a 'dream' wife for the homosexual poet, or are we to read the ambivalent union as that of the poet wedded to his Muse? Whether 'Nature' or 'Art', or a composite of both, Merrill's dramatization of the anxious relation between artistic and biological posterity begins with the personification of the homosexual poet as traitor to this Gaia-like figure. While Nature has her 'enviable blooms', Merrill's garden is, in sharp contrast, unseeded and empty. The poem opens as its speaker wakes from a dream. However, as with the trilogy's constant traffic between the worlds of the living and the dead, the delineations

---

[98] Merrill, 'Childlessness', *Collected Poems*, 148.

between the unconscious and waking worlds are blurred; the 'dream-wife' is also present in the poet's waking reality as the cause of his stirring. If Merrill intended her as a straightforward personification of Nature, his portrait is unusual for its distinctly urban or industrial associations. The 'dull lead foil' of her cloak, and 'asphalt' landscape have more in common with the speaker's barren plot than traditional personifications of Mother Nature. Domestic antagonisms echo in the background of the poet's punning play on the 'ranting and raining' female harpy, recalling the marital frictions of 'The Broken Home' (1966), where 'Father Time and Mother Earth,' have 'A Marriage on the rocks'.[99]

The mysterious cloaked figure is both muse and mother – she is capable of both imaginative *and* actual 'blooms' on which the poet must rely and by which he is enraptured.[100] The futile '*trick*lings' (my emphasis) of the attempts to irrigate the poet's unplanted 'little plot' suggest the double-dealings of an 'enchantress' who is not to be trusted and only 'masked as friend', who will later unfurl the sublime 'bolts' of nightmare that 'burst along' the poet's limbs, 'like buds,/Like bombs'. These imaginative 'buds' are the only blooms that the poet-speaker can create, and they too are bound up with a suspicion of the generative task, with their sinister metamorphosis from 'buds' to 'bombs' across the end of a line. The idea of verse as a garment to clothe the body has several incarnations in the poem. The colours of sunset that 'clothe', before penetrating the body to 'burst' as pulsing 'buds', transmute into a shirt of Nessus that visits punishment upon the poet's parents in the last lines of the poem:

The cloak thrown down for it to wear
In token of past servitude
Has fallen onto the shoulders of my parents
Whom it is eating to the bone.[101]

Condemned to be the child of his parents, a fate that he figures as 'past servitude', the guilt of this abstention from the cycle of life finds expression in the surfacing reminders of the generative task – the 'toddlers, holy dolls, dead ancestors' that populate the speaker's nightmares. This unspoken guilt for the childlessness bound up with the poet's homosexuality takes

[99] Merrill, 'The Broken Home', *Collected Poems*, 198.
[100] According to Robert Graves, the muse is also always a maternal figure. See Graves, *The White Goddess: A Historical Grammar of Poetic Myth* (London: Faber, 1952).
[101] Merrill, 'Childlessness', *Collected Poems*, 149.

form in the tumult of images that close the poem. Haunted by his inability
to partake of the generative task of biology, Merrill is wedded instead to a
'dream-wife' or muse of poetry. The speaker finds himself punished by the
feverish imaginings in which the poisoned cloak that Deianira unknow-
ingly gives to Hercules is figured eating his parents' flesh.

As it broods on the parallels between the tasks of artistic and biological generation, this earlier poem of Merrill's has much to tell us about
the development of the poet's thinking on the childlessness shared by
JM and the figures that populate *Sandover*. The idea of humanity as
God Biology's 'Greenhouse' finds its faint roots in the generative metaphors that shape 'Childlessness'. The transplantation 'for the common
good/Of certain rare growths' prefigures the cloning of 'PLANT-SOUL
DENSITIES'[102] in *Sandover*'s heavenly 'Research Lab'. In Merrill's lyric,
however, where the reproductive imperative is symbolized by the horti-
cultural, the familial presents itself in the poem through the figure of a
lit room, observed through an open window:

> Houses
> Look blindly on; one glimmers through a blind.
> . . . .
> But in my garden
> Nothing is planted. Neither
> Is that glimmering window mine.[103]

If the 'glimmering window' is momentarily offered as a consolation to the
speaker's barren plot, its suggestions of a privileged perception, as the single glimmering eye in a row of 'blind' houses, are quickly overridden. This
trope recurs in Merrill's much-anthologized lyric, 'The Broken Home',
where the 'parents and child' stand at the window 'gleaming like fruit':

> Crossing the street,
> I saw the parents and the child
> At their window, gleaming like fruit
> With evening's mild gold leaf.
>
> In a room on the floor below,
> Sunless, cooler – a brimming

---

[102] Merrill, *Sandover*, 151
[103] Merrill, 'Childlessness', *Collected Poems*, 148.

Saucer of wax, marbly and dim –
I have lit what's left of my life.[104]

The speaker, 'on the floor below', in his 'Sunless, cooler' room, seeks reassurance that 'you and I are as real/At least as the people upstairs' – those who have engaged in successful reproduction. By the time Merrill comes to write the poems that will become *Sandover*, the poet seeks no such reassurance. While the overall movement within the poem (from childlessness to a meditation on Nature and Art) is repeated in Book 7 of *Mirabell*, Merrill no longer displays the antagonism expressed in the earlier lyric. Rather, if a conflict between Nature and the mind dedicated to art persists in the trilogy, it is an 'enchanting interpenetration',[105] as Merrill, 'like any atom', remains 'Two-minded'.[106] Although the trope of the raging storm recurs again in *Sandover*, Nature's 'lashing hail' is no longer the guilty punishment of 'Childlessness', but 'rapturous' ecstasies that 'Flagstad herself'[107] cannot rival.[108] Nature is no longer antagonistic but 'Mind's equal': the 'dream-wife' is now 'mother, sister, bride' in a 'marriage' that the poet is meant to 'save', in a generational inversion where, Merrill jokes, 'the kids stay/Together for their parents' sake'.[109]

One of the central tenets of *Sandover*'s cosmology is the revelation that the 'childless' possess privileged access to the 'spiritual' life, or 'MIND VALUES' that are associated in the trilogy with poetry and music. While painters and sculptors are said to be excluded from this 'LIFE OF/THE MIND' as they are tied to what is implied to be a heterosexual compulsion to 'PRODUCE AT LAST/BODIES', the homosexual is predisposed to 'SUCH MIND VALUES AS PRODUCE THE BLOSSOMS/OF POETRY & MUSIC'.[110]

When Auden questions their second spirit guide, Mirabell, 'Why the four of us?/Because we're musical?' (misreading the shared quality amongst the four), the board answers: 'KEEP IN MIND THE CHILDLESSNESS WE SHARE THIS TURNS US/OUTWARD TO THE

[104] Merrill, 'The Broken Home', *Collected Poems*, 197–200.
[105] David Kalstone, *James Merrill: Essays in Criticism*, ed. Lehman and Berger, 142.
[106] Merrill, *Sandover*, 232–3.
[107] Kirsten Flagstad (1895–1962) was a celebrated Norwegian soprano, noted for her Wagnerian roles.
[108] Merrill, *Sandover*, 233.
[109] Ibid., 229.
[110] Ibid., 156.

LESSONS & THE MYSTERIES'.[111] The 'childless' are, for the most part, the male homosexuals that populate both JM's real-life and afterlife. The chief exception to this rule – Maria Mitsotàki or 'MM' (who is revealed, significantly, to be a reincarnation of Plato) forms the centre around which the poem's claims of happy childlessness are made. Her 'insouci-ance' about her lack of progeny is echoed in 'The Emerald' (1972). The scene focuses on Merrill's receiving of his dead father's ring, 'For when you marry. For your bride', his mother adds:

> I could not tell her, it would sound too theatrical,
> *Indeed this green room's mine, my very life.*
> *We are each other's; there will be no wife,*
> *The little feet that patter here are metrical.*[112]

'The Emerald' expresses significantly less anxiety about this exclusion from the marital and reproductive realm than Merrill's earlier explo-rations of childlessness. Here, biological procreation is displaced to accommodate the poetic offspring, a move that foreshadows *Sandover*'s trade-off between reproduction and a receptivity to acts of aesthetic cre-ation. JM's responsibility to his 'metrical' offspring is, by this time, felt as a freedom. Hence, in *Sandover*: 'EXCEPT AS MESSENGERS WE HAVE NO COMMITMENT TO A YOUNGER GENERATION'.[113] As White has noted, writing before adoption was widely viable for the would-be gay parent, 'childless homosexuals become the natural transmitters of wis-dom to the next generation – as spiritual, since never, biological par-ents'.[114] Significantly, the 'FIVE' immortal souls that 'PURSUE THEIR LEADERSHIP' of the human race 'UNDER VARIOUS GUISES'[115] (including Einstein and Plato) are 'LARGELY CHILDLESS'.[116] As DJ perceptively notes of the dead and living gathered for the *Script*'s 'les-sons'; 'You realize, Robert is the one/Parent among us'.[117]

Mirabell relates to a somewhat incredulous JM and DJ, that the homo-sexual, the poet, and the musician are naturally inclined towards the production of 'V WORK':

---

[111] Ibid., 216.
[112] Merrill, 'The Emerald', *Collected Poems*, 342.
[113] Merrill, *Sandover*, 206.
[114] White, 'The Inverted Type', 50.
[115] Merrill, *Sandover*, 142.
[116] Ibid., 468.
[117] Ibid., 413.

LOVE OF ONE MAN FOR ANOTHER OR LOVE BETWEEN WOMEN
IS A NEW DEVELOPMENT OF THE PAST 4000 YEARS
ENCOURAGING SUCH MIND VALUES AS PRODUCE THE
    BLOSSOMS
OF POETRY & MUSIC, THOSE 2 PRINCIPAL LIGHTS OF
GOD BIOLOGY. LESSER ARTS NEEDED NO EXEGETES:
ARCHITECTURE SCULPTURE THE MOSAICS & PAINTINGS THAT
FLOWERED IN GREECE & PERSIA CELEBRATED THE BODY.
POETRY MUSIC SONG INDWELL & CELEBRATE THE MIND. . .
HEART IF U WILL
[. . .]
NOW MIND IN ITS PURE FORM IS A NONSEXUAL PASSION
OR A UNISEXUAL ONE PRODUCING ONLY LIGHT.
FEW PAINTERS OR SCULPTORS CAN ENTER THIS LIFE OF THE
    MIND.
THEY (LIKE SO-CALLD NORMAL LOVERS) MUST PRODUCE AT
    LAST
BODIES   THEY DO NOT EXIST FOR ANY OTHER PURPOSE[118]

Not only does Merrill's connoisseurial cosmology deem the visual arts 'LESSER', it is also problematic for its representation of homosexuality as a sanitized and idealized arrangement of two minds, rather than bodies. Edmund White has noted that Merrill's dichotomous formulations are somewhat uneasy: homosexuality is reduced to a 'NONSEXUAL PASSION', while heterosexuality is little more than a 'stud service'.[119] In this respect, Merrill refuses the explicit physicality of Ginsberg's poetry, claiming instead that the 'Mind in its pure form' is 'a unisexual one'.[120]

Sex enters Merrill's cosmology only as a mischievous metaphor for JM and DJ's willing ears and pen:

DJ:

What part, I'd like to ask Them, does sex play
In this whole set-up? Why did They choose *us?*
Are we more usable than Yeats or Hugo,
Doters on women, who then went ahead
To doctor everything their voices said?

---

[118] Ibid., 156.
[119] White, 'The Inverted Type', 50.
[120] Merrill, *Sandover*, 156

We haven't done that. JM: No indeed.
Erection of theories, dissemination
Of thought – the intellectual's machismo.
We're more the docile takers-in of seed.
No matter what tall tale our friends emit,
Lately – you've noticed? – we just swallow it.[121]

Where JM and DJ's passive transcription of the spirit voices is framed as
an act akin to fellatio, Yeats and Victor Hugo's heterosexuality is 'blamed'
for their dilution of the spirit's messages to their own ends. The misuse
of the spirit conversation is playfully spun out as analogous to the power
differential within the act of oral sex – a phallic metaphor continued in
JM's questioning of his 'ex-shrink' as to the roots of these 'Inseminations
by psycho roulette?':

     What underlies these odd
Inseminations by psycho-roulette?"
I stared, then saw the light:
"Somewhere a Father Figure shakes his rod
At sons who have not sired a child?
Through our own spirit we can both proclaim
And shuffle off the blame
For how we live – that good enough?"[122]

From the moment JM's psychiatrist suggests that the whole scenario is
nothing more than a 'folie à deux',[123] Merrill provides the reader with
a convenient new framework through which to read the poem's occult
underpinnings. If the voices that speak through the board are no more
than an elaborate Wildean mask through which the 'truth' can be spoken, then the trilogy's elaborate cosmology of the privileged homosexual
becomes the mitigating argument for a life well lived. The childless life is
validated when the 'blame' for having not 'sired a child' is offset by the
commitment to produce 'V WORK'.

As previously noted, Helen Vendler identifies a displacement of 'the
civic and familial' in Merrill's trilogy. However, *Sandover* proposes an
intimate relationship between the familial and the virtues identified as

[121] Ibid., 154.
[122] Ibid., 30.
[123] Ibid.

those of the 'mind and heart', with these concerns converging at the very centre of its vision. While Vendler follows Merrill's initial cue in seeing a dichotomous relationship between the poetic arts and the reproductive impulses of heterosexual relations, the trilogy reveals the relationship to be a more dialectical one, in which the artistic legacies of 'V WORK' are enmeshed with the biological legacies of reproduction.

As in Ginsberg's later poems about the 'sterility' of homosexuality (in lyrics such as 'This Form of Life Needs Sex'), the bonds of art and homosexuality in *Sandover* are inextricably, but uneasily, linked. 'I will have to accept women/if I want to continue the race', Ginsberg laments; accept, that is not the symbolic female of 'the Muse but living meat phantom' (*GCP*, 284–5). Struggling with these anxieties about the non-procreativity of being gay, Ginsberg concludes that homosexuality is

> . . . no more answer to life
> than the muscular statue
> I felt up its marbles
> envying Beauty's immortality in the
> museum of Yore –
> You can fuck a statue but you can't
> have children.

(*GCP*, 285)

Ginsberg's sterile vision is linked to the traditional aesthetic implications of homosexuality; Greek statues, the cult of beauty – all recurring tropes in Merrill's oeuvre. However, where Ginsberg feels irremediably cut-off from the reproductive realm, in *Sandover*, JM and DJ find themselves participating, somewhat unconventionally, in the generative task. When Ephraim is looking for 'any strong sane women/In early pregnancy' whose unborn child might be a fitting home for the soul of his earthly 'representative', JM and DJ direct him to an ex-roommate whose wife 'is on the nest'.[124] While these ill-advised conspiracies to transport newly reincarnated souls into the unborn babies of friends and associates go (rightly) awry, the poem does build up a successful surrogate family made up of queer (or 'honorary' queer, in the case of MM) members. This is headed up by the 'family constellation'[125] of JM & DJ, WHA & MM that propels the narrative of the poem. However, if *Sandover* is read

---

[124] Merrill, *Sandover*, 20.
[125] Merrill, *Recitative*, 51

as a long farewell to the paternal WHA (who calls JM and DJ 'MY BOYS') and 'Maman' MM (as she is ironically known to her 'ENFANTS'), these parental substitutes are also no more than creations of Merrill's fictional imagination; reflections of JM's spiritual and artistic investments.

(viii) Ego fragmentation and the bardic voice

The dispersal of JM's consciousness through the component characters of the trilogy epitomizes *Sandover's* fracturing of a central, bardic voice, where 'the point remained, to be always of two minds'.[126] The world of *Sandover* is one of paradoxical doublings and confusing reflections. The trilogy's propensity to uncover equivalencies is framed by Robert Morse's objection in the poem:

> Everything in Dante knew its place.
> In this guidebook of yours, how do you tell
> Up from down? Is Heaven's interface
>
> What your new friends tactfully don't call Hell?[127]

In Merrill's vision, Heaven and Hell 'come, even now at times, to the same thing'. This is echoed in the recollection of Merrill's childhood error, in which 'hell' was mis-identified with the German word for 'bright'.[128] This reflective cancelling also operates on the generative level, where JM and DJ's meddling in the reincarnation of souls, 'Had bypassed religion . . . / Had left heredity, Narcissus bent/Above the gene pool'.[129]

Many critics have responded to this insistent doubling in the poem, which is accompanied by recurrent mirror imagery that goes beyond the recapitulation of the Narcissus myth. This propensity extends to Merrill's love of puns and word play – the linguistic equivalent of this recurring trope. However, few have commented on the ways in which such divisions of the self may be seen to relate to the psychosexual models of homosexual subjectivity. *Sandover* explores the myth of Narcissus as an archetype for the poet's identity, for the idea of the self-reflected and refracted echoes in the trilogy's persistent duality and mirror reflections.

---

[126] Merrill, *Sandover*, 51.
[127] Ibid., 256.
[128] Merrill, *Recitative*, 274.
[129] Merrill, *Sandover*, 20.

Sandover is haunted by M's – JM, MM ('Maman'), Mimi, Maya Deren, Mary Jackson, Charles Merrill, as well as Mirabell's moniker, closely resembling Merrill's own. Not only is the 'antiworld' a mirror image of its earthly counterpart, the mirror also provides the only means by which the dead can see the living, as well as the means of their final release.[130] As JM and DJ shatter the mirror in the closing sections of *Sandover* to release WHA and MM to his/her new 'life', so the poem also fragments its centralizing consciousness into innumerable shards.

The myth of Narcissus has historically been employed as a symbolic figure for same-sex desire; the myth of a young man absorbed in desire for his own reflection operates as an allegory for a rather narrow definition of homosexual attraction as defined by sameness. Freud took this one step further, conceiving of the 'narcissistic' process of object-choice (when the individual 'seeks for [their] own ego and finds it again in other people') as 'of particularly great importance in cases where the outcome is a pathological one'.[131] For Freud, Narcissus' passion for his own reflection serves as a model for the pathology of the homosexual. Although the problem remains with how such models reduce the homosexual experience to an ahistorical experience, whether analytic or symbolic, literary uses of the myth abound and, for this reason, are of relevance to a discussion of literary representations of homosexuality. The incidence of mirrors in homosexual poetry also takes on new resonance in a post-Lacanian age. Take, for example, John Ashbery's 'The Thinnest Shadow' (1956):

A face looks from the mirror
As if to say,
'Be supple, young man,
Since you can't be gay'.[132]

The injunction from the reflected self to 'be supple' operates on several levels. In concurrence with some conceptions of homosexual ego formation, the subject seems to articulate the problems with 'normative' responses of self-definition in the Lacanian mirror stage. Looking at his reflection, not only does the homosexual subject gain a sense of an individuated self, but also one of internal division and fragmentation from a self-differentiated and marginalized, historically, by virtue of its desires.

---

[130] Ibid., 150, 152–3.
[131] Sigmund Freud, *On Sexuality: Three Essays on the Theory of Sexuality*, Vol. 7, ed. Angela Richards (London: Penguin, 1977), 145.
[132] John Ashbery, *Some Trees* (New Haven, CT: Yale University Press, 1956), 46

This negative cultural definition is articulated in Ashbery's poem by the images of a decaying vessel: 'His heart is full of lies/And his eyes are full of mold'. This internalized disgust reappears later in Ashbery's 'The Skaters' (1966),[133] where the 'half-man' look inspires 'the disgust of honest folk', recalling Elizabeth Bishop's 'half looking glass' man in 'The Gentleman of Shalott'.[134] The doubleness offered by reading 'mold' as both an image of decay and as an ability to be shaped, is characteristic of Ashbery's multiple layers of possible meaning. However, where John Shoptaw's reading of this passage sees the reflection offering 'subtlety as the alternative to openly gay behaviour', counselling 'resourceful evasive action',[135] the parental instructions of the mirror remain seditious, in light of the poem's historical context.

David Bergman also employs psychosexual models of homosexuality in his discussion of 'gay egolessness' in relation to *Sandover*. He suggests that the numerous transfigurations that take place in the poem arise out of the absence of a homosexual model for the construction of gay identity.[136] This 'egolessness', Bergman contends, develops out of the homosexual's relation to society, rather than the 'vicissitudes of the Oedipal crisis'.[137] It is a negative as well as an absent identity that, for Bergman, stands in contrast to heterosexual male poets such as Robert Lowell, who are self-assertively preoccupied with the acquisition of a voice and poetic identity. Although Bergman's model reduces the polyvalence of homosexual experience to a single ahistorical model of identity formation, his discussion of the differing approaches to the poetic voice in Lowell and Merrill's work is noteworthy in terms of its canny characterization of Merrill's dispersal of the bardic voice. Comparing the strongly autobiographical foundations of both *Sandover* and Lowell's *History*, Bergman contends:

> History is a mirror in which Lowell finds pieces of his ever more fragmented but omnipresent face. Merrill's mirror is a history which takes him further and further from himself . . . Merrill is an artist of transfiguration; his bats become peacocks, and male prostitutes, angels. Everyone is subordinated to the larger work. Merrill becomes the

---

[133] John Ashbery, *Rivers and Mountains* (New York: Holt, Rinehart and Winston, 1966), 40.
[134] Bishop, *Complete Poems*, 9.
[135] Shoptaw, *On the Outside Looking Out*, 5.
[136] Bergman, *Gaiety Transfigured*, 44.
[137] Ibid., 45.

instrument through which history is articulated, whereas Lowell is the figure to whom History has come to be enacted.[138]

As Bergman's reading suggests, Merrill is able to transform the autobiographical weight of *Sandover* into a grand act of self-dispersal and erasure, as History is articulated through the numerous friends, characters and literary figures that the poem takes in.

Sandwiched between the McCarthyite homophobia of the 1950s that 'Howl' registers, and the cataclysm of AIDS that would eventually come to take Merrill's life, *Sandover* harnesses the camp clichés and the Wildean pun to create an epic education in connoisseurship. While never as theatrically prophetic as Whitman or Crane, Merrill presents childlessness as crucial to the justification of his (and his fellow homosexuals') 'ways to men'. The poem's dazzlingly complex cosmology not only validates but also privileges 'how we live'.[139] In doing so, far from 'a warmed up' version of 'Milton, Dante, Genesis',[140] the trilogy recasts the epic for a moment of time, although short-lived, when homosexuality could dare to assume universal relevance.

---

[138] Ibid., 47.
[139] Merrill, *Sandover*, 30.
[140] Ibid., 136.

Chapter 4

'The natural noise of the present': John Ashbery's *Flow Chart*

(i) 'A great deal of thinking went into it and out/the other side'[1]

John Ashbery began his poem *Flow Chart* (1991) after the artist Trevor Winkfield suggested that he write a 100-page poem about his recently deceased mother.[2] Accordingly, he set about composing at the rate of a page-a-day between 8 December 1987 and 28 July 1988, the latter date being the poet's 61st birthday. *Flow Chart* was not only inspired, then, by the loss of Ashbery's mother but also reached towards Ashbery's own 61st anniversary, with the movement of the poem 'flowing/backward into an origin' (*FC*, 10).

While *Flow Chart*'s diaristic evolution is sandwiched between these two 'originary' events, the body of the poem busies itself with the ordinary and the everyday. The speakers record a life that 'becomes a description of every second of the time it took' (*FC*, 7), putting into the poem 'whatever happened to be around, at any given moment' (*FC*, 96). *Flow Chart* exists in a dynamic that shifts between these two axes of operation; the systemic charting of the quotidian, alongside the ebb and flow of birth and death. This dual focus characterizes what I perceive to be Ashbery's

---

[1] Ashbery, *Flow Chart* (London: Carcanet, 1991), 213. Hereafter, all references to this edition will appear in the body of the text as *FC*, followed by the page reference, i.e. (*FC*, 213).

[2] 'Trevor Winkfield, the English Painter . . . who did the book's cover, came to visit at Hudson some time in '87, and asked what I'd been writing. I said I'd been writing some very short poems, and he said, 'Why don't you write a hundred-page poem about your mother?', who had died earlier that year. I retained the idea of writing a hundred-page poem, as something to try and do, but I didn't really think about making it about my mother, since I don't write poems about subjects – but she does occasionally make a cameo appearance' (*John Ashbery in Conversation with Mark Ford* (London: Between the Lines, 2003), 64).

approach to the epic mode – holding the minutiae of life firmly in sight, while attending to the 'big things' of nation and history with which the epic is traditionally concerned. Certainly, the poem does not immediately set itself up as an epic in the traditional sense. As with much of Ashbery's poetry, it is its 'difficulty' that presents itself most strongly to the reader in the first instance.

As its title suggests, *Flow Chart* is not 'about' anything that can be firmly anchored down. The poem is a 'freight train of associations' (*FC*, 196) in which readers are invited to immerse themselves. As with Ashbery's work in general, *Flow Chart* resists critical models that seek to elucidate meaning through 'close reading'. Instead, to make sense of *Flow Chart*, the reader must take on board the advice delivered by the poem itself:

> . . . For the discourse [. . .]
> to take place on a meaningful level, that is, outside someone's brain,
>   a state of artificial
> sleep would have to be induced, first of all.

(FC, 198)

As Keith Cohen has noted, the issue of authorial positioning in Ashbery's poetry is a slippery one; his poetry simultaneously signals and celebrates the collapse in the distinction between high and low culture. As Cohen remarks, 'the voice of the poems seems at one moment to be mouthing the discourse, at the next moment to be mocking it'.[3] Nowhere is this truer than in *Flow Chart*'s ventriloquization of multiple discourses and voices, the consequence of which is a poetic surface that is difficult to penetrate. In this chapter, I want to establish the ways in which *Flow Chart* might be made to operate on this 'meaningful level' if we consider it as a text that engages with the tradition of the autobiographical epic. As a work concerned with tracing and recapturing beginnings and sources, *Flow Chart* taps into the epic tradition's concern with founding myths. At times, the Hudson River can be seen to operate in the poem as an updated version of Wordsworth's Derwent from *The Prelude*. However, if Ashbery began with the idea of writing a poem all about his mother, the 'current of daily activity'[4] (as Shoptaw has described the compositional

---

[3] Keith Cohen, 'Ashbery's Dismantling of Bourgeois Discourse', *Beyond Amazement: New Essays on John Ashbery*, ed. David Lehman (Ithaca: Cornell University Press, 1980), 130.

[4] John Shoptaw, 'James Merrill and John Ashbery', *The Columbia History of American Poetry*, ed. Jay Parini with the assistance of Brett C. Miller (New York: Columbia University Press, 1993), 773.

practice for this poem) soon sweeps the poem's initial donnée into more indistinct terrain:

> And the river threaded its way best it could through sharp obstacles
> and was sometimes not there.
>
> (*FC*, 96)

The Hudson River performs this game of hide-and-seek throughout the poem, periodically emerging in the metaphors of flow and irrigation that appear amidst the stream of the poem's voices. If we think of the river as a symbol of Ashbery's original intentions to compose a poem concerned with his own origins, it is apt that the poem narrates the diversion of its own original focus.[5]

While the opening sections of the poem are full of aquatic imagery, the maternal foundations of *Flow Chart*'s composition disappear as the poem negotiates the 'obstacles' of Ashbery's surroundings and imagination. Similarly, any sense that what we are reading is purely autobiographical soon gets lost amidst the chorus of voices paraded before the reader. The numerous personae that make up the 'collective memory' (*FC*, 27) of the poem constitute a formal recasting of the Whitmanian 'multitude': Ashbery's poem contains multitudes not by utilizing the poet as a conduit to observe the full range of American life, but by filtering a multitude of voices and discourses.[6] If we compare Ashbery's approach to that of *The Changing Light at Sandover*'s multi-voiced narrative, it is clear that *Flow Chart* embodies a more democratic poetics. Turning away from the homotextual coded-ness of Merrill's connoisseurial work, Ashbery's poem follows Whitman's example in seeking an audience of the many:

> you can browse through this catalog and, who knows, perhaps come
> up with a solution that will apply
> to your complicated case . . .
>
> (*FC*, 40)

---

[5] Ashbery bought a house in Hudson in 1978 with a view to replicating his beloved grandfather's house of his Rochester childhood. See David Lehman, *The Last Avant-Garde: The Making of the New York School of Poets* (New York: Doubleday, 1998), 123.

[6] 'Do I contradict myself?/Very well then I contradict myself,/(I am large, I contain multitudes)' (Whitman, 'Song of Myself', *Complete Poetry and Selected Prose and Letters*, 84).

In offering this poetic 'catalog' of experiences that might resonate with the reader's own, Ashbery's poem follows Whitman in renegotiating the relationship between the public and the private in the epic mode.

Expanding upon James McCorkle's reading of Ashbery as a grand re-visioner of the lyric mode, I will argue that through his formal recasting of the Whitmanian 'multitude', Ashbery moves away from lyric solipsism and towards what McCorkle has called, the 'polyphonic social'.[7] As part of this discussion, I consider Ashbery's *Three Poems* (1972) as a precursor text to *Flow Chart,* both for the ways in which it incorporates multiple popular discourses, and for its engagement with epic themes. 'The System', I suggest, presents an earlier working through many of the ideas that dominate *Flow Chart,* particularly those concerning the interpenetration of autobiographical and public discourses.

In order to identify the ways in which critics have already begun to think of his experimentalism as taking place in terms of the public and the private dialectic, I consider in detail some of the critical work surrounding Ashbery. S. P. Mohanty and Jonathan Monroe's 1987 reappraisal of Ashbery as a 'social poet', opened the way for a re-evaluation of his representation by critics such as Helen Vendler and Harold Bloom, who had championed the poet as a follower in the American Transcendentalist tradition. Mohanty and Monroe's article contends that Ashbery had undergone a serious misreading by those such as Bloom, who, they claimed, had ignored the 'social' dimension of the poet's concern with the 'self-world relationship'.[8]

(ii) 'And the river threaded its way best it could through sharp obstacles and was sometimes not there' (*FC,* 96)

As already noted, Ashbery has spoken of beginning *Flow Chart* with the idea of recasting Wordsworth's *The Prelude,* figuring his mother as the 'river's temporal flow' and then 'charting it as an autobiography'.[9] There

---

[7] See James McCorkle, 'Nimbus of Sensations: Eros and Reverie in the Poetry of John Ashbery and Ann Lauterbach', *The Tribe of John: Ashbery and Contemporary Poetry,* ed. Susan Schultz (Tuscaloosa & London: The University of Alabama Press, 1995), 101–25.

[8] S. P. Mohanty and Jonathan Monroe, 'John Ashbery and the Articulation of the Social', *Diacritics* 17.2 (Summer 1987), 37.

[9] Shoptaw, 'James Merrill and John Ashbery', 773.

is certainly much to compare between the two poems.[10] However, where Wordsworth's Derwent functions as a narrative vehicle for the return of memories through which to trace the growth of a poet's mind, Ashbery's Hudson River is concerned to record its daily outpourings:

> . . . I put my youth and middle
>   age into it,
> and what else? Whatever happened to be around, at a given moment,
>   for that is the best
> we have; no one can refuse it, and, by the same token, everyone must
>   accept it,
> for it is like a kind of music that comes in sideways and afterwards you
>   aren't sure
> if you heard it or not . . .

(*FC*, 96–7)

With the poem's focus upon the 'music' of the everyday, Ashbery's river soon diverges into a multitude of tributaries, presenting a plethora of narratives and stories. This polyphony of voices puts paid to any sense that Ashbery is engaging in the 'autobiographical myth-making'[11] of a Wordsworthian-styled epic.[12] Rather than attempting the retrograde autobiographical flow of *The Prelude*,[13] Ashbery's poem emerges as a chart or template for a 'one-size-fits-all' autobiography.[14] Places and names that might anchor the narrative to Ashbery's own history are omitted or replaced by the usual cast of pop culture figures or stock characters that

---

[10] Mutlu Blasing undertakes a lengthy comparative study of *Flow Chart* and *The Prelude* in the final section of her chapter, 'John Ashbery: The Epidemic of the Way We Live Now', *Politics and Form in Postmodern Poetry* (Cambridge: Cambridge University Press, 1995), 146–55.

[11] Harold Bloom, *The Visionary Company: A Reading of English Romantic Poetry* (Garden City, NY; London, England: Doubleday; Faber and Faber, 1961).

[12] For a discussion of Ashbery's relationship with the Romantic tradition, see Stephen Clark, '"Uprooting the Rancid Stalk": Transformations of Romanticism in Ashbery and Ash', *Romanticism and Postmodernism*, ed. Edward Larrissy (New York & Cambridge: Cambridge University Press, 1999), 157–78.

[13] When asked by Mark Ford about *Flow Chart's* relationship with Wordsworth's epic, Ashbery replied, 'I would never have the temerity to compare it to *The Prelude*', *John Ashbery in Conversation with Mark Ford*, 65.

[14] Ashbery uses this phrase in reference to his poem, 'Soonest Mended'. 'These are not autobiographical poems, they're not confessional poems . . . what I am trying to get at is a general, all-purpose experience – like those stretch socks that fit all sizes', A. Poulin Jr, 'The Experience of Experience: A Conversation with John Ashbery', *The Michigan Quarterly Review* 20.3 (1981), 250–1.

populate his shorter poems: 'Alvin and the chipmunks' (*FC*, 133) and 'Red Riding Hood' (*FC*, 216) jostle with 'Miss Winslow' (*FC*, 45), 'Fred', 'Joan', 'John' and 'Judson L. Whittaker' (*FC*, 61), while 'Superstition Mountain', and 'the Lost Dutchman Mine' (*FC*, 110) coexist alongside Clapham Common, and an American landscape that takes in New York, Minnesota, San Francisco and 'Main Street' (*FC*, 88). The specificities of Ashbery's childhood are nowhere to be seen:[15]

> . . . Early on
> was a time of seeming: golden eggs that hatched
> into regrets, a snowflake whose kiss burned like an enchanter's
> poison; yet it all seemed good in the growing dawn.
>
> (*FC*, 5)

In their place, we get a fairytale allegory of loss of innocence; a landscape populated by enchanters and golden eggs that gestate 'regrets'. Childhood is metaphorically homogenized as 'the growing dawn': we return to a point of origin, but it is merely marked as 'early on' – a kind of 'once upon a time' that cannot be anchored down in Ashbery's own specific history.

Reframing Wordsworth's 'correspondent breeze'[16] as the 'breeze that always nurtures' (*FC*, 5), *Flow Chart* ironizes *The Prelude*'s sense of nature as a guiding force:

> Whither shall I turn,
> By road or pathway, or through open field,
> Or shall a twig or any floating thing
> Upon the river point me out my course[17]

> The breeze that always nurtures us (no matter how dry,
> how filled with complaints about time and the weather is the air)
> pointed out a way that diverged from the true way without negating it,
> to arrive at the same result by different spells,
> so that no one was wiser for knowing the way we had grown.
>
> (*FC*, 5)

---

[15] For instance, Ashbery spent the majority of the first 7 years of his life living with his grandparents in Rochester.

[16] William Wordsworth, *The Prelude: A Parallel Text*, 1805 edition (London: Penguin, 1971), 37.

[17] Wordsworth, *The Prelude*, 34–6.

Ashbery parodically transforms Wordsworth's predestined 'course' into the 'true way'. However, *Flow Chart*'s narrator takes a Frostian 'road less travelled' that only 'arrives at the same result' or destination, just 'by different spells'.[18] Ashbery's breeze can only direct the poet to equally benign alternative routes. This 'way' has no potential to negate or disturb what is suggested in the quasi-Christian phrasing of 'the true way', as the normative path. In this sense, we might think of Ashbery's Frostian parable as speaking not only about sexual norms, but also as parodying the idea of the epic quest or journey. Here, Ashbery's assertion that choice is merely illusory undermines the notion of the fated or heroic journey that is central to the narrative of the classical epic poem.[19]

Mutlu Blasing has read *Flow Chart* alongside *The Prelude* as texts that both 'give a minute account of subjective responses to events, whether cataclysmic or barely registrable' (*sic*).[20] While Wordsworth's epic offers 'an instructive companion'[21] to Ashbery's poem (e.g. Wordsworth's hope of fixing 'the wavering of balance of my mind' strongly prefigures the forces at work in the phrase 'flow chart'), I am also interested in the differences in approach of the two poets and where Ashbery's project moves beyond, as Blasing also notes, being merely a 'parodic simulacrum of a Romantic poem'.[22] Alongside the 'unrelenting irony' that Blasing recognizes *Flow Chart* offers, Ashbery refuses the Wordsworthian 'egotistical sublime' by diffusing his own voice through the multiplicity of voices on offer in the poem. Where *The Prelude* is unrelenting in its project to create an 'outline of the poet's mind', Ashbery's poem is, it seems to me, more concerned with the way in which his own life is a larger reflection of what John Bayley has called, 'the natural noise of the present'.[23] The poem doesn't offer 'mere signifier[s] of what is most personal',[24] but a series of reflections of the 'collective memory' (*FC*, 27), heard through the 'music that comes in sideways' (*FC*, 97). Rather than focusing on the

---

[18] For a comparison of the operations of syntax in Wordsworth's *The Prelude* and *Flow Chart*, see Geoff Ward, 'Teleotropic syntax in Ashbery and Wordsworth', *Romanticism and Postmodernism*, ed. Edward Larrissy, 86–97.

[19] '[T]his other way, necessarily the only choice, is the route of artistic and homosexual experimentation. The sexual choice (if it is one) is so fundamental, so meaningful, that it cannot be understood otherwise than as no choice, as the way it was meant to be' (Shoptaw, 'James Merrill and John Ashbery', *The Columbia History of American Poetry*, 69).

[20] Blasing, *Politics and Form in Postmodern Poetry*, 148.

[21] Ibid.

[22] Blasing, *Politics and Form in Postmodern Poetry*, 153.

[23] Bayley, 'Richly Flows Contingency', 3.

[24] Blasing, *Politics and Form in Postmodern Poetry*, 154–5.

unique nature of the poet's receptivity, Ashbery is concerned with the applicability of his experiences to everyone: 'You'll find your story isn't so different from any honest man's, nor less/bizarre and compelling' (*FC*, 43).

As well as ironizing the benevolent forces of nature, Ashbery's poem also refuses Wordsworth's emphasis upon the importance of childhood. The formative experiences of youth are recast as archetypal fairytale occurrences that leave the reader none the wiser about the way the poet has grown, but rather create a generalized narrative of childhood. The 'system of repeatable, programmed events' that make up a scientific flow chart become, in Ashbery's poetic translation of the form, the interchangeable details of a life – 'anybody's autobiography', as Shoptaw puts it.[25]

Ashbery rehearsed this autobiographical template in 'Soonest Mended' (1970):

These then were the hazards of the course,
Yet though we knew the course *was* hazards and nothing else
It was still a shock when, almost a quarter of a century later,
The clarity of the rules dawned on you for the first time.
They were the players, and we who had struggled at the game
Were merely spectators . . .[26]

As a 'one-size-fits-all confessional poem', 'Soonest Mended' foreshadows *Flow Chart* in the way that it offers us hospitable scenarios that accommodate and echo our own subjective experiences. If, however, 'Soonest Mended' suggests that the 'distinctiveness' of our lives and memories is illusory, it simultaneously creates a sense of a shared history and consciousness that allows us to read the poem as a fragment of our own confessions. This communal consciousness is comparable to *Flow Chart*'s 'bloodstream of our collective memory' (*FC*, 27), where the flow of the nation's memory is given voice by the epic mode:

          . . . It occurs to me in my home on the beach
sometimes that others must have experiences identical to mine
and are also unable to speak of them, that if we cared
enough to go into each other's psyche and explore

---

[25] Shoptaw, 'James Merrill and John Ashbery', 773.
[26] Ashbery, 'Soonest Mended', *Selected Poems* (London: Carcanet, 1986), 88.

around, some of the canned white entrepreneurial brain food
could be reproduced in time to save the legions
of the dispossessed . . .

(FC, 23)

Ashbery discards the idea of one's individuality and uniqueness without exclamation. Other people's lives are not so much similar as 'identical'. Here, Ashbery foregrounds the role of the poet as quasi-analyst for
the community: Ashbery's hero is the one who shares in the inability to
'speak' of things, but paradoxically can also give voice to those experiences that the others are 'unable to speak of' (*FC*, 14). Ashbery paro-
dies the prophetic voice that we have observed at work in the poems of
Merrill and Ginsberg; his narrator strives to give voice to a warning that
cannot be heard 'except by speaking in tongues' (*FC*, 22).

The frustrations of the mediatory role – 'taking dictation/from on
high' (*FC*, 216) – are positioned at the very forefront of Merrill's *Sandover*.
However, while Merrill's dissatisfaction stems from his feelings of insig-
nificance in the 'cosmic carpool'[27] of recorders, Ashbery's frustrations
centre on a sense of the futility of producing anything at all:

> . . . But though reams of work do get done
> not much listens. I have the feeling my voice is just for me,
> that no one else has ever heard it, yet I keep mumbling the litany
> of all that has ever happened to me . . .

(FC, 81)

It is noteworthy that Ashbery objectifies his listener – he laments that
'not *much* listens', rather than 'not many'. Ashbery's typical verbal slippage serves to emphasize the loneliness of his performance. While
Wordsworth could be certain of an audience in Coleridge, as both his
friend and the addressee of *The Prelude*, Ashbery's concern that his poem
will remain without an audience seems to echo Shoptaw's contention
that 'no modern epic can mean to the culturally diverse population of
the United States what the *Iliad* and the *Divine Comedy* or even *Paradise
Lost* meant to their nations'.[28] Shoptaw is right to note the shift in the
cultural importance of the epic poem in the twentieth century. However,
the mumbled litany of *Flow Chart* reinvigorates the epic mode for the

---

[27] Merrill, *Sandover*, 262.
[28] Shoptaw, 'James Merrill and John Ashbery', 758.

modern world by reinterpreting, as Ginsberg had before him, Williams' contention that 'news offers the precise incentive to epic poetry'.[29]

(iii) 'I'm more someone else, taking dictation/from on high, in a purgatory of words' (*FC*, 216)

At first glance, *Flow Chart* would seem to take up where *Sandover* left off. With its author's mediating of a symphony of voices 'from on high', Ashbery's poem, like Merrill's, spins its tale in a dizzying array of accents. This multiplicity of dialects de-centres Ashbery's authorial presence, echoing Rimbaud's 'Je est un autre'. 'I'm more someone else' (*FC*, 216), Ashbery says, echoing Merrill's anxiety at ventriloquizing the dictées from the afterlife. As well as sharing a broader concern with the mystery of one's origins and death, the two poems explore the poet's role as medium. 'I see I am as ever/a terminus of sorts . . . lots of people arrive in me' (*FC*, 127), Ashbery laments, recalling Merrill's experience as poet-medium in *Sandover*. However, in other ways, *Flow Chart*'s 'purgatory of words' (*FC*, 216) departs significantly from the cosmological vision that *Sandover* presents. Unlike Merrill's camp cacophony of supernatural voices, Ashbery's polyvocalism is very much of this world, its discourses culled from 'our everyday thoughts and fantasies' (*FC*, 1). As David Herd has suggested in his reading of the poem, *Flow Chart* stands as a 'monument to the everyday', as it undertakes a quasi-epic treatment of the banal and the commonplace.[30] This fascination with quotidian life is to be found everywhere in Ashbery's *oeuvre*, the 'small accidents and pleasures/Of the day' in 'Self-Portrait in a Convex Mirror'; the 'newspaper and the garbage/Wrapped in it, the over, the under' of 'The Explanation';[31] 'our daily quandary about food and the rent and bills to be paid' in 'Soonest Mended'.[32] Ashbery's world is one where 'Nothing is too 'unimportant'/or too important for that matter.'[33]

Flow Chart focuses that fascination more sharply, asking us to interrogate again and again 'the still-fertile ground of our once-valid compact/with the ordinary and the true' (*FC*, 9). As we have already

---

[29] William Carlos Williams, 'Review of Ezra Pound's *A Draft of XXX Cantos*', quoted in Mike Weaver, *William Carlos Williams: The American Background*, 120.

[30] David Herd, *John Ashbery and American Poetry* (New York: Palgrave, 2001), 212.

[31] Ashbery, *Houseboat Days: Poems* (New York: Viking, 1977), 14.

[32] Ashbery, *Selected Poems*, 87.

[33] Ashbery, *Houseboat Days*, 14.

seen, this dramatization on an epic scale of the 'small things' of life is not only fertile ground for a mock-epic project. Both Ginsberg and Merrill's poems have already shown that such fascination with the minutiae of everyday life is not incompatible with a serious and modern approach to the American epic. As a poem that systematically charts the daily flow of the speaker's thoughts and perceptions, *Flow Chart*'s attempt to articulate the multifaceted experiences of ordinary Americans finds Ashbery engaging in a distinctly modern incarnation of the epic project.

By situating the ambitions of *Flow Chart* within the traditional epic function of giving voice to 'the tribe', one can see how Ashbery's achievement is, as John Bayley argues, 'to have sounded, in poetry, the standard tones of the age'.[34] Ashbery is a poet who, as Douglas Crase remarks, 'writes with the stereo on'.[35] In this sense *Flow Chart* shares with *The Fall of America* a concern with the current pulse of contemporary culture. Where Ginsberg's epic journey is sound-tracked by 'Radio the soul of the nation' (*GCP*, 369), Ashbery's poetry is also full of the sounds of 'America calling/. . . The force of colloquial greetings'.[36] In presenting the multiplicity of contemporary American culture, *Flow Chart* fulfils Aristotle's insistence that the epic poet give his work 'appropriate magnitude', achieving a successful imitation of life in its full diversity by presenting a wealth of detail, even if it means that the reader cannot apprehend every facet of it at any given moment.[37]

This technique of poetic 'excess' (both in form and content) is at the very heart of *Flow Chart*'s ambitious effects. In his essay comparing the excessive syntactical turns in Ashbery's poetry to Wordsworth's technique in *The Prelude*, Geoff Ward writes that both poets produce such 'teleotrophic syntax' in an effort to 'suture over trauma':

> . . . these incessant reformulations add to each other, pile upon words, more or less repeating themselves in an accurate recreation of the ways in which, after a shocking incident, we babble our way back and forth over the same ground, using slightly altered terms.[38]

---

[34] John Bayley, 'Richly Flows Contingency', 3.

[35] Douglas Crase, 'The Prophetic Ashbery', *Beyond Amazement: New Essays on John Ashbery*, ed. David Lehman, 65.

[36] Ashbery, 'Pyrography', *Selected Poems*, 212.

[37] Aristotle, *Poetics*, trans. Malcolm Heath (London: Penguin, 1996), 30.

[38] Ward, 'Teleotrophic Syntax in Ashbery and Wordsworth', *Romanticism and Postmodernism*, ed. Larrissy, 90.

Writing *A Wave* (1984) in the aftermath of his near-death experience in 1982, Ward argues, Ashbery began to write a poetry focused on the excesses of syntax, moving away from a poetics primarily concerned with the surrealism of images. The syntactical rhythm and tone of this body of work that includes *Flow Chart* is one that works by 'riddling through self-doubt' and one that is 'striated by moments of near-derailment, near-resolution'.[39] For Ward, *Flow Chart* 'risks all on the long syntactical reach . . . encrypting Barbara Johnson's suspicion that knowledge is an effect of syntax', as reflected by its endlessly unrolling qualifications. In *Flow Chart* 'meaning is where we are going', and the reader is bombarded with elaborate syntactical meanderings as the poem journeys to a centre or moment of revelation that is never reached.[40]

In a 1972 interview in the *New York Quarterly*, Ashbery described his formal approach to the poetic line in terms of the expressive potential of 'excess'. Comparing the 'prolongation and improvisation of time' in the 'sexual act' to the expressive potential of the long line, Ashbery sexualizes the formal choices he makes in his poetry, talking about the 'expansiveness of eroticism' as a comparable experience to the formal transgressions of the long line.[41] Its disruptive potential resides in this excessive quality in terms of the long line as the site of an overflow of meaning that can, as Barthes has said of the 'text of bliss', 'discomfort (perhaps to the point of boredom)'.[42] These are the 'plaited lines that extend/ like a bronze chain into eternity' (*FC*, 3) in the opening sequence of the *Flow Chart*. Gently mocking the extensive quality of his own poetics here, Ashbery evokes the 'chained bay waters of Liberty' of Crane's 'To Brooklyn Bridge'; his own lines echoing the 'arching path' of the 'cable strands' of its architecture[43] as they unfold in sequences of syntactic qualification in what can seem to the reader like an 'eternity'.[44]

---

[39] Ibid., 92.

[40] Ibid.

[41] Janet Bloom and Robert Losada, 'Craft Interview with John Ashbery', *New York Quarterly* 9 (Winter 1972), 25–6.

[42] Roland Barthes, *The Pleasure of the Text*, trans. Richard Miller (New York: Hill & Wang, 1975), 14.

[43] Crane, 'Atlantis', *CPHC*, 105.

[44] The idea of poetic excess, however, has also been theorized by feminists in terms of the Kristevan *semiotique*, so cannot be deemed an exclusively homotextual effect. However, Roland Barthes' definition of the text of bliss closely describes a parallel relationship between the disruptive potential of homosexuality and a disjunctive text: 'The text that imposes a state of loss, the text that discomforts (perhaps to the point of boredom), unsettles the reader's historical, cultural, psychological assumptions, the consistency of his tastes, values, memories, brings to a crisis his relation to language' (Barthes, *The Pleasure of the Text*, 14).

Attempting to 'chart', and thus to bring meaning through order to the 'melting pot' of American experience, *Flow Chart* enacts the difficulty of imposing epic coherence on American multiplicity. The poem registers the difficulty of tackling the epic amidst the sheer volume of history and incident in the modern world, yet still insists upon attempting to juggle them into provisional patterns and soar above the obstacles of the age: 'It's impossible/to keep abreast of the times', Ashbery concedes, 'and yet we still think of wings' (*FC*, 43). The loss of bearings experienced amidst the unanchored flow of history and landscape that constitutes 'America' is re-enacted by the disorienting vastness of the poem itself. *Flow Chart*'s 'shifting banks of words rising like steam/out of someplace into something' registers the absence of navigational markers (*FC*, 9). We are 'someplace', lost in an anonymous landscape that, while being a classic Ashberian strategy of non-descriptiveness – think of the 'somewhere, someone' of 'At North Farm' – also evokes a sense of being lost in the uncharted territory of a New World.[45]

It seems to me that the experience of reading *Flow Chart* approximates the crisis of identity (of both origin and home) that lies at the heart of American national identity. The difficulty in retrieving a sense of ancestral belonging, and the inevitable improvisation of an identity that follows in America's assimilatory culture, are reflected in the poem's polyphonous performance. In this sense, the aesthetic dilemmas of Ashbery's poem mirror the existential dilemmas of a modern American identity: the poem is, as Shoptaw has put it, simultaneously 'everybody's' and 'nobody's' story.[46]

(iv) Is *Flow Chart* an epic?

Upon its publication in 1991, Frank Muratori pronounced *Flow Chart* to be 'as close to an epic poem as our postmodern, nonlinear, deconstructed sensibilities will allow'.[47] Muratori's caveatic celebration of *Flow Chart*'s achievement foregrounds the late twentieth century hostility to strict generic forms. Muratori's comments suggest that the meandering flow of Ashbery's 'nonlinear' narrative is the product of

---

[45] John Ashbery, 'At North Farm', *A Wave* (New York: Noonday Press, 1998), 1.

[46] For a discussion of *Flow Chart* as a 'one-size-fits-all autobiography', see Shoptaw, *On the Outside Looking Out*, 302.

[47] Frank Muratori, Review of *Flow Chart*, *Library Journal* 116.8 (1 May 1991), 79.

a post-modern age that cannot accommodate the epic's expression
'self-determination' without taking a 'scissors-and-paste' approach to
the mode (*FC*, 129).

There is, of course, a long and well-documented history of poets questioning the viability of an age for the production of an epic. From Crane's
concerns about the order of 'our present stage of cultural development'
in the late 1920s,[48] to Merrill's contention over 50 years later that 'psychological action is more interesting than epic',[49] the texts I consider
here are no exception to the unspoken rule that the viability of the modern American epic must be continually re-questioned if it is to remain a
vital site for the contention of what it means to be American.

Muratori's review recognizes that *Flow Chart*'s epic status is not without its problems. Ashbery's characteristic genre-bending precludes the
poem's easy classification, as he melds the formal complexity of the
poem's embedded double sestina (after Swinburne's 'The Complaint
of Lisa') with prose, oral autobiography, stream of consciousness, confession, 'high' and 'low' diction, pop culture and mythological references. Like *Sandover*, *Flow Chart* does not wear its national or epic
concerns on its sleeve. Ashbery's meditation on the interrelation
between 'free will/and predestination' doesn't come until the 129th
page of the poem:

> . . . how about free will
> and predestination, to say nothing of self-determination? Just how
>   do they fit together? I know I explained this once but
> that was a cold while ago and now this upstart rephrasing of it seems
>   to be
> causing a lot of attention, I don't know why. It's only a re-working, a
>   scissors- and-paste
> job; the wording is almost identical.
>
>   (*FC*, 129)

Ashbery's confession here, however, does seem to suggest that there is
an element of conscious engagement in his poetry with the idea of epic.
Seemingly bemused by all the 'attention' he is getting for what he sees
as nothing more than an 'upstart rephrasing' of the same old story, the
narrator pleads the case for his unoriginality – 'the wording is almost

---

[48] Crane to Winters, 4 June 1930, *O My Land*, 427–30.
[49] Merrill, 'An Interview with Ashley Brown', *Recitative*, 46.

identical', he points out (*FC*, 129). However, if Ashbery is merely re-hashing the old Miltonic themes of 'free will/and predestination' ('though with a joke or two added as leavening, or gilding the/pill as you might say') (*FC*, 129), like its seventeenth-century predecessor, alongside those more universal concerns *Flow Chart* is also preoccupied with the issues of the political present.

The echoing fall-out from the privacy debates of the late 1980s resounds in *Flow Chart*'s sifting of 'sexual practices? Proclivities? The right to kill and maim?/. . . buggery' (*FC*, 131).[50] These are the pressing issues of Ashbery's contemporary America, which was mired in the Iran-Contra hearings as he was writing. The scandal of the arms-for-hostages negotiations first broke in the news in November of 1986, and the televised hearings of the Tower Commission followed thereafter, providing the source of the title for Ashbery's poem.[51] Earlier that year, the Supreme Court had also delivered its ruling on *Bowers* vs *Hardwick*, upholding the constitutionality of sodomy law in Georgia, and decreeing that the implicit constitutional right to privacy did not extend to consensual sex between homosexual adults.[52]

Both events make their appearances in amputated phrases or references in the poem, and the 'daily news stories behind this poetry' are palpable.[53] The US Congress issued its final report on the Iran-Contra affair on 18 November 1987, and several government aides were indicted on 16 March 1988. These issues would have been at the forefront of the Ashbery's mind as he engaged in the daily composition of *Flow Chart*. '[W]hen are we going to get together?' the poem asks of its reader, and 'invade each other's privacy in a significant way' (*FC*, 27):

> Latest reports show that the government
> still controls everything but the location of the blond captive
> has been pinpointed thanks to urgent needling from the backwoods
>   constituency
> and the population in general is alive and well. But can we dwell

---

[50] For a discussion of the privacy wars of the 1980s, see Nelson, *Pursuing Privacy*, 112–59.

[51] 'Ashbery first learned the term "flow chart" from watching the Iran-Contra hearings on television, where the organizational, informational and material flow of the national security Council, a "secret government" within the US government, was charted on enlarged placards for a national audience', Shoptaw, *On the Outside Looking Out*, 334.

[52] See www.law.cornell.edu/supct/html/historics/USSC_CR_0478_0186_ZS.html for a summary of the case and its rulings, site visited 3 July 2011.

[53] Shoptaw, *On the Outside Looking Out*, 335.

on any of it ? Our privacy ends where the clouds' begins, just here,
    just at
this bit of anonymity on the seashore.

(FC, 14)

In putting into the poem, 'whatever happened to be around, at any given moment' (*FC*, 96), *Flow Chart* registers the very real sense of conspiracy ('the government still controls everything'), while the 'blond captive' as a vision of an archetypal helpless female victim de-politicizes and eroticizes what would perhaps have been its real-life inspiration – the hostage situation in the Lebanon. 'Can we dwell/on any of it?' the poem asks. Skilfully punning here, Ashbery questions not only the poetic potential of these contemporary events but also their capacity to provide some kind of resting or dwelling place. Can we feel at home in a nation that is rife with conspiracy and refuses our right to privacy, the poem seems to ask.

Flow Chart returns insistently to this idea of home and origin and 'how . . . they/all fit together': 'Home becomes more than a place, more even than/a concept for this elite minority' (*FC*, 23–4). In order to grasp the ways in which Ashbery plays with both the location and concept of 'home' to suggest the improvisatory nature of one's origins, we must join this 'elite minority' for a moment. While, theoretically speaking, the construct of 'home' is a more private locus of belonging, connoting one's domicile or family dwelling, the idea of 'origin' tends towards questions of national, or biological 'homes'. *Flow Chart* plays with the inter-relation of both these ideas. Attempting 'a re-working' of the old epic forms, Ashbery's 'rephrasing' of the old themes of 'free will', 'predestination' and 'self-determination' (*FC*, 129) recasts the American epic project as a way of rethinking these constructs of both public and private kinds of 'home'.

'*This* is the frontier', the poem tells us; 'Beyond lies civility, a paradise of choices – maybe' (*FC*, 134). From the vantage point of the poet's avant-garde locale, Ashbery surveys the fascinating banality of suburban life, the uncertain 'paradise of choices' in which 'home' offers a white picket-fence idyll of consumerism. These are the suburbs that appear in 'The System',[54] 'through which one makes one's way to where the country is':[55]

---

[54] 'The System' is not only the central poem from the 1972 collection *Three Poems*. Ashbery also made it the centre piece of his *Selected Poems* in 1985.
[55] John Ashbery, *The Mooring of Starting Out: The First Five Books of Poetry* (New York: Ecco Press, 1997), 341.

The system was breaking down. The one who had wandered alone past so many happenings and events began to feel, backing up along the primal vein that led to his center, the beginning of a hiccup that would, if left together, explode the center to the extremities of life, the suburbs through which one makes one's way to where the country is.[56]

For Ashbery, the suburbs are the thoroughfares of complacence through which one must travel in order to reach the heart and 'center' of the urban body politic. They are 'connected' to Ashbery's version of America but, as he states in 'The One Thing that Can Save America', 'the juice is elsewhere'.[57]

The quasi-epic hero that opens 'The System' ('the one who had wandered') perceives these 'overgrown suburbs' as the 'extremities of life'. Ironically, these idyllic domiciles are less 'homely' to the wanderer than the eventful pulse of the metropolis. However, if the suburbs are some kind of peripheral paradise, they are also always connected to 'the country'[58] – that is, America at large. Being connected, they are also threatened by the arterial backup in the 'primal vein' that was beginning to make itself heard at the end of the 1960s, just as Ashbery was beginning *Three Poems*. As Shoptaw notes, the composition of *Three Poems* took place against the backdrop of highly charged domestic and international politics. The 'urban hiccup' was also felt in the revolutionary changes that were beginning to take place in both race relations and gay rights.[59]

Twenty years on from writing *Three Poems*, connection can only be achieved through Cranean masochistic gestures, by 'placing your hand in the fire' (*FC*, 17). The narrator of *Flow Chart* reprises the role of the epic wanderer that we see in 'The System' – he has 'no real home', or 'no one to inhabit it except you' (*FC*, 27). However, home has now become interchangeable with the idea of a soul or identity – one can be inhabited

---

[56] Ibid.

[57] Ashbery, 'The One Thing That Can Save America', *Self-Portrait in a Convex Mirror*, 44.

[58] Here, country connotes both the rural and the national, in a typical example of Ashberian verbal slippage.

[59] The recent Stonewall riot of June 1969 cannot have failed to have an impact upon Ashbery, who had returned to New York from Paris in 1965 to be an associate editor at *ArtNews* as he began 'The System'. Shoptaw notes, 'writing in the middle of domestic and foreign upheavals, Ashbery reconstructs the systemic fission of American society' (*On the Outside Looking Out*, 148).

by a beloved – and even if the false comforts of home are revealed to be merely 'a diagram' (*FC*, 136):

> . . . The fullness in the house at night
> is only a diagram (but cling to it, anyway) of where things were, and though
> we can remember what things, they are gone now; only their relation to one another subsists.
>
> (*FC*, 136)

Recalling the close of Elizabeth Bishop's poem 'Over 2,000 Illustrations . . .' where 'Everything' is 'only connected by "and" and "and"',[60] the connectedness in Ashbery's poem is, like the 'diagram' that simulates a false sense of 'fullness', meagre, and ultimately empty.

The idea that identity and home are intimately bound up with eroticism is borne out by an early confession in the poem: 'Can I deny my true origin and nature even if it's going to get me into a lot of / trouble later?' (*FC*, 29). This rare moment of political resistance recalls Crane's own doubting of the advantages of disguising his sexual proclivities.[61] In the context of Ashbery's time, however, while the poet seems to acknowledge the dangers of 'coming-out', the phrase, 'my true origin and nature' recalls the 'true way' of *Flow Chart*'s opening parody of the Romantic quest (*FC*, 5).[62] The idea of an essential core to same-sex desire is also suggested by Ashbery's phrase 'my true origin and nature'. These words assert quite directly that the narrator's sexual identity is not a matter of preference, but a matter of 'nature'. If there is any question of choice, it is whether to affirm ('Can I deny . . .?'). The association between 'trouble' and homosexuality is reprised later in the poem, in the 'suspicious' conversation overheard between 'two boys in the next row of lockers' that the narrator feels he should report to the McCarthyist-sounding 'office' (*FC*, 99). In this latter instance, Ashbery hints at a confrontation with contemporary politics, but even then does so indirectly, as if the writing of the poem is a process of overcoming resistance to its deeper subject matter that could still land him in trouble, years after the fact.

---

[60] Bishop, 'Over 2,000 Illustrations and a Complete Concordance', *Complete Poems*, 58.
[61] 'Let my lusts be my ruin, then, since all else is a fake and a mockery' (Hart Crane to Wilbur Underwood, 1 July 1926, *O My Land*, 261).
[62] Stephen Clark has identified Ashbery's poetry with the romantic 'interior quest for a lost paradise' (Clark, 'Transformations of Romanticism in Ashbery and Ash', 158).

(v) Situating Ashbery: The critical response

If Ashbery's *oeuvre* does not present an explicit exposition of national identity, then the response to his work has certainly engaged fully with ideas
about what it means to be American. Both Mohanty and Monroe have
claimed an emblematic role for 'Ashbery criticism', asserting that 'the
business of explaining Ashbery [has become] a significant kind of cultural
definition'.[63] His 'rise to the status of representative national poet' after
the success of *Self-Portrait in a Convex Mirror*, has meant that 'what is at stake
in the criticism of Ashbery . . . Is the meaning and status of what it is to be
"American" '.[64] This is no small claim indeed.[65] However, if postmodernism is, as Stuart Hall has suggested, partly a way to describe 'how the world
dreams itself to be "American" ',[66] it is perhaps no surprise that as the foremost practitioner of postmodern poetics, Ashbery has been taken up as
the battleground for contesting modern notions of American citizenship.

Such statements encourage us to think about just how important the
idea of nation might be to a poet who has produced poems entitled
'The One Thing That Can Save America' and ' "They Dream Only of
America" ' (1957). In the latter poem, Ashbery works to upset the famil-
iar sense of well-known signifiers, by returning insistently to figures from
American literature and popular mythology:

> They dream only of America
> To be lost among the thirteen million pillars of grass:
> 'This honey is delicious
> *Though it burns the throat.*'

> And hiding from darkness in barns
> They can be grownups now
> And the murderer's ash tray is more easily –
> The lake a lilac cube.[67]

---

[63] Mohanty and Monroe, 'John Ashbery and the Articulation of the Social', 37.
[64] Ibid.
[65] Martin Kevorkian has also argued that Ashbery 'exploits the generative power of scho-
lastic chatter' in *Flow Chart*, as yet another discourse through which to filter the 'natural
noise of the present' (as John Bayley puts it). See 'John Ashbery's *Flow Chart*: John
Ashbery and the Theorists on John Ashbery against the Critics against John Ashbery',
New Literary History 25.2, 'Writers on Writers' (Spring 1994), 459–76.
[66] The implicit equation of Hall's comment is the association of America and modernity. Stuart Hall, cited in Andrew Ross, *Universal Abandon? The Politics of Postmodernism*
(Minneapolis, MN: University of Minnesota Press, 1988), xii.
[67] Ashbery, ' "They Dream Only of America" ', *The Mooring of Starting Out*, 63.

Evoking the clichés of the 'New World' as a place of freedom and liberation, Ashbery subverts the idea of the American Dream, equating this
with a desire to be '*lost* among the thirteen million pillars of grass' (my
emphasis). Both misrepresenting and punning here on the 'multitudes'
that make up the landscape of Whitman's *Leaves of Grass*, Ashbery's
phrasing also suggests the biblical story of Lot and the transformation
of his wife into a pillar of salt. This combination of references resonates
with the poem's expression of yearning to be an erased or anonymous
presence among the masses (an idea we have already seen at work in
'Soonest Mended'), while harbouring suggestions of illicit sexual activity with the story's palpable associations with Sodom. Building on these
resonances, Ashbery continues in a Whitmanian register with the seminal 'honey' that '*burns the throat*'[68] before working through a mêlée of
American mythotypes that David Herd has identified: hiding in barns
(as in Mark Twain), Raymond Chandler's pulp fiction or *film noir*-esque
'murderer's ash tray', the Stevensian 'lake as lilac cube', Kerouac's cross-
country car journeys of 'hundreds of miles'.[69] Ashbery, however, confounds traditional metaphors to suggest that the barn is a safe-house
from the dangers of the world where sexual freedoms can be discov-
ered; 'They can be grownups now', he tells us, as the unnamed pair hide
'from' rather than *in* darkness.

   Despite its evocation of a collage of American literary references, the
poem ends with a disruption of the expectations of national signifiers.
Ashbery represents these clichés in the quotation marks of the title of
the poem itself, suggesting that they are only figures of speech:

There is nothing to do
For our liberation, except wait in the horror of it.

And I am lost without you.[70]

Ultimately defying the founding tenets of the American life it has evoked,
the poem suggests that the promised liberation is, in fact, something to
fear. Similarly, the 'wise' message or prophecy anticipated in 'The One
Thing That Can Save America' arrives too early and is misrecognized;
'you have ripped it open not knowing what it is', the narrator tells us.[71]

---

[68] Ashbery claims to have overheard this phrase spoken by his friend Pierre Matory.
[69] Herd, *John Ashbery and American Poetry*, 84–5.
[70] Ashbery, ' "They Dream Only of America" ', *The Mooring of Starting Out*, 63.
[71] Ashbery, 'The One Thing That Can Save America', *Self-Portrait in A Convex Mirror*, 44.

Both poems ultimately deny the salvation or liberation promised by their titles, evoking Stuart Hall's take on the American postmodern 'dream', only to undermine it.

Mohanty and Monroe's somewhat hyperbolic assertion about the significance of 'Ashbery criticism' is prompted by their quest to recast him as a social rather than a private poet. In this sense, their reading owes much to Douglas Crase's essay from 1980, which championed Ashbery 'not as our most private poet, but as our most public one'.[72] Mohanty and Monroe's review also sought to bring into question dominant critical narratives of genealogy (namely the one disseminated by Harold Bloom) that identified Ashbery as the inheritor of a Romantic canon that includes Whitman, Stevens and Crane. However, while Mohanty and Monroe's reading did much to institute a watershed in the representation of Ashbery as a poet who only operates in a mode of lyric solipsism, their thesis has some problems; chiefly that their argument is founded upon an uneasy dichotomy between the 'social' and the 'private'. Placing these terms in strict opposition to one another, Mohanty and Monroe's methodology creates, for me, an overly simplistic and rhetorical dichotomy, where, as we have seen in the preceding chapters, there exists a complex and co-interdependent relationship between the public and the private realms.

What remains helpful, however, about Mohanty and Monroe's thesis is that it has encouraged critics to think about Ashbery as a poet who also operates in the social realm. A notable example of this phenomenon can be seen in Helen Vendler's more recent book, *Invisible Listeners: Lyric Intimacy in Herbert, Whitman and Ashbery* (2005). Vendler paints a portrait of Ashbery not as a 'socially apathetic, solipsistic or narcissistic' voice but as a poet who 'allows the ethics of social life to enter the verbal space of lyric'.[73] As part of a study that looks at the relationship between the poet and addressee in the lyric, Vendler's conception of the form is that it is not always engaged in the representation of the lone, solipsistic voice,[74] but that the 'intimate lyric' is, at heart, concerned with mediation between the poet and an 'invisible listener'.[75] For Vendler,

---

[72] Crase, 'The Prophetic Ashbery', in *Beyond Amazement: New Essays on John Ashbery*, ed. David Lehman, 1.

[73] Helen Vendler, *Invisible Listeners: Lyric Intimacy in Herbert, Whitman and Ashbery* (Princeton, NJ: Princeton University Press, 2005), 57.

[74] Vendler terms this kind of lyric 'the lyric of solitary meditation' (Vendler, *Invisible Listeners*, 80).

[75] Ibid.

Ashbery's achievement in the genre has been to wrest language from its context; 'to bring into lyric a vast social lexicon of both English English [*sic*] and American English – common speech, journalistic cliché, business and technical and scientific language, allusion to pop culture as well as to canonical works'.[76] Conducting a mediation between the 'I' of the poet and the 'you' of the reader',[77] Vendler argues that Ashbery's poems make us readers 'co-creators'. In this sense, Vendler firmly disassociates the lyric form from its solipsistic caricatures.

In his essay, 'Nimbus of Sensations: Eros and Reverie in the Poetry of John Ashbery and Ann Lauterbach', James McCorkle joins Mohanty and Monroe in proposing that there is something essentially 'social' about Ashbery's poetry. McCorkle argues that this 'socialization' takes place as Ashbery 're[-]visions the lyrical ideals of self and voice', 'reinscrib[ing] the property of *melopoeia*, that the poem be sung, as central to lyric form'.[78] Invoking the musical element of Greek tragedy, McCorkle returns to the Classical roots of lyric in order to talk about the ways in which Ashbery confounds generic expectations. He suggests that Ashbery's poetry puts into question 'lyricism's subjectivity'[79] by proffering a polyphonic, disjunctive voice that refuses the 'hermetic' character usually ascribed to the lyric's traditional incarnation. McCorkle turns to this caricature of the traditional lyric voice in order to make a point about how much more 'social' it is now and the interchange that takes place between the 'space of the poem, the poet/singer, and the audience'.[80]

McCorkle's discussion of Ashbery's long poems, including *Flow Chart*, produce some interesting questions about the relationship between the lyric mode and what might come to emerge as an approach to the modern American epic poem in the age of mass distribution and a potential global audience. He argues that, while Ashbery's thematic concerns remain 'thoroughly those defining the lyric', his voice breaks through the confines of the genre. Both *Flow Chart* and 'Self-Portrait', McCorkle proposes, 'are fluid mnemonic structures that move from the personal to include the polyphonic social'.[81] Although McCorkle is unclear as to the nature of the new dynamic that exists between this 'social' Ashbery as poet/singer, and his imagined audience, he attributes this idiosyncratic

---

[76] Vendler, *Invisible Listeners*, 57.
[77] Ibid., 60.
[78] McCorkle, 'Nimbus of Sensations', 101.
[79] Ibid., 108.
[80] Ibid., 101.
[81] Ibid., 103.

orientation to the homosexual realm, where Ashbery's collage of voices and decentred pronouns function as an 'implicit critique of heterosexuality's exclusivity and centrality'.[82] By disrupting the panoptical narrative 'I', McCorkle argues that Ashbery's poetry disputes the codes of normalcy that restrict some to the sidelines where, under such a normalizing gaze, otherness appears 'misshapen, misfit'.[83]

Ashbery's engagement with discourses of homosexuality is unlike that which we have observed at work in Merrill, where many of the poet's puns and jokes rely on the reader being familiar with homosexual codes and references, and thereby excludes the uneducated and/or heterosexual reader from fully participating in *Sandover*'s rich store of allusions. Instead, McCorkle's reading situates *Flow Chart*'s 'homotextuality' on a conceptual level, where Ashbery's non-normative poetic strategies are seen as an analogue to (and a critique of) the place of the homosexual in society. For McCorkle, Ashbery's questioning of lyricism's subjectivity, 'parallels the disruptive quality homosexuality has within the ideological demands of our culture',[84] and in support he cites Roland Barthes' definition of the 'text of bliss' as being resonant with the apocalyptic, excessive effects of Ashbery's disjunctive techniques.[85]

In this respect, McCorkle's reading chimes with my own observations about Ashbery's excessively long line. Ashbery's polyphony and syntactical excessiveness are certainly formally disruptive, the porousness of *Flow Chart*'s saturated lines having emerged after his initial experiments in *Three Poems*. The chorus of voices in 'Litany' (1979) could also be seen as an earlier working through of an impulse that comes to the fore in *Flow Chart*. In this sense, there is an ambition in Ashbery's poetry in general that works to see through the limitations of traditional thinking. The transgressive forms of the prose poems that comprise *Three Poems*, and *Flow Chart*'s long lines, point to a consistent impulse in Ashbery's work to challenge Anglo-American traditions, and while our discussion is centred upon the epic poem, it might be argued that Ashbery's poetry seems determined to play with all genres.

In approaching the question of how homosexuality manifests itself in Ashbery's poetry, McCorkle can be seen to take something from John Shoptaw's approach. Shoptaw's *On the Outside Looking Out* (1994) has

---

[82] Ibid., 107.
[83] Ibid., 108.
[84] Ibid.
[85] Roland Bathes, *The Pleasure of the Text*, 14.

been the only full-length study (to date) to approach Ashbery's poetry with the focus on the poet's homosexuality.[86] Although Ashbery's verse rarely addresses his sexual orientation directly, Shoptaw argues that his poetry is, at the very heart, 'homotextual' (a phrase he borrows from Jacob Stockinger).[87] Founded upon his contention that 'Ashbery's poetry is not so much representative as "misrepresentative" ',[88] Shoptaw's discussion of Ashbery is centred on the idea of 'crypt words' and buried meanings. He argues that Ashbery's poems 'behave' in a way that reflects the poet's homosexuality, even if their subject matter aspires to be as representative as possible. Shoptaw's work relies, in part, on manuscript drafts of poems that reveal subtle revisions of words.[89] However, the majority of these 'sonic revisions' are the critic's own suggestions, where he posits echoes of familiar words or phrases, for example, 'blurred version' for 'blurred vision',[90] or more pertinently, 'mincing flag' for 'mincing fag'.[91]

While Shoptaw's study throws up some interesting analyses of Ashbery's word-games and compositional thought processes, my enquiry here is not so much interested in Ashbery's 'mis-representational' strategies (as Shoptaw sees them), as his representational ambitions. Talking about *The Vermont Notebook* (1975), Shoptaw reflects that, 'in these samples Ashbery *represents* American talk and writing with an eerie lack of telltale exaggeration, so that his *simulations* become indistinguishable from *actual* American discourses . . .' (my emphasis).[92] It is here, in Ashbery's re-presentation of contemporary American speech, that *Flow Chart* engages in a distinctly epic project. With its incessant raking together of individual anecdotes and histories, *Flow Chart* offers us Bayley's 'natural noise of the present', attempting to create a poetic fabric that simulates both a history and an immanent present at the same time.

This democratizing impulse extends to Ashbery's stance on his own sexuality. As has been noted, Ashbery's poetry rarely makes explicit

---

[86] Articles which have considered Ashbery from a queer perspective include Catherine Imbriglio, ' "Our Days Put On Such Reticence": The Rhetoric of the Closet in John Ashbery's *Some Trees*', *Contemporary Literature* 36.2 (1995), 249–88, and John Vincent, 'Reports of Looting and Insane Buggery behind Altars: John Ashbery's Queer Politics', *Twentieth Century Literature* 44 (Summer 1998), 155–75.
[87] Stockinger, 'Homotextuality: A Proposal', *The Gay Academic*, 27.
[88] Shoptaw, *On the Outside Looking Out*, 2.
[89] Shoptaw's first example is from Ashbery's unpublished poem 'Games in the Sun', where he substitutes 'boarders' for 'borders'. See Shoptaw, *On the Outside Looking Out*, 6.
[90] Ashbery, *Three Poems*, 36.
[91] Ashbery, 'A Boy' (1953). Cited in Shoptaw, *On the Outside Looking Out*, 6.
[92] Shoptaw, *On the Outside Looking Out*, 16.

reference to his own homosexuality,[93] and he has himself claimed that 'I do not think of myself as a gay poet',[94] stating in an interview with John Koethe in 1982 that, 'you should try to make your poem as representative as possible'.[95] By refusing to let his sexual identity define his writing, Ashbery eschews factional politics in favour of all-embracing democratic ambitions. This desire, for his poetry to speak beyond himself and his own circumstances, is an inclusive manifesto that makes him an excellent candidate to write in the epic mode. However, it does not preclude a role for Ashbery's gay identity.

Thinking about the representative potential of homosexuality, Ashbery has spoken about the resonance of an 'odd, exceptional, damaged sensibility':

> It's rather strange to me, that the people who get taken up as spokespersons for everybody living at a certain time . . . But it seems odd to me and something I wonder about it a great deal: why is it that the average Joe when writing poetry doesn't really illuminate the experience of a number of readers the way a very odd, exceptional, damaged sensibility does?[96]

The idea of being a 'spokesperson for everybody living' echoes quite clearly the traditional role of the poet in the epic mode; to 'illuminate the experience' of a community or nation is at the heart of the mediatory role of the epic poet. Ashbery, talking here in 1985, was clearly thinking about such matters in the period immediately preceding the composition of *Flow Chart*.

(vi) *Flow Chart* and polyphony

No poet since Whitman has tapped into so many different American voices, and, at the same time, so preserved his utterance against the jangle of influence.[97]

---

[93] Shoptaw notes the sole occurrence of the word 'homosexual' in the poem 'Halibun': 'I'm hoping that homosexuals not yet born get to inquire about it, inspect the whole random collection as though it were a sphere' (Ashbery, *A Wave*, 39).

[94] Conversation with Shoptaw, *On the Outside Looking Out*, 4.

[95] John Koethe, 'An Interview with John Ashbery', *SubStance* 37–38 (1983), 183.

[96] John Murphy, 'John Ashbery: An Interview with John Murphy', *Poetry Review* 75.2 (August 1985), 23.

[97] Schultz, *The Tribe of John*, 1.

'I'm just a copier', Ashbery laments towards the close of *Flow Chart*: 'You are the history, the book' (*FC*, 204). As I have already suggested, there is much about Ashbery's numerous allusions to his status as a medium in *Flow Chart* that evokes the role claimed by Merrill in the composition of *The Changing Light at Sandover*. However, in sharp contrast to the occult structure and connoisseurial coded-ness of *Sandover*, *Flow Chart*'s everyday, contemporary, cultural references aim at a more Whitmanian ideal; a poem which can be read by 'everyone':

> I want the reader to be able to experience the poem without having to refer to outside sources to get the complete experience as one has to in Eliot sometimes or Pound. This again is a reflection of my concern for communicating which as I say many people don't believe I have – but for me a poem has to be all there and available to the reader and it of course is very difficult to decide at certain moments what the ideal reader is going to know about and what he isn't going to know about.[98]

While there is recognition of the consensus of opinion that does not regard him as a poet with a 'concern for communicating', Ashbery maintains that the will is there to make the poem 'available for the reader', in a way that does not require the extensive knowledge of, say, Merrill, Pound or Eliot's 'ideal reader'. Although Ashbery's poems are undeniably packed full of obscure references, it is (arguably) not necessary to have read *Orlando Furioso* in order to comprehend 'Soonest Mended' (in the way that a preliminary acquaintance with *The Golden Bough* is essential to a clear understanding of *The Waste Land*). The poem itself provides an explanation of the connection between our own predicament and the heroine of this fifteenth-century Italian epic poem: 'always having to be rescued'.[99]

In the same way, *Flow Chart* eschews the partisan politics and connoisseurial referencing of *Sandover*, presenting itself instead as equally disorientating to all readers. Ashbery's democratic ambition refuses the marginal voice of homotextuality that Merrill's coded poetics often embrace with their camp parody of poetic forebears such as W. H. Auden. As I have proposed, *Flow Chart*'s polyphony manifests

---

[98] Richard Wilbur, 'Craft Interview with John Ashbery', *New York Quarterly* 9 (Winter 1972), 122–3.

[99] Ashbery, 'Soonest Mended', *Selected Poems*, 87.

itself instead as a *formal* way of enacting Whitman's 'multiplicities' –
the variety of dictions and types of American speech place Ashbery's
poem in a tradition of oral autobiography or recorded talk. It is this
reproduction of oral utterance that also largely shapes the structures
of the poem's long sentences and lines – a feature we also observed in
'Howl', with Ginsberg under the influence of both the Whitmanian
long line and Olson's 'breath unit'. *Sandover*'s reproduction of the
recorded 'talk' between JM, DJ and the voices from the other world
does not resemble the loose forms of Ginsberg and Ashbery's long
poems, retaining Merrill's fascination with formal frames. Merrill's
transcription of the Ouija dialogue is a dazzling display of rhyme and
pun, whereas Ashbery's formal finesse is restricted to *Flow Chart*'s care-
fully embedded double sestina.

Ashbery's take on Henry James' classic imperative also discards Merrill's
message of intellectual elitism, for an interpretation that emphasizes
instead the loss (and retention) of valuable thoughts:

> . . . be one of those
> on whom nothing is lost. Organize your thoughts in random lines,
>   and, later on
> down the road, paginate them.
>
> (*FC*, 158–9)

Ashbery shifts the emphasis here onto an anxious need to retain each
and every detail of the day; it is *thoughts* that must not be lost, rather than
meanings or inferences; each thought process is as potentially valuable
as another as material for Ashbery's diaristic poem. They must all be collected in order to be sifted, organized, and 'later on', paginated in the
final form that *Flow Chart* takes.

As I proposed in my introduction to this chapter, the democratic
impulse of Ashbery's multi-voiced vision seems to me to be very much
like a formal incarnation of the Whitmanian 'multitude': 'Do I contradict myself?/Very well then I contradict myself,/I am large, I contain
multitudes'.[100] There is something very similar present in the way in
which *Flow Chart* registers the full range of American diction, including
'multitudes' of styles of talking, storytelling, remembering and declaim-
ing. In place of the plethora of types that populate Whitman's poetry,

---

[100] Whitman, 'Song of Myself', *Complete Verse, Selected Prose*, 84.

Ashbery works to express the full range of 'forms of expression' available to contemporary Americans:

> My idea is to democratise all forms of expression, an idea which comes to me from afar, perhaps from Whitman's *Democratic Vistas* – the idea that both the most demotic and the most elegant forms of expression deserve equally to be taken into account.[101]

As Mark Ford has noted, like Whitman, Ashbery feels 'most fully himself when he contains multitudes'.[102] Susan Schultz also concurs with this portrait of Ashbery as a poet who can simulate many voices, while maintaining the distinctness of his own. As Schultz takes care to point out, while Ashbery flirts with an array of different American voices, his own 'utterance' is not lost among the 'jangle of influence'.[103] Quite what is at stake here in championing Ashbery as a poet who, while trying on so many other voices, can maintain a clear and cogent poetic identity, needs clarification. Clearly, in the course of *Flow Chart*, Ashbery tries on a series of chameleon identities and voices, bringing to mind Keats' delineation of the powers of 'negative capability'.[104] However, while *Flow Chart* strongly recalls Wordsworth's autobiographical epic project in some respects, Ashbery ultimately refuses the Wordsworthian 'egotistical sublime' for a rather more Keatsian conception of the poetic ego, which moves towards Eliot's 'escape from personality'.[105]

Furthermore, while *Sandover*'s chorus of Ouija-mediated messages reflect Merrill's quest to find and fashion his own poetic personae through the voices of tradition (specifically those of Auden and Proust), Ashbery's multiple tones and dictions do not give any sense that he is engaging in an urgent dialogue with tradition. Rather, *Flow Chart* reads like the present meanderings of the poet's thoughts, taking in the voices of poet's past only when they intrude upon his mind. 'Pick a channel,

[101] Andre Bleikasten 'Entretien avec John Ashbery', *La Quinzaine littéraire* (16–28 February 1993), 7. Cited in Shoptaw, *On the Outside Looking Out*, 1.
[102] Mark Ford, review of *Flow Chart*, *Times Literary Supplement* (27 December 1991), 9.
[103] Schultz, *The Tribe of John*, 1.
[104] Keats defined negative capability as 'when a man is capable of being in uncertainties, mysteries, doubts, without any irritable reaching after fact and reason'. John Keats, letter to George and Thomas Keats, Sunday, 21 December 1817. *John Keats: Selected Poems and Prose*, ed. Elizabeth Cook (Oxford & New York: Oxford University Press, 1990), 370.
[105] T. S. Eliot, 'Tradition and the Individual Talent', *The Sacred Wood* (London: Faber, 1997), 58.

explore, document it', *Flow Chart* seems to direct its author: 'please take all the evidence into account in your report when you write it' (*FC*, 43).

(vii) A new kind of epic

I'm very particular about the trivia I associate with.

(*FC*, 196)

How many bridges between here and the/other end of that journey?

(*FC*, 43)

One of the functions of the modern epic poems we have looked at has been to articulate the spirit of the age. For example, Crane hoped that the 'mechanical manifestations of today' might be a suitable 'subject for lyrical, dramatic and even epic poetry'.[106] However, Crane's visions of a 'mystical synthesis'[107] of America's past and present floundered under his self-conscious labouring to transform a Victorian bridge into a potent symbol of 'today'. Ashbery, however, is rather more successful at mining the resources of popular culture to poetic ends. Speaking of *Flow Chart*'s absorption in the 'dense technology of modern living',[108] John Bayley has contrasted Ashbery's 'effortless' immersion in the present-day with Crane's self-conscious paean to the Brooklyn Bridge. In doing so, Bayley not only draws attention to Ashbery's ability to amalgamate successfully a hotch-potch of cultural references, but also highlights an important precursor for *Flow Chart*. As Ginsberg has claimed the importance of Crane to the writing of 'Howl', so *The Bridge* might also be thought of a 'Model Text' for Ashbery's poem.

Ashbery begins *Flow Chart* with an invocation that also strongly recalls Crane's epic project:

Still in the published city but not yet
overtaken by a new form of despair, I ask
the diagram: is it the foretaste of pain
it might easily be? Or an emptiness
so sudden it leaves the girders
whanging in the absence of wind,

(*FC*, 1)

---

[106] Crane to Gorham Munson, 18 February 1923, *O My Land*, 132.
[107] Ibid., 131.
[108] Bayley, 'Richly Flows Contingency', 3.

Crane's hymn to a modern metropolis is recast here in Ashbery's 'published city'. It is a phrase that suggests both the loss of privacy (as the
poet becomes published, and thus enters the public domain) and a
reality determined by the parameters of one's work. Ashbery's New
York is, like O'Hara's, a city whose bricks and mortar are literally the
poems and stories that make up his *oeuvre*. However, Ashbery's poetry
refuses to be engulfed by the 'despair' that cut short Crane's poetic
career. At first, the 'girders' and 'the plaited lines' of Ashbery's bridge
seem to follow in a pastiche of Cranean Romanticism, as they 'extend/
like a bronze chain into eternity' before Ashbery's meditation breaks
off absent-mindedly:

> *. . . It seems I was reading something,*
> I have forgotten the sense of it or what the small
> role of the central poem made me want to feel. No matter.
>
> (*FC*, 1)

The promise of a transcendent symbol and what it 'made me want to feel'
is lost to the amnesia of both the poet and the people. Just as Ashbery
loses his train of thought, the people have forgotten the rejuvenating
role of the 'river god' (a figure that recalls Eliot's symbolic Fisher King)
and the gesturing of Crane's bridge towards a time not anchored in the
'here-and-now' is lost once again:

> Sad grows the river god as he oars past us
> downstream without our knowing him: for if, he reasons,
> he can be overlooked, then to know him would be to eat him,
> ingest the name he carries through time to set down
> finally, on a strand of rotted hulks. And those who sense something
> squeamish in his arrival know enough not to look up
> from the page they are reading, the plaited lines that extend
> like a bronze chain into eternity.
>
> (*FC*, 3)

Like Merrill's yearning for 'the kind of unseasoned telling found/In legends, fairy tales',[109] *Flow Chart* sees Ashbery nostalgic for a past mode of
literature where the storytelling is undiluted by the cosmetics of 'our

---

[109] Merrill, *Sandover*, 3.

age's fancy narrative concoctions',[110] preferring the bare bones of 'the ordinary and the true':

> . . . the coat I wear,
> woven of consumer products, asks you to pause and inspect
> the still-fertile ground of our once-valid compact
> with the ordinary and the true.

(FC, 9)

Easily mis-read as 'compost', 'compact' suggests here the degradation, both semantically and literally, of a 'contract' between reader and subject. The 'still-fertile ground' implies a different landscape than that of Eliot's sterile wasteland; Ashbery does not want to compose a late twentieth-century version of Eliot's poem. Here, it is neither the mythic connection of past and present that can regenerate, nor the potency of consumerism, but the 'shards of common crockery' and the 'stuff of ordinary heresy' (*FC*, 11). In *Flow Chart*, river gods pass unnoticed and 'overlooked': 'Forget the promises the stars made you', the narrator implores, they are 'twinned to no notion that can have an impact/on our way of thinking, as crabbed now/as at any time in the past' (*FC*, 9).

If these astrological systems of ordering the universe are bankrupt, a new chart or vision must be found to make sense of the fabric of a world which is 'woven of consumer products' (*FC*, 9) and 'our everyday thoughts and fantasies' (*FC*, 5). Ashbery seems to be ironically voicing the view of a modern secular society that such archaic systems of 'belief' are worn-out and redundant. Astrology, as the means of decoding the 'promises' of the stars', has always been a way to talk about the 'ordinary and the true' by de-familiarizing the substance of our everyday lives. *Flow Chart* works to foreground what has ever been present in the mythic mechanism; the estrangement of the everyday. This circular process of cultural renewal is clearly so central to the purpose of the poem that Ashbery evokes it in the title of the poem itself.

Flow Chart's narrative is also, broadly speaking, circular. Its opening lament – 'now the bridge will never be built' (*FC*, 25), is converted into a direct invitation in the poem's last lines: 'It's open: the bridge, that way' (*FC*, 216). Ashbery begins by offering a vision of cultural sterility that recalls Eliot's *The Waste Land*: ritual deities are not recognized or

---

[110] Ibid.

ignored in a world where 'a god has bungled it again' (*FC*, 5). There is also something of a Tiresian consciousness who has 'seen it all' (*FC*, 214) embedded in the poem's ever-shifting central voice. However, while there has been remarkably little critical ink spilt over Eliot's sexuality and claims that *The Waste Land* is an elegy for his friend Jean Verdenal,[111] Ashbery's poem is as uninterested in establishing Eliot as the 'prime ram' of a homosexual 'flock',[112] as he is in heralding himself as any kind of spokesperson for a sexual minority.

The Eliotic echoes of the poem's references to river gods and the dried up shoots of the willow (*FC*, 11) bump up against Whitmanian invocations to 'generations of aspiring lovers and writers before me' (*FC*, 191) and the poem's Cranean invocations, but they do so to hint at those from whom he differentiates himself, rather than necessarily affirming them, or signalling a continuity. The strength of Ashbery's poetry (and of *Flow Chart* itself) is the poet's chameleonic capacity to inhabit a multitude of voices and personae that are not restricted by tribal politics. Instead, the poem aspires to speak for and of the 'bloodstream/of our collective memory' (*FC*, 27) in a modern recasting of the American epic project that I propose had been rehearsed in *Houseboat Days*:

> Might I just through proximity and
> Aping of postures and attitudes communicate this concern of mine
> To them? That their jagged attitudes correspond to mine
> That their beefing strikes anniversary silver bells within
> My own chest . . .?[113]

Flow Chart works through a similar mechanism of 'aping' the postures of contemporary American life and culture, working to emphasize a correspondence between the poet and his listeners that could be, like the quests of the great epic heroes of the past, 'exemplary':

> . . . I had begun working on something like
> my autobiography, I was going to distil whatever happened to me, not
>   taking into account

---

[111] John Peter was the first to suggest a homosexual reading of the poem in his essay, 'A New Interpretation of *The Waste Land*' (1952), *Essays in Criticism* 19.2 (April 1969), 140–75.

[112] Crane to Allen Tate, 12 June 1922, *O My Land*, 90.

[113] Ashbery, *Houseboat Days*, 25.

the terrific things that didn't, which were the vast majority, and
    maybe if I reduced it
all sufficiently, somebody would find it worth his while, i.e., exemplary.
                                                              (*FC*, 135)

In this sense, John Shoptaw's proposal that we might read *Flow Chart* as
'anybody's autobiography'[114] seems an apt interpretation of the poem's
ambiguous title. Shoptaw argues that the poem provides a 'schematic
outline of an autobiography into which readers may process their own
manufactured lives'.[115] Placing Ashbery in an Augustinean tradition of
recording 'what I am now, at this moment, as I set down my confessions',[116]
Shoptaw focuses on the diary-like process of the poem's composition.
The poem is, in Ashbery's own words,

> the result of what I had to say on certain days over a period of 6 months,
> during the course of thinking about my past, the weather outside. I
> free-associate and come up with all kinds of extra material that doesn't
> belong – but it does.[117]

As a poet well-versed in the Surrealist tradition, it is unsurprising that
Ashbery allows the unconscious to speak by employing a technique akin
'automatic writing'. The American analogue to this practice could be
seen as the democratization of poetry, through the inclusion of the random trivia of everyday life. Ashbery's poem gives equal weight to both
these practices, and in doing so brings his own personal touch to the epic
mode.

In terms of Ashbery's autobiographical agenda in the poem, the relationship between the '*culte de moi*'[118] and the epic mode is one that is
also at the heart of *Flow Chart*'s arrangement of discourses. The poem
journeys through a first-person narrative that shifts character and gender, time and location, charting 'the ebb and flow of life perceived'.[119]
As Wordsworth himself contended in *The Prelude*, 'the history of a Poet's

---

[114] Shoptaw, *On the Outside Looking Out*, 302.
[115] Ibid., 307.
[116] St Augustine, *Confessions*, trans. R. S. Pine-Coffin (New York: Penguin, 1961), 209.
[117] Dinitia Smith, 'Poem Alone', *New York* (20 May 1991), 48. Quoted in Shoptaw, *On the Outside Looking Out*, 308.
[118] Ashbery, *Flow Chart*, 187. Ashbery also uses this phrase in his obituary for Frank O'Hara.
[119] Shoptaw, *On the Outside Looking Out*, 306.

mind/Is labour not unworthy of regard',[120] and *Flow Chart* both revisits and questions the unfolding of a poet's mind as a subject fit for
poetic consumption. However, while putting into the poem 'whatever
happened to be around, at any given moment' (*FC*, 96), and returning insistently to themes of origin and home, the poem can be seen to
contribute to the ongoing transformation of the modern American epic
poem.

The traditional invocation beginning the epic is recast by *Flow Chart's*
opening reference to the chart or 'diagram': the poem's muse is sys-
tematized and ordered – it can be known, and thus, it is implied, mas-
tered. The 'absence of wind' (*FC*, 3) stands in contrast to Wordsworth's
'gentle breeze', suggesting the absence of traditional inspiration which
can only return, belatedly, if 'I drop, humbled, eating from the red-clay
floor': 'only then does inspiration come: late, yet never too late' (*FC*,
6). This humble pose of the poet is reprised in *Flow Chart's* closing section where the 'outline of your head', once detected in the rich though
tepid layers of America's history, must be passed over: 'you know it's
time to read on'. 'We are/merely agents', Ashbery stresses, 'taking dic-
tation/from on high' (*FC*, 216) and repeating 'the formulas that have
come to us so many times/in the past'. Returning to the vision of the
'published city', Ashbery meditates on the 'rich though tepid layers' of
the city. If 'the past' is the 'overlay' of 'the legend of our rabid ancestors', this sedimentation of layers forms a deep foundation for Ashbery's
reappraisal of the epic mode for modern times. Although he identifies
himself as the scribe for the 'purgatory of words' that forms the rich
and various discourses of modern American life, what Ashbery achieves
is not slavish transcription but the reinvigoration of 'the legend of our
rabid ancestors'.

Helen Vendler has argued for Ashbery as a public poet in terms of his
operating as a 'barometer of contemporary language'[121] and it is here that
I locate *Flow Chart's* contribution to the genealogy this study has traced.
Reverberating with the 'natural noise of the present', Ashbery's poem tries
to chart in its 'freight train of associations' (*FC*, 196) the very melting pot
of modern America. As it fails at times to rise above the 'satisfying chatter'
(*FC*, 195) of its dense poetics, in enacting the difficulty of imposing an
epic coherence on the multiplicities of contemporary America, *Flow Chart*
stands as a record of the difficulties of the modern epic project.

---

[120] Wordsworth, *The Prelude*, 481.
[121] Schultz, introduction to *The Tribe of John*, 3.

'I'm just a copier. You are the history, the book', one voice in the poem contends, noting the paradox of Ashbery's ambitions in *Flow Chart* (*FC*, 204). Ultimately, Ashbery delegates the task to his readers (and critics). With his closing directive he offers only the trace of a solution that suggests that the individual should not only acknowledge his or her own place in the flow of American history but also participate in it: 'It's open: the bridge, that way' (*FC*, 216).

Postscript

Flow Chart's closing invocation of *The Bridge* illustrates the intertextual nature of the genealogy that this study has traced, where each poem develops a dialogue not only with its European epic precursors but also with an epic American tradition. The poetry of Whitman stands at the very heart of this homosexual tradition, providing (in the case of Crane and Ginsberg especially) an important poetic dialogue, prefiguring the way that these poets have fashioned a voice to speak about homosexual desire. Following the work of James E. Miller and Robert K. Martin, I hope to have demonstrated the importance of Whitman's melding of the private and the public realms where Whitman's suggestion that 'the common is personal'[1] functions as a crucial foundation for the modern homosexual epic. The post-war poems considered here create a complex web of interconnection and cross-referencing in the ways in which they develop the Whitmanian legacy, and also draw upon the influence of Crane to develop their own vision of a modern epic poem that can accommodate homosexuality at its very centre.

If, as Bakhtin notes, 'the world of epic is the national heroic past. It is a world . . . of fathers and of founders of families',[2] each of the poets considered here has confronted this ideological exclusion, rethinking the epic in different ways in order to authorize himself as a suitably 'representative' voice. In *The Bridge*, for example, Crane challenges his exclusion by flagrantly recasting one of the founding myths of America as a homoerotic union between himself and a Native American man, utilizing contemporary discourses of citizenship to imagine the homosexual as the 'ideal' American citizen. In turn, both Ginsberg and Ashbery's poems reimagine the collective experience of the epic. In *The Fall of America*, Ginsberg harnesses the potential of the collective voice of radio as part of his bid to recast the traditional epic descent to the underworld as an encounter with the collective unconscious. Similarly, in *Flow Chart*,

---

[1] Creeley, introduction to *Whitman: Poems Selected by Robert Creeley*, 7.
[2] Bakhtin, *The Dialogic Imagination: Four Essays*, 13.

Ashbery utilizes a wide variety of popular culture references as a cast of voices through which he can disperse himself in order to articulate the multiplicity of the American experience – the 'multitudes' of Whitman's *Leaves of Grass* recast as a formal multiplicity of voices and discourses. However, although the poem draws strongly on *The Prelude, Flow Chart* refuses to offer the reader a central autobiographical voice akin to that of Wordsworth's poem. Instead, Ashbery proffers an autobiographical template that can accommodate the reader's own story, undermining the traditional centrality of the epic voice.

The Changing Light at Sandover also works towards a decentralization of the epic voice, with Merrill doubling, refracting and mirroring his own poetic avatar 'JM' through the host of 'spirit voices' that the poem encompasses to bring new resonance to the traditional epic *nekyia*. However, unlike Ginsberg's poetry, which relies heavily upon the Whitmanian long line, Merrill's poem incorporates a dizzying array of traditional forms and metres, demonstrating that the reinvigoration of the epic tradition does not necessarily demand a complete departure from formal traditions. By focusing in the latter part of the book on three east-coast poets, all born in 1920s America (Ginsberg, Merrill and Ashbery), I hope to have demonstrated the variousness of the contemporary American response to the tradition of the epic poem.

While Ginsberg's coupling of an avant-garde aesthetic with his radical politics suggests that the 'homosexual epic' might be best expressed via formally progressive means, the indebtedness of Merrill's poetry to a formal tradition reinforces a long-standing coupling of High Culture with homosexuality, indicating instead that the expression of homosexuality (or indeed any other 'liberal' subject matter) need not be married to the breaking of the pentameter. Indeed, Crane, Merrill and Ashbery's poems all incorporate traditional poetic forms to some extent; while Merrill careers through an impressive catalogue of forms in *Sandover,* *Flow Chart*'s embedded double sestina nestles happily within the poem's larger concern to explore the expressive potential of the long line. Although *The Bridge* appears quite formally traditional to us now, its dislocated narratives of America past and present within the ordinarily cohesive framework of epic instantiates Crane's modernist ambitions, as well as setting a precedent for the genealogy I trace here.

Although each of the poems establishes a distinct mode of engaging with poetic tradition and of rethinking the relationship between the public and the private spheres, there are also some recurring themes and shared preoccupations that have emerged from my readings. Both

Crane and Merrill go so far in their quest to authorize their own sexuality as to envisage the homosexual poet as the *very definition* of the American citizen, or, as Merrill proposes in *Sandover*, the *ideal* example of a human being. In *The Bridge*, Crane's use of the figure of the Native American allegorizes his own erasure from the nation as a homosexual utilizing contemporary citizenship discourse and literary precedents to imagine the 'counter-matrimony' of himself and the Native in order to cast the homosexual as the emblematic American citizen. Challenging those who ignore Crane's homosexuality as a significant factor in his placement in the tradition of the American verse epic, I have argued with Thomas Yingling's otherwise refreshing reading of Crane, challenging his claim that homosexuality only maintains an unconscious presence in Crane's texts, proposing instead that homosexuality functions quite centrally in *The Bridge*, as Crane insists upon the legible inscription, rather than encryption, of his sexuality.

Following Crane's example, homosexuality stands at the very centre of the cosmology that Merrill constructs in *Sandover*, as the poem suggests that the childless (and by extension, the homosexual) are uniquely privileged in an aesthetic and spiritual sense. While Merrill's 'self-shattering' presents *Sandover* (on the one hand) as a grand act of self-dispersal and erasure, the central message of the poem also controversially suggests that homosexuality and a creative gift are the markers of a privileged 'soul' that can not only make up for the losses of childlessness, but are in some way the product of it. Although Merrill operates within a very different kind of sexual subculture to that presented in Ginsberg's work, both poets cast themselves as the central characters of their poems, with Merrill bringing new meaning to the mediatory role of the epic poet in his role as occult medium, while Ginsberg recasts himself as the epic hero of his own modern-day Odyssey across America. However, whereas Ginsberg speaks with new force for the centrality of the homosexual in America by drawing fully upon the richness of contemporary culture, Merrill confines himself to a world of coded high-cultural reference and camp puns, reserving admission to his afterlife to those significantly educated, homosexual and (most crucially) childless.

Crane, Ginsberg and Merrill all demonstrate a shared concern with lack of progeny, or with the difficulties of reconciling their sexuality with a desire for family. If classical epics such as *The Odyssey* and *The Aeneid* are dominated by biological genealogies, the American homosexual epic seems preoccupied with finding a new way to negotiate this idea of 'legacy'. In this sense, where Ashbery's poem expresses nostalgia for origins (as imagined by *Flow Chart*'s preoccupation with 'sources', 'beginnings' and 'belonging') it signals a return to the classical epics' concern with foundations and origins. Ashbery perceives connections and continuities in the echoes of history and culture as the voices of his poem chorus into a hymn to popular culture.

Ashbery's use of multiple voices also incites us to draw comparisons between *Flow Chart* and *Sandover*. The polyvocalism of these two poems might be read as an allegory for the poets' concern with the afterlife, both literally and figurally speaking (i.e. through Art). However, while both poems share an epic frame of encyclopaedic reference, *Flow Chart* reaches more towards the 'mainstream', and in doing so responds more successfully to what we might see as the shifting demands of the epic mode in the late twentieth century. As a 'poem including history', the modern American epic poem must act as a barometer of its surrounding culture. In terms of the epic project, this is reflected in Ashbery's move to reconcile an epic expression of popular culture with the narration of more traditional historical or allegorical narratives – a move anticipated 60 years previously in Crane's attempt to combine the expression of the beauty of the modern technological age with his own mystical vision of America in *The Bridge*.

Far more than the other poets discussed here, Allen Ginsberg was responsible for bringing homosexuality to the forefront of American literature in the twentieth century. In firmly anchoring his poetic experiments in the subject matter of his carnal exploits, Ginsberg advanced the cause of homosexual subject matter as fit for epic treatment, drawing on the legacy of Whitman to authorize his political agenda. If the epic of the New World demanded a shift away from its European forebears, the epics of the late twentieth century also saw a modification of the mode in order to respond to the changes in modern communication. In this sense, the shift in the relationship between the public and the private in these poems can be attributed, in part, to the ways in which each poet has incorporated contemporary media into his epic project. While Crane utilized a symbol of public architecture (the Brooklyn Bridge) alongside discourses of public legislation regarding citizenship to articulate his private feelings in *The Bridge*, Ginsberg's poetry embraces whole-heartedly the full range of contemporary mediums of communication, with the radio, newspaper headlines and popular song permeating the lines of *The Fall of America* in a poem that seeks to reclaim language for the People, wresting it back from its misuse by politicians and Generals. Conversely, Merrill's confession that 'I rarely buy a newspaper, or vote' in 'The Broken Home'[3] is continuous with the somewhat personal vision of history and philosophy that *Sandover* presents. However, Merrill's poem seems to suggest that the private parlour game between himself and David Jackson can reveal 'truths' that resonate beyond his elite coterie.

In choosing to focus upon these poems, I hope not only to have begun the task of unravelling the anxious relationship between the homosexual and his American home, but also to have illustrated in some way the centrality of such a discussion to the ongoing evaluation of these poets, who stand at the very centre of the American literary canon. As evinced by William Logan's 2007 review of the Library of America edition of Crane's work, homosexuality and canonicity are still uncomfortable bedfellows for some critics, and the homosexual subject remains a controversial figure in some quarters.[4] However, while Logan's damning report on Crane's work claims that 'the hope for a homegrown American epic that died with him has never entirely revived', the poems considered here suggest otherwise.[5] They stand as a testament to the existence of a rich and vital genealogy of works that not only engage with the idea of a 'homegrown' epic poem (nourished by the examples of Crane and Whitman), but also one that continues a dialogue with its European precursors, mining the epic tradition to reimagine an America that can embrace, in Ginsberg's words, the 'crooked' along with the 'straight'.

---

[3] Merrill, 'The Broken Home', *Collected Poems*, 199.
[4] William Logan, 'Hart Crane's Bridge to Nowhere', Review of Hart Crane's *Complete Poems and Selected Letters*, 28 January 2007, *New York Times Book Review*, http://query.nytimes.com/gst/fullpage.html?res=990CE0D71130F93BA15752C0A9619C8B63. Site accessed on 14 March 2010.
[5] Ibid.

Bibliography

Anderson, Benedict. *Imagined Communities: Reflections on the Origin and Spread of Nationalism*. London: Verso, 1983.

Aristotle, *Poetics*. Trans. Malcolm Heath. London: Penguin, 1996.

Ashbery, John. *Some Trees*. New Haven: Yale University Press, 1956.

———. *Rivers and Mountains*. New York: Holt, Rinehart and Winston, 1966.

———. *Self-Portrait in a Convex Mirror*. Harmondsworth: Penguin Books, 1976.

———. *Houseboat Days: Poems*. New York: Viking, 1977.

———. *April Galleons: Poems*. New York: Viking, 1987.

———. *Flow Chart*. London: Carcanet, 1991.

———. *The Mooring of Starting Out: The First Five Books of Poetry*. New York: Ecco Press, 1997.

———. *A Wave*. New York: Noonday Press, 1998.

———. *John Ashbery in Conversation with Mark Ford*. London: Between the Lines, 2003.

———. *A Worldly Country*. Manchester: Carcanet, 2007.

Augustine. *Confessions*. Trans. R. S. Pine-Coffin. New York: Penguin, 1961.

Bakhtin, M. M. *The Dialogic Imagination: Four Essays*. Ed. Michael Holquist. Trans. Caryl Emerson and Michael Holquist. Austin: University of Texas Press, 1981.

Barthes, Roland. *The Pleasure of the Text*. Trans. Richard Miller. New York: Hill & Wang, 1975.

Bataille, Georges. *Eroticism: Death & Sensuality*. Trans. Mary Dalwood. San Francisco, CA: City Lights Books, 1986.

Bayley, John. 'Richly Flows Contingency', Review of *Flow Chart*, *New York Review of Book*, Vol. 38, No. 14 (August 1991): 3.

Bercovitch, Sacvan. *The Puritan Origins of the American Self*. New Haven: Yale University Press, 1975.

———. *The American Jeremiad*. Madison, WI: University of Wisconsin Press, 1979.

Bergman, David. *Gaiety Transfigured: Gay Self-Representation in American Literature*, Madison, WI: University of Wisconsin Press, 1991.

Berlant, Lauren and Elizabeth Freeman. 'Queer Nationality', *Boundary* 2, Vol. 19, No. 1, 'New Americanists 2: National Identities and Postnational Narratives' (Spring 1992): 149–80.

Bernstein, Michael. *The Tale of the Tribe: Ezra Pound and the Modern Verse Epic*. Princeton, NJ: Princeton University Press, 1980.

Bersani, Leo. *Homos*. Cambridge & London: Harvard University Press, 1995.

Berthoff, Warner. *Hart Crane: A Reintroduction*. Minneapolis, MN: University of Minnesota Press, 1989.

Bhabha, Homi K., ed. *Nation and Narration.* London & New York: Routledge, 1990.

Bishop, Elizabeth. *Complete Poems.* London: Chatto & Windus, 1991.

Blackmur, R. P. *The Double Agent: Essays in Craft and Elucidation.* New York: Arrow, 1935.

Blasing, Mutlu Konuk. *Politics and Form in Postmodern Poetry: O'Hara, Bishop, Ashbery, and Merrill.* New York & Cambridge: Cambridge University Press, 1995.

Blasius, M. and S. Phelen, eds. *We Are Everywhere: A Historical Sourcebook of Gay and Lesbian Politics.* London & New York: Routledge, 1997.

Bloom, Clive and Brian Docherty, eds. *American Poetry: The Modernist Ideal.* New York: St Martin's Press, 1995.

Bloom, Harold. *The Visionary Company: A Reading of English Romantic Poetry.* Garden City, NY, London, England: Doubleday; Faber and Faber, 1961.

Bloom, Janet and Robert Losada. 'Craft Interview with John Ashbery', *New York Quarterly,* No. 9 (Winter 1972): 25–6.

Borges, Jorge Luis. 'The Telling of the Tale', *The Atlantic Monthly,* Vol. 86, No. 3 (September 2000): 63–5.

Brown, Wendy. *States of Injury: Power and Freedom in Late Modernity.* Princeton, NJ: Princeton University Press, 1995.

Brunner, Edward. *Splendid Failure: Hart Crane and the Making of the Bridge.* Urbana, IL: University of Illinois Press, 1985.

Buckley, C. A. 'Exploring the Changing Light at Sandover: An Interview with James Merrill', *Twentieth Century Literature,* Vol. 38, No. 4 (Winter 1992): 415–35.

Buckton, Oliver. *Secret Selves: Confession and Same-Sex Desire in Victorian Autobiography.* Chapel Hill & London: University of North Carolina Press, 1998.

Butterfield, R. W. *The Broken Arc: A Study of Hart Crane.* Edinburgh: Oliver & Boyd, 1969.

Byron, Glennis and Andrew J. Sneddon, eds. *The Body and the Book: Writings on Poetry and Sexuality.* Amsterdam & New York: Rodopi, 2008.

Cady, Joseph. 'Not Happy in the Capitol: Homosexuality in the *Calamus* Poems', *American Studies,* Vol. 19 (1978): 5–22.

Caldicott, Helen. *Missile Envy: The Arms Race and Nuclear War.* New York: William Morray, 1984.

Canaday, Margot. 'Building a Straight State: Sexuality and Social Citizenship under the 1944 G.I. Bill', *The Journal of American History,* Vol. 90, No. 3 (December 2003): 935–5.

Caron, David. *AIDS in French Culture: Social Ills, Literary Cures.* Wisconsin & London: University of Wisconsin Press, 2001.

Charters, Ann, ed. *The Portable Beat Reader.* London: Penguin Books, 1993.

——. *Beat Down to Your Soul: What Was the Beat Generation?* London: Penguin Books, 2001.

Chauncey, George. '"Christian Brotherhood" or Sexual Perversion? Homosexual Identities and the Construction of Sexual Boundaries in the World War I Era'. *Hidden from History.* Ed. Duberman, Vicinus and Chauncey. London: Penguin Books, 1989: 294–317.

——. *Gay New York: The Making of the Gay Male World 1890–1940*. London: Flamingo, 1994.

Cherkovski, Neeli. *Whitman's Wild Children*. Venice & San Francisco: Lapis Press, 1998.

Clark, David R., ed. *Critical Essays on Hart Crane*. Boston: G.K. Hall & Co, 1982.

Clark, Stephen. ' "Uprooting the Rancid Stalk": Transformations of Romanticism in Ashbery and Ash'. *Romanticism and Postmodernism*. Ed. Edward Larrissy. Cambridge & New York: Cambridge University Press, 1999: 157–79.

Clark, Tom. *Charles Olson: The Allegory of a Poet's Life*. Berkeley, CA: North Atlantic Books, 2001.

Cole, Merrill. 'Empire of the Closet', *Discourse*, Vol. 19. No. 3 (Spring 1997): 67–91.

Corber, Robert J. *In the Name of National Security: Hitchcock, Homophobia and the Political Construction of Gender in Postwar America*. Durham, NC: Duke University Press, 1993.

Coviello, Peter. 'Intimate Nationality: Anonymity and Attachment in Whitman', *American Literature: A Journal of Literary History, Criticism, and Bibliography*, Vol. 73, No.1 (March 2001): 85–119.

Crane, Hart. *The Letters of Hart Crane: 1916–1932*. Ed. Brom Weber. Berkeley & Los Angeles: University of California Press, 1965.

——. *The Complete Poems and Selected Letters and Prose of Hart Crane*. Ed. Brom Weber. Garden City, NY: Doubleday, 1966.

——. *O My Land, My Friends: The Selected Letters of Hart Crane*. Ed. Langdon Hammer and Brom Weber. New York & London: Four Walls Eight Windows, 1997.

——. *The Complete Poems*. Ed. Marc Simon. New York & London: Liveright, 2000.

——. *Hart Crane: Complete Poems & Selected Letters*. Ed. Langdon Hammer. New York: The Library of America, 2006.

Creeley, Robert. Introduction to *Whitman: Poems Selected by Robert Creeley*. Baltimore, MD: Penguin Books, 1973.

Dante, Alighieri. *The Inferno of Dante*. Trans. Robert Pinsky. New York: Farrar, Straus and Giroux, 1994.

Dean, Tim. 'Hart Crane's Poetics of Privacy', *American Literary History*, Vol. 8, No.1 (Spring 1996): 83–109.

Dembo, L. S. *Conceptions of Reality in Modern American Poetry*. Berkeley, CA: California University Press, 1966.

D'Emilio, John. *Sexual Politics, Sexual Communities*. London & Chicago: Chicago University Press, 1983.

Doody, Terence. *Confession and Community in the Novel*. Baton Rouge & London: Louisiana State University Press, 1980.

Dickinson, Peter. *Here Is Queer: Nationalisms, Sexualities, and the Literatures of Canada*. Toronto, Buffalo & London: University of Toronto Press, 1999.

DiPrima, Diane. *Memoirs of a Beatnik*. New York: Traveller's Companion, 1969.

Dollimore, Jonathan. *Sexual Dissidence: Augustine to Wilde, Freud to Foucault*. Oxford: Clarendon Press, 1991.

——. *Death, Desire, and Loss in Western Culture*. New York: Routledge, 1998.

——. *Sex, Literature and Censorship*. Cambridge & Malden: Polity Press, 2001.

Duncan, Robert. *Opening of the Field.* New York: Grove Press, 1960.

Edelman, Lee. *Transmemberment of Song: Hart Crane's Anatomies of Rhetoric and Desire.* Stanford: Stanford University Press, 1987.

———. *Homographesis: Essays in Gay Literary and Cultural Theory.* New York & London: Routledge, 1994.

Edinger, Edward F. *Melville's Moby-Dick: A Jungian Commentary, an American Nekyia.* New York: New Directions, 1978.

Ehrenpreis, Irvin. 'Otherworldly Goods', *New York Review of Books,* 22 January 1981: 47–51.

Eliot, T. S. *Collected Poems 1909–1962.* London: Faber, 1963.

———. *Selected Prose of T. S. Eliot.* Ed. Frank Kermode. New York: Harcourt Brace Jovanovich, 1975.

———. *The Sacred Wood.* London: Faber, 1997.

Escoffier, Jeffrey. *American Homo: Community and Perversity.* Berkeley, Los Angeles & London: University of California Press, 1998.

Evans, David T. *Sexual Citizenship: The Material Construction of Sexualities.* New York & London: Routledge, 1993.

Fiedler, Leslie. *An End to Innocence: Essays on Culture and Politics.* Boston: Beacon, 1955.

———. *Love and Death and the American Novel.* New York: Criterion, 1960.

Fisher, Clive. *Hart Crane: A Life.* New Haven & London: Yale University Press, 2002.

Fletcher, Angus. *A New Theory for American Poetry: Democracy, the Environment, and the Future of Imagination.* Cambridge & London: Harvard University Press, 2004.

Fone, Byrne R. S., ed. *Hidden Heritage: History and the Gay Imagination.* New York: Irvington, 1981.

Ford, Mark. 'Review of *Flow Chart*', *Times Literary Supplement,* 27 December 1991: 9.

Foucault, Michel. *The History of Sexuality.* Vol. 1. *An Introduction.* Trans. Robert Hurley. New York: Pantheon, 1978.

Fowlie, Wallace. *Love in Literature.* Bloomington, IN: Indiana University Press, 1965.

Fowlie, Wallace. *Love in Literature: Studies in Symbolic Expression.* Bloomington, IN: Indiana University Press, 1965.

Frank, Waldo. *The Rediscovery of America: An Introduction to the Philosophy of American Life.* New York & London: C. Scribner's Sons, 1929.

Freud, Sigmund. *On Sexuality: Three Essays on the Theory of Sexuality.* Ed. Angela Richards. London: Penguin, 1977.

Fuss, Diana, ed. *Inside/Out: Lesbian Theories, Gay Theories.* London & New York: Routledge, 1991.

Gabriel, Daniel. *Hart Crane and the Modernist Epic.* Basingstoke: Palgrave Macmillan, 2007.

Gans, Eric. *The End of Culture: Toward a Generative Anthropology.* Berkeley, Los Angeles & London: University of California Press, 1985.

———. *Originary Thinking: Elements of Generative Anthropology.* Stanford: Stanford University Press, 1993.

——. 'Originary Thoughts on Sexuality', *Chronicles of Love & Resentment*, No. 220, November 2000, www.anthropoetics.ucla.edu

Gardner, Jared. ' "Our Native Clay": Racial and Sexual identity and the Making of Americans in *The Bridge*', *Arizona Quarterly*, Vol. 44, No. 1 (March 1992): 24–50.

——. *Master Plots: Race and the Founding of an American Literature 1797–1854.* Baltimore & London: Johns Hopkins University Press, 1998.

——. 'Review of *The Homosexual Tradition in American Poetry: An Expanded Edition*', *American Literature*, Vol. 71, No. 4 (1999): 817–18.

Geis, Deborah R. and Steven F. Kruger, eds. *Approaching the Millennium: Essays on Angels in America.* Ann Arbor: University of Michigan Press, 1997.

Giles, Paul. *Hart Crane: The Contexts of The Bridge.* Cambridge: Cambridge University Press, 1986.

——. *Virtual Americas: Transnational Fictions and the Transatlantic Imaginary.* Durham & London: Duke University Press, 2002.

Gilman, Richard. *Decadence: The Strange Life of an Epithet.* New York: Farrar Straus & Giroux, 1979.

Ginsberg, Allen. *Allen Verbatim: Lectures on Poetry, Politics, Consciousness.* Ed. Gordon Ball. New York: McGraw Hill Book Company, 1974.

——. *Collected Poems 1947–1980.* New York: Harper Row, 1984.

——. *Allen Ginsberg 'Howl': Original Draft Facsimile, Transcript & Variant Versions, Fully Annotated by Author, with Contemporaneous Correspondence, Account of First Public Reading, Legal Skirmishes, Precursor Texts & Bibliography.* Ed. Barry Miles. New York: Harper Perennial, 1995.

——. *Journals Mid-Fifties 1954–1958.* Ed. Gordon Ball. New York: Harper Collins, 1996.

——. *Deliberate Prose.* Ed. Bill Morgan. London: Penguin, 2000.

——. *Spontaneous Mind: Selected Interviews 1958–1996.* Ed. David Carter. London: Penguin, 2001.

——. *The Book of Martyrdom and Artifice: First Journals and Poems 1937–1952.* Ed. Bill Morgan and Juanita Liebermann-Plimpton. Cambridge, MA: Da Capo Press, 2006.

Ginsberg, Allen and Louis Ginsberg. *Family Business: Selected Letters Between a Father and Son.* Ed. Michael Schumacher. London: Bloomsbury, 2001.

Girard, René. *Violence and the Sacred.* Trans. Patrick Gregory. Baltimore & London, Johns Hopkins University Press, 1972.

——. *'To double business bound': Essays on Literature, Mimesis, and Anthropology.* Baltimore & London: Johns Hopkins University Press, 1978.

Graves, Robert. *The White Goddess: A Historical Grammar of Poetic Myth.* 3rd amended and enlarged. London: Faber, 1952.

Greenberg, David F. *The Construction of Homosexuality.* Chicago & London: University of Chicago Press, 1988.

Gunn, Thom. *Collected Poems.* London: Faber, 1993.

——. *Boss Cupid.* London: Faber, 2000.

Gwiazda, Piotr, *James Merrill and W. H. Auden.* Basingstoke: Palgrave Macmillan, 2007.

Hall, Donald, ed. *Contemporary American Poetry*. Baltimore: Penguin Books, 1974.

Halperin, David. *One Hundred Years of Homosexuality, and Other Essays on Greek Love*. New York & London: Routledge, 1990.

———. *How to Do the History of Homosexuality*. Chicago & London: University of Chicago Press, 2002.

———. 'Pal O' Me Heart', in *London Review of Books*, 22 May 2003: 32.

Hammer, Langdon. *Hart Crane and Allen Tate: Janus-Faced Modernism*. Princeton, NJ: Princeton University Press, 1993.

Hartman, Anne. 'Confessional Counterpublics in Frank O'Hara and Allen Ginsberg', *Journal of Modern Literature*, Vol. 28, No. 4 (2005): 40–56.

Herendeen, Warren and Donald G. Parker, eds. 'Wind-Blown Flames: Letters of Hart Crane to Wilbur Underwood', *Southern Review*, Vol. 16, No. 1 (April 1980): 360–2.

Herd, David. *John Ashbery and American Poetry*. New York: Palgrave, 2001.

Homer. *The Odyssey*. Trans. E. V. Rieu. Middlesex, Baltimore & Victoria: Penguin Books, 1946.

———. *The Iliad*. Trans. E. V. Rieu. Middlesex, Baltimore & Victoria: Penguin Books, 1950.

———. *The Odyssey of Homer*. Trans. Richard Lattimore. New York: Harper Collins, 1975.

Hyde, Lewis, ed. *On the Poetry of Allen Ginsberg*. Ann Arbor: University of Michigan Press, 1984.

Imbriglio, Catherine. ' "Our Days Put On Such Reticence": The Rhetoric of the Closet in John Ashbery's *Some Trees*', *Contemporary Literature*, Vol. 36, No. 2 (1995): 249–88.

Ingebretsen, Edward. 'Frost as Virile Poet: The Queer Politics of Heterosexuality', *European Contributions to American Studies*, Vol. 44 (2000): 313–25.

Irigaray, Luce. *Sexes and Genealogies*. Trans. Gillian C. Gill. New York: Columbia University Press, 1993.

Irwin, John T. 'Naming Names: Hart Crane's "Logic of Metaphor" ', *Southern Review*, Vol. II, No. 2 (1975): 284–99.

———. "Foreshadowing and Foreshortening: The Prophetic Vision of Origins in Hart Crane's *The Bridge*', *Word & Image: A Journal of Verbal/Visual Enquiry*, Vol. 1, No. 3 (1985): 288–312.

Iser, Wolfgang. *The Fictive and the Imaginary: Charting Literary Anthropology*. Baltimore & London: Johns Hopkins University Press, 1993.

Jacobsen, Thorkild. "How did Gilgamesh Oppress Uruk?", *Acta Orientalia*, Vol. 8 (1930): 62–74.

———. *The Treasures of Darkness: A History of Mesopotamian Religion*. New Haven & London: Yale University Press, 1976.

Jay, Gregory. 'Catching up with Whitman: A Review Essay', *South Atlantic Review*, Vol. 57, No. 1 (January 1992): 89–102.

Johnson, David K. *The Lavender Scare: The Cold War Persecution of Gays and Lesbians in the Federal Government*. Chicago: University of Chicago Press, 2006.

Johns-Putra, Adeline. *The History of the Epic*. Hampshire & New York: Palgrave Macmillan, 2006.

Johnston, Devin. 'Resistance to the Message: James Merrill's Occult Epic', *Contemporary Literature*, Vol. 41, No.1 (Spring 2000): 87–116.

Jung, Carl. 'On Picasso' (1932), *The Spirit in Man, Art, and Literature, Collected Works*, Vol. 15. London: Routledge & Kegan Paul, 1953: 135–41.

——. *Psychology and Alchemy*. Trans. R. F. C Hull. *Collected Works*, Vol. 12. London: Routledge & Kegan Paul, 1953.

Kantorowicz, E. H. *The King's Two Bodies*. Princeton, NJ: Princeton University Press, 1957.

Keats, John. *John Keats: Selected Poems and Prose*. Ed. Elizabeth Cook. Oxford & New York: Oxford University Press, 1990.

Keenaghan, Eric. 'Vulnerable Households: Cold War Containment and Robert Duncan's Queered Nation', *Journal of Modern Literature*, Vol. 28, No. 4 (Summer 2005): 57–90.

Kevorkian, Martin. 'John Ashbery's *Flow Chart*: John Ashbery and the Theorists on John Ashbery against the Critics against John Ashbery', *New Literary History*, Vol. 25, No. 2, Writers on Writers (Spring 1994): 459–76.

Koethe, John. 'An Interview with John Ashbery', *SubStance*, Vol. 37–38 (1983): 181–2.

Korg, Jacob. *Ritual and Experiment in Modern Poetry*. New York: Macmillan, 1995.

Kramer, Jane. *Allen Ginsberg in America*. New York: Fromm International Publishing Corp, 1970.

Kristeva, Julia. *Nations without Nationalism*. New York: Columbia University Press, 1993.

Kummings, Donald D. *Approaches to Teaching Whitman's Leaves of Grass*. New York: MLA, 1990.

Kushner, Tony. *Angels in America: A Gay Fantasia on National Themes*. New York: TCG, 1992.

Lardis, John. *The Bop Apocalypse: The Religious Visions of Kerouac, Ginsberg, and Burroughs*. Urbana & Chicago: University of Illinois Press, 2001.

Larrissy, Edward, ed. *Romanticism and Postmodernism*. Cambridge & New York: Cambridge University Press, 1999.

Lawrence, D. H. *Studies in Classic American Literature*. Garden City, NY: Doubleday, 1953.

Lehman, David. *Beyond Amazement: New Essays on John Ashbery*. Ed. David Lehman. Ithaca & London: Cornell University Press, 1980.

——. *The Last Avant-Garde: The Making of the New York School of Poets*. New York: Doubleday, 1998.

Lehman, David and C. Berger. *James Merrill: Essays in Criticism*. Ithaca & London: Cornell University Press, 1983.

Lindsay, Vachel. *Selected Poems*. Ed. Mark Harris. New York: Macmillan, 1963.

Logan, William. 'Hart Crane's Bridge to Nowhere', *New York Times Book Review*, Review of Hart Crane's *Complete Poems and Selected Letters* (Library of American, 2006), January 28, 2007. www.query.nytimes.com/gst/fullpage.html?res=990 CE0D71130F93BA15752C0A9619C8B63. Site accessed 14 March 2007.

Loughery, John. *The Other Side of Silence: Men's Lives and Gay Identities*. New York: Henry Holt & Co, 1998.

Lowell, Robert. *Robert Lowell: Collected Poems.* Ed. Frank Bidart and David Gewanter. New York: Farrar, Straus and Giroux, 2003.

Lynch, Michael. 'Here is Adhesiveness: From Friendship to Homosexuality', *Victorian Studies*, Vol. 29, No. 1 (Autumn 1985): 67–96.

MacPhail, Scott. 'Lyric Nationalism: Whitman, American Studies, and the New Criticism', *Texas Studies in Literature and Language*, Vol. 44, No. 2 (Summer 2002): 133–60.

Martin, Robert K. 'Whitman's Song of Myself: Homosexual Dream and Vision', *Partisan Review*, Vol. 41, No. 2 (1975): 80–96.

——. *The Homosexual Tradition in American Poetry.* Austin, TX: University of Texas Press, 1979.

——. *The Homosexual Tradition in American Poetry, Expanded.* Iowa: University of Iowa Press, 1998.

——. 'Myths of Native Masculinity: Hart Crane and the Poem of the Nation'. *American Modernism across the Arts.* Ed. Jay Bochner and Justin D. Edwards. New York & Canterbury: Peter Lang, 1999: 205–17.

Materer, Timothy. *James Merrill's Apocalypse.* Ithaca, NY: Cornell University Press, 2000.

McHale, Brian. *The Obligation toward the Difficult Whole: Postmodernist Long Poems.* Tuscaloosa: University of Alabama Press, 2004.

Merrill, James. *Recitative: Prose by James Merrill.* San Francisco, CA: North Point Press, 1986.

——. *Collected Poems.* Ed. J. D. McClatchy and Stephen Yenser, New York: Alfred J. Knopf, 2001.

——. *The Changing Light at Sandover: Including the Whole of The Book of Ephraim, Mirabell's Books of Number, Scripts for the Pageant and a New Coda, The Higher Keys.* 3rd edn. New York: Alfred J. Knopf, 2003.

Merrill, Thomas. F. *Allen Ginsberg.* Boston: Twayne Publishers, 1969.

Meyers, Jeffrey. *Homosexuality and Literature, 1980–1930.* London: Athlone Press, 1977.

Miller, James E. *T. S. Eliot's Personal Waste Land: Exorcism of the Demons.* University Park, London: Pennsylvania State University Press, 1977.

——. *The American Quest for a Supreme Fiction: Whitman's Legacy in the Personal Epic.* Chicago & London: University of Chicago Press, 1979.

——. *Leaves of Grass: America's Lyric-Epic of Self and Democracy.* New York: Twayne, 1992.

——. *T. S. Eliot: The Making of an American Poet: 1888–1922.* University Park, London: Pennsylvania State University Press, 2005.

Milton, John. *Paradise Lost.* Ed. Christopher Ricks. London & New York: Penguin, 1989.

Mizruchi, Susan L. *The Science of Sacrifice: American Literature and Modern Social Theory.* Princeton, NJ: Princeton University Press, 1998.

Mohanty, S. P. and Jonathan Monroe. 'John Ashbery and the Articulation of the Social', *Diacritics*, Vol. 17, No. 2 (Summer 1987): 37–63.

Moon, Michael. *Disseminating Whitman: Revision and Corporeality in Leaves of Grass.* London: Harvard University Press, 1991.

Mosse, George. *Nationalism and Sexuality: Middle-Class Morality and Social Norms in Modern Europe.* Madison, WI: University of Wisconsin Press, 1985.

Muratori, Frank. 'Review of *Flow Chart*', *Library Journal*, Vol. 116, No. 8 (1 May 1991): 79.

Murphy, John. 'John Ashbery: An Interview with John Murphy', *Poetry Review*, Vol. 75, No. 2 (August 1985): 20–5.

Murphy T. F. and S. Poirier. *Writing AIDS: Gay Literature, Language and Analysis.* New York: Columbia University Press, 1993.

Nadel, Alan. 'Replacing the Waste Land – James Merrill's Quest for Transcendent Authority', www.english.uciuc.edu/maps/poets/m_r/merrill/nadel.htm. Site accessed 25 September 2005.

Nealon, Christopher. *Foundlings: Lesbian and Gay Historical Emotion Before Stonewall.* Durham: Duke University Press, 2001.

Nelson, Deborah. *Pursuing Privacy in Cold War America.* New York: Columbia University Press, 2002.

New, Elisa. *The Regenerate Lyric: Theology and Innovation in American Poetry.* Cambridge: Cambridge University Press, 1993.

——. *The Line's Eye: Poetic Experience, American Sight.* Cambridge & London: Harvard University Press, 1998.

Nickowitz, Peter. *Rhetoric and Sexuality.* New York, NY & Basingstoke: Palgrave Macmillan, 2006.

Nilsen, Helge Normann. *Hart Crane's Divided Vision: An Analysis of The Bridge.* Oslo & London: Universitetsforlaget & Global Book Resources Ltd, 1980.

O'Hara, Frank. *The Collected Poems of Frank O'Hara.* Ed. Donald Allen. Berkeley, Los Angeles & London: University of California Press, 1995.

——. *'Why I am Not a Painter' and Other Poems.* Ed. Mark Ford. Manchester: Carcanet, 2003.

O'Murray, Stephen. *American Gay.* Chicago & London: Chicago University Press, 1996.

Parker, Andrew, Russo, Mary et al., eds. *Nationalism and Sexualities.* New York & London: Routledge, 1992.

Parkinson, Thomas. *Hart Crane and Yvor Winters: Their Literary Correspondence.* Berkeley & London: University of California Press, 1978.

Patton, Cindy. *Sex and Germs: The Politics of AIDS.* Boston: South End Press, 1985.

Pearce, Roy Harvey. *The Continuity of American Poetry.* Middletown, CT: Wesleyan University Press, 1987.

Pease, Donald E., ed. *National Identities and Post-Americanist Narratives.* Durham & London, Duke University Press, 1994.

Perloff, Marjorie. *Poetic License: Essays on Modernist and Postmodernist Lyric.* Evanston: Northwestern University Press, 1990.

Peter, John. 'A New Interpretation of *The Waste Land*' (1952), *Essays in Criticism*, Vol. 19, No. 2 (April 1969): 140–75.

Phillips, Siobhan. *The Poetics of the Everyday.* New York & Chichester: Columbia University Press, 2010.

Polito, Robert, ed. *A Reader's Guide to James Merrill's A Changing Light at Sandover.* Ann Arbor: University of Michigan Press, 1994.

Poulin, A. Jr. 'The Experience of Experience: A Conversation with John Ashbery', *The Michigan Quarterly Review*, Vol. 20, No. 3 (1981): 232–55.

Pound, Ezra. *ABC of Reading*. London: Faber, 1951.

——. *Selected Cantos*. New York: New Directions, 1970.

——. *The Cantos*. London: Faber, 1986.

Raskin, Jonah. *American Scream: Allen Ginsberg's Howl and the Making of the Beat Generation*. Berkeley, Los Angeles & London: University of California Press, 2004.

Reed, Brian. *Hart Crane: After His Lights*. Tuscaloosa: University of Alabama Press, 2006.

Riddel, Joseph. 'Hart Crane's Poetics of Failure', *ELH*, Vol. 33, No. 4 (December 1966): 487.

Robinson, Paul. *Gay Lives*. Chicago & London: University of Chicago Press, 1999.

Rehder, Robert. Stevens, *Williams, Crane, and the Motive for Metaphor*. Basingstoke: Palgrave Macmillan, 2005.

Rofes, Eric. *Dry Bones Breathe: Gay Men Creating Post-AIDS Identities and Cultures*. New York & London: Haworth Press, 1998.

Rogin, Michael Paul. *Ronald Reagan, the Movie and Other Episodes in Political Demonology*. Berkeley, Los Angeles & London: University of California Press, 1987.

Ross, Andrew. *Universal Abandon? The Politics of Postmodernism*. Minneapolis: University of Minnesota Press, 1988.

Rother, James. 'Merrill the Prodigal', Review of *James Merrill's Collected Poems*. 2001, *Contemporary Poetry Review*, www.cprw.com/Rother/Merrill.htm. Site accessed 24 March 2011.

Rowe, William. *Poets of Contemporary Latin America: History and the Inner Life*. Oxford: Oxford University Press, 2000.

Sanders, Edward. *The Poetry and Life of Allen Ginsberg: A Narrative Poem*. London: Scribner, 2002.

Sarkonak, Ralph. *Angelic Echoes: Hervé Guibert and Company*. Toronto & London: University of Toronto Press, 2000.

Savage, D. S. 'The Americanism of Hart Crane'. *The Personal Principle: Studies in Modern Poetry*. London: Routledge, 1944.

Scharnhorst, Gary. 'Moodie, My Dad, Allen Ginsberg and Me: Reflections on Wichita and "Wichita Vortex Sutra" ', *Midwest Quarterly: A Journal of Contemporary Thought*, Vol. 45, No. 4 (2004): 369–80.

Schellenberg, Ken, ed. *The Gay Herman Melville Reader*. Arlington, VA: Gival Press, 2002.

Schumacher, Michael. *Dharma Lion: A Critical Biography of Allen Ginsberg*. New York: St Martin's Press, 1992.

Schultz, Susan M., ed. *The Tribe of John: Ashbery and Contemporary Poetry*. Tuscaloosa & London: University of Alabama Press, 1995.

Schweizer, Bernard. *Approaches to the Anglo and American Female Epic, 1621–1982*. Aldershot: Ashgate, 2006.

Sedgwick, Eve Kosofsky. *Between Men: English Literature and Male Homosocial Desire*. New York: Columbia University Press, 1985.

——. *Epistemology of the Closet*. Berkeley, CA: University of California Press, 1992.

Shoptaw, John, 'John Ashbery and James Merrill'. *The Columbia History of American Poetry*. Ed. Jay Parini with the assistance of Brett C. Miller. New York: Columbia University Press, 1993: 750–75.

——. *On the Outside Looking Out: John Ashbery's Poetry*. Cambridge: Harvard University Press, 1994.

Shover, John L., ed. *Politics of the Nineteen Twenties*. Waltham: Ginn-Blaisdell, 1970.

Sinfield, Alan. *Cultural Politics-Queer Reading*. London: Routledge, 1994.

Snediker, Michael D. 'Hart Crane's Smile', *Modernism/Modernity*, Vol. 12, No. 4 (2005): 629–58.

——. *Queer Optimism*. Minneapolis, MN & London: University of Minnesota Press, 2009.

Sontag, Susan. *Illness & its Metaphors/AIDS & its Metaphors*. London: Penguin, 1991.

Stockinger, Jacob. 'Homotextuality: A Proposal'. *The Gay Academic*. Ed. Louie Crew. Palm Springs: Etc. Publications, 1979: 135–51.

Sundquist, Eric J. 'Bringing Home the Word: Magic, Lies and Silence in Hart Crane', *ELH*, Vol. 44, No. 2 (Summer 1977): 376–98.

Svonkin, Craig. 'Manishevitz and Sake, the Kaddish and Sutras: Allen Ginsberg's Spiritual Self-Othering', *College Literature*, Vol. 37, No. 4 (Fall 2010): 166–93.

Tambling, Jeremy. *Confession: Sexuality, Sin and the Subject*. Manchester & New York: Manchester University Press, 1990.

Tapper, Gordon A. *The Machine that Sings*. London: Routledge, 2006.

Tate, Allen. *Essays of Four Decades*. Chicago, IL: Swallow, 1968.

Tate, Michael L. 'From Scout to Doughboy: The National Debate over Integrating American Indians into the Military, 1891–1918', *Western Historical Quarterly*, Vol. 17, No. 4 (October 1986): 417–37.

Tillyard, E. M. W. *The English Epic and its Background*. London: Chatto & Windus, 1954.

Tóibín, Colm. *Love in a Dark Time: Gay Lives from Wilde to Almodovar*. London: Picador, 2002.

Torgovnick, Marianna. *Gone Primitive: Savage Intellects, Modern Lives*. Chicago, IL: Chicago University Press, 1990.

Trachtenberg, Alan, ed. *Hart Crane: A Collection of Critical Essays*. Englewood Cliffs, NJ: Prentice Hall, 1982.

Trigilio, Tony. '*Strange Prophecies Anew': Rereading Apocalypse in Blake, H.D. and Ginsberg*. Madison: Fairleigh Dickinson University Press, 2000.

——. *Allen Ginsberg's Buddhist Poetics*. Carbondale: Southern Illinois University Press, 2007.

Unterecker, John. *Voyager: A Life of Hart Crane*. New York: Blond, 1970.

Van Ghent, Dorothy. 'Comment'. *Wagner Literary Magazine* (Spring 1959): 27.

Vendler, Helen. *Part of Nature, Part of Us*. Cambridge: Harvard University Press, 1980.

——. *Invisible Listeners: Lyric Intimacy in Herbert, Whitman, and Ashbery*. Princeton, NJ: Princeton University Press, 2005.

Vincent, John. "Reports of looting and insane buggery behind altars: John Ashbery's queer politics", *Twentieth Century Literature*, Vol. 44 (Summer 1998): 155–175.

——. *Queer Lyrics: Difficulty and Closure in American Poetry.* Palgrave Macmillan, 2003.

Virgil. *The Aeneid.* Trans. W. F. Jackson Knight. London, New York, Victoria & Ontario Auckland: Penguin Books, 1956.

Vogler, Thomas A. *Preludes to Vision: The Epic Venture in Blake, Wordsworth, Keats and Hart Crane.* Berkeley, CA: University of California Press, 1971.

Walker, Jeffrey. *Bardic Ethos and the American Epic Poem.* Baton Rouge & London: Louisiana State University Press, 1989.

Wallace, Michelle. 'Critical Fictions'. *Critical Fictions: The Politics of Imaginative Writing.* Ed. Philomena Mariani. Seattle: Bay Press, 1991: 139–42.

Walls, Neal. *Desire, Discord and Death: Approaches to Ancient Near Eastern Myth* Boston: Asor Books, 2001.

Warner, Michael. 'Thoreau's Bottom', *Raritan*, Vol. 11 (Winter 1992): 25.

Weaver, Mike. *William Carlos Williams: The American Background.* Cambridge: Cambridge University Press, 1971.

White, Edmund. *States of Desire: Travels in Gay America.* London: André Deutsch, 1980.

——. 'The Inverted Type: Homosexuality as a Theme in James Merrill's Prophetic Books'. *Literary Visions of Homosexuality.* Ed. Stuart Kellogg. New York: Haworth Press, 1983: 47–52.

Whitman, Walt. *Complete Poetry and Selected Prose and Letters.* Ed. Emory Holloway. London: The Nonesuch Press, 1938.

——. *Leaves of Grass.* New York: Grossett & Dunlap, 1976.

Whitmer, Peter O. *Aquarius Revisited: Seven Who Created the Sixties Counterculture that Changed America.* New York: Citadel Press, 1991.

Wiegman, Robyn. *American Anatomies: Theorizing Race and Gender.* Durham & London: Duke University Press, 1995.

Wilbur, Richard. 'Craft Interview with John Ashbery', *New York Quarterly*, No. 9 (Winter 1972): 122–23.

Wilkie, Brian. *Romantic Poets and Epic Tradition.* Madison, WI: University of Wisconsin Press, 1965.

Williams, Alan. 'A Cold Spring: The Poet of Feeling'. *Elizabeth Bishop and Her Art.* Ed. Lloyd Schwartz and Sybill P. Estess. Ann Arbor: University of Michigan Press, 1983.

Williams, William Carlos. *Paterson.* New York: New Directions, 1963.

Winters, Yvor. *The Anatomy of Nonsense.* Norfolk: New Directions, 1943.

Wittig, Monique. *The Lesbian Body.* Trans. David Le Vay. New York: Viking Press, 1971.

Woods, Gregory. *Articulate Flesh: Male Homo-eroticism and Modern Poetry.* New Haven & London: Yale University Press, 1987.

——. 'Hart Crane'. *American Poetry: The Modernist Ideal.* Ed. Clive Bloom and Brian Docherty. Basingstoke: Palgrave Macmillan Press, 1995.

——. *A History of Gay Literature: The Male Tradition.* New Haven & London: Yale University Press, 1998.

Wordsworth, William. *The Prelude: A Parallel Text.* Ed. J. C. Maxwell. London: Penguin, 1971.

Yenser, Stephen. *The Consuming Myth: The Work of James Merrill.* Cambridge, MA & London: Harvard University Press, 1987.

Yingling, Thomas. *Hart Crane and the Homosexual Text: New Thresholds, New Anatomies.* Chicago & London: University of Chicago Press, 1990.

——. *AIDS and the National Body.* Ed. Robyn Wiegman. Durham & London: Duke University Press, 1997.

Zeiger, M. *Beyond Consolation: Death, Sexuality, and the Changing Shape of Elegy.* Ithaca & London: Cornell University Press, 1997.

Index